D0983464

Motivational Interviewing and Stages of Change in Intimate Partner Violence

Christopher M. Murphy, PhD, is a Professor of Psychology and Director of Clinical Psychology Training at the University of Maryland, Baltimore County. He also directs the New Behaviors Program at the Domestic Violence Center of Howard County, Maryland, a comprehensive clinical service, training, and research program focused on perpetrators of intimate partner abuse. Dr. Murphy's research focuses on the efficacy of cognitive-behavioral and motivational treatments for perpetrators of intimate partner abuse, the role of alcohol and drugs in partner abuse, motivation to change abusive behavior, and psychological abuse in dating and marital relationships. His work on intimate partner violence has received support from the National Institute of Alcohol Abuse and Alcoholism, National Institute of Mental Health, and Centers for Disease Control and Prevention. Dr. Murphy has previously co-authored, with Christopher Eckhardt, *Treating the Abusive Partner: An Individualized Cognitive-Behavioral Approach* (2005).

Roland D. Maiuro, PhD, is the Clinical Director of the Seattle Anger Management, Domestic Violence, and Workplace Conflict Programs located at the Cabrini Medical Tower in Seattle. He was a Henry Rutgers Scholar at Rutgers University, earned his doctoral degree in clinical psychology at Washington University in St. Louis, and served as both a post-doctoral fellow and faculty member at the University of Washington School of Medicine. Dr. Maiuro is currently an Adjunct Research Scientist for the Moss Rehabilitation Research Institute and the Albert Einstein Health Care Network. He is the recipient of the Social Issues Award from the Washington State Psychological Association, a Lifetime Achievement Award from the Northwest Domestic Violence Treatment Provider Association, and the Gold Achievement Award from the American Psychiatric Association for program development, teaching, and applied research in the areas of anger and interpersonal violence. Dr. Maiuro is currently the Editor-in-Chief of *Violence and Victims*, an internationally distributed research journal devoted to theory, practice, and public policy related to perpetrators, victims, and the trauma associated with interpersonal violence.

Motivational Interviewing and Stages of Change in Intimate Partner Violence

CHRISTOPHER M. MURPHY, PhD
ROLAND D. MAIURO, PhD

Editors

SPRINGER PUBLISHING COMPANY

New York

Springer Publishing Company, LLC
11 West 42nd Street
New York, NY 10036
www.springerpub.com

Acquisitions Editor: Jennifer Perillo
Project Manager: Mark Frazier
Cover design: David Levy
Composition: Apex CoVantage, LLC

Ebook ISBN: 978-0-8261-1978-0

09 10 11 12 / 5 4 3 2 1

The author and the publisher of this Work have made every effort to use sources believed to be reliable to provide information that is accurate and compatible with the standards generally accepted at the time of publication. The author and publisher shall not be liable for any special, consequential, or exemplary damages resulting, in whole or in part, from the readers' use of, or reliance on, the information contained in this book. The publisher has no responsibility for the persistence or accuracy of URLs for external or third-party Internet Web sites referred to in this publication and does not guarantee that any content on such Web sites is, or will remain, accurate or appropriate.

Library of Congress Cataloging-in-Publication Data

Motivational interviewing and stages of change in intimate partner violence / [edited by] Christopher Murphy, Roland Maiuro.
    p. cm.
  Includes bibliographical references and index.
  ISBN 978-0-8261-1977-3 (alk. paper)
  1. Family violence—Psychological aspects. I. Murphy, Christopher M. (Christopher Mark) II. Maiuro, Roland D.
    RC569.5.F3M68   2009
    362.82'92—dc22   2009003788

Printed in the United States of America by Hamilton Printing

Contents

Contributors

Pamela C. Alexander, PhD
Senior Research Scientist
Wellesley Centers for Women
Wellesley, MA

Audrey Begun, PhD
Professor
Helen Bader School of Social Welfare,
    Center for Addiction and Behavioral
    Health Research
University of Wisconsin-Milwaukee
Milwaukee, WI

Daniel Bolt, PhD
Professor, Department of Educational
    Psychology
University of Wisconsin-Madison
Madison, WI

Serge Brochu, PhD
Professor, School of Criminology
University of Montreal
Montreal, Canada

Normand Brodeur, PhD
Assistant Professor, School of Social
    Service
Université Laval
Quebec City, Canada

Michael J. Brondino, PhD
Associate Professor
Helen Bader School of Social Welfare,
    Center for Addiction and Behavioral
    Health Research
University of Wisconsin-Milwaukee
Milwaukee, WI

Kelly H. Burkitt, PhD
Director of Research Development
Center for Health Equity Research
    and Promotion
VA Pittsburgh Healthcare System
Pittsburgh, PA

Melissa Cahill, PhD
Chair, Probation and Parole
Collin County Community Supervision
    and Corrections Department
McKinney, TX

Norman Cobb, PhD, LCSW
Associate Professor
School of Social Work
University of Texas at Arlington
Arlington, TX

Mary-Margaret Driskell, MPH
Senior Project Manager
Pro-Change Behavior Systems, Inc.
Kingston, RI

Christopher Eckhardt, PhD
Associate Professor of Psychology
Purdue University
West Lafayette, IN

Jeffrey Edleson, PhD
Professor, School of Social Work
Director, Minnesota Center Against
    Violence and Abuse (MINCAVA)
University of Minnesota
St. Paul, MN

Andrea Gielen, ScD, ScM
Professor and Deputy Director
Center for Injury Research and Policy
Johns Hopkins Bloomberg School of
    Public Health
Johns Hopkins University
Baltimore, MD

Jessica Griffin Burke, PhD
Assistant Professor
Graduate School of Public Health
University of Pittsburgh
Pittsburgh, PA

Amy Holtzworth-Munroe, PhD
Professor of Psychology
Indiana University
Bloomington, IN

Barbara R. Kistenmacher, PhD
Director of Addictions Treatments
Bronx-Lebanon Hospital Center
New York, NY

Gregory L. Larkin, MD, MSPH, FACEP
Professor of Surgery and Associate
    Director of Emergency Medicine
Department of Surgery
Section of Emergency Medicine
Yale University School of Medicine
New Haven, CT

Peter Lehmann, PhD, LCSW
Associate Professor
School of Social Work
University of Texas at Arlington
Arlington, TX

Deborah A. Levesque, PhD
Senior Vice President of Research and
    Product Development
Pro-Change Behavior Systems, Inc.
Kingston, RI

Jocelyn Lindsay, PhD
Professor of Social Work
Laval University
Quebec City, Canada

Patricia Mahoney, MA
Research Associate
Johns Hopkins Bloomberg School of
    Public Health
Johns Hopkins University
Baltimore, MD

Lyungai Mbilinyi, MSW, MPH, PhD
Research Assistant Professor
SSW Co-Director
Innovative Programs Research Group
University of Washington
Seattle, WA

Karen A. McDonnell, PhD
Associate Professor
George Washington University School
    of Public Health and Health Services
Washington, DC

Eugene Morris, LCSW-C
Manager
Montgomery County Abused Persons
    Program
Rockville, MD

Peter H. Musser, PhD
Research Associate in Psychology
University of Maryland, Baltimore
    County
Baltimore, MD

Clayton Neighbors, PhD
Associate Professor
Psychiatry and Behavioral Sciences
University of Washington
Seattle, WA

Bradley Norlander, PhD
Psychologist
Texas Youth Commission
Giddings State School
Giddings, TX

Patricia O'Campo, PhD
Director
Centre for Research on Inner City
    Health
St. Michael's Hospital
Toronto, Canada

Jason Phelps, MSW
Montreal, Canada

James O. Prochaska, PhD
Director
Cancer Prevention Research Center
Professor of Clinical and Health
   Psychology
University of Rhode Island
Kingston, RI

Janice M. Prochaska, PhD
President & Chief Executive Officer
Pro-Change Behavior Systems, Inc.
Kingston, RI

Roger Roffman
Professor, School of Social Work
University of Washington
Seattle, WA

Gilles Rondeau, PhD
Program Coordinator
School of Social Service
University of Montreal
Montreal, Canada

Joshua N. Semiatin, MA
Graduate Student in Psychology
University of Maryland, Baltimore
   County
Baltimore, MD

Gene Shelley, PhD
Behavioral Scientist
Centers for Disease Control and
   Prevention
Atlanta, GA

Ashley Sibley, PhD
Department of Psychology
Southern Methodist University
Dallas, TX

Catherine A. Simmons, PhD, LCSW
Assistant Professor
College of Social Work
University of Tennessee
Knoxville, TN

Terri Strodthoff, PhD
Director
Alma Center
Milwaukee, WI

Casey T. Taft, PhD
Associate Professor
Boston University School of Medicine
National Center for Posttraumatic
   Stress Disorder
Boston VA Medical Center
Boston, MA

Denise Walker, PhD
Research Assistant Professor
SSW Co-Director
Innovative Programs Research Group
University of Washington
Seattle, WA

Benjamin Weinstein, PhD
Clinical Psychologist
Graduate School of Psychology
Assumption University of Thailand
Bangkok, Thailand

Robert L. Weiss, PhD
Professor Emeritus of Psychology
University of Oregon
Eugene, OR

Joan Zegree, PhD
Adjunct Assistant Professor
School of Social Work
University of Washington
Seattle, WA

Introduction

1

Understanding and Facilitating the Change Process in Perpetrators and Victims of Intimate Partner Violence: An Introduction and Commentary

CHRISTOPHER M. MURPHY AND ROLAND D. MAIURO

One of the main contributions of the transtheoretical model of behavior change (TTM; Prochaska & DiClemente, 1984) has been to sharpen our conceptual focus on motivation and readiness to change. The idea that individuals (and larger systems as well) proceed through an orderly set of stages in preparing for, accomplishing, and maintaining behavior change has been a major insight with wide applicability to addictive behaviors, psychotherapy, and health behavior promotion (Prochaska & DiClemente, 2005; Prochaska, DiClemente, & Norcross, 1992; Prochaska, Johnson, & Lee, 1998).

THE STAGES OF CHANGE

The TTM explains intentional behavior change along a temporal dimension that utilizes both cognitive and performance-based components. Existing research has found that individuals move through a series of stages (precontemplation, contemplation, preparation, action, and maintenance) in the adoption of healthy behaviors or cessation of unhealthy ones (Prochaska & Velicer, 1997).

Precontemplation is the stage in which an individual has no intent to change behavior in the near future, usually measured as the next

3

6 months. With respect to behavior change, precontemplators are characterized as resistant, unmotivated, or demoralized. They tend to avoid information, discussion, or thoughts with regard to changing the targeted health behavior.

In the *contemplation* stage individuals express an intention or desire to change without a clear and immediate plan to enact the desired changes. They are aware of the benefits of changing, but remain aware of the costs, risks, or drawbacks. Contemplators are often seen as either ambivalent to change or as procrastinators.

Preparation is the stage in which individuals express a clear intention to change, usually within the next month, and may have begun taking initial steps. Given its shorter time frame, the preparation stage is often viewed as a transition rather than stable stage, with individuals intending to take imminent and concrete steps toward the target goal.

Action is the stage in which an individual has been making overt and measurable lifestyle changes, typically for a period of less than 6 months. Finally, in the *maintenance* stage, individuals have successfully altered their behavior and may need to take additional steps to prevent relapse and consolidate gains secured during the action stage. Those in maintenance are also distinguishable from those in action in that they tend to report higher levels of self-efficacy and resistance to relapse.

Approximately a decade ago, several scholars recognized the potential utility of the TTM for understanding the change process in both perpetrators (Daniels & Murphy, 1997; Dutton, 1995) and victims (Brown, 1997) of intimate partner abuse. With respect to perpetrators, the need for greater emphasis on motivation and readiness to change was starkly apparent in the tendency of many perpetrators to deny or minimize personal problems, blame others for their behavioral difficulties, failure to attend court-ordered services, overt resistance to counseling, and noncompliance with directive behavior change interventions. Clinical observations with both victims and perpetrators further revealed frequent cycling through periods of separation and reunification, a steady accrual of negative consequences associated with relationship problems and abuse, and the need for a lengthy period of self-evaluation and support prior to significant life change. Such circumstances resemble the change process facing those with addictions and the challenges of health behavior promotion, both instances in which the TTM had been successfully applied.

MOTIVATIONAL INTERVIEWING

Motivational interviewing (MI) is a therapeutic strategy and counseling approach that is based on the recognition that clients who need to make changes approach counseling at different levels of readiness to change (Miller & Rollnick, 2002). As such, it is intimately related to models of change that delineate different phases or stages such as the TTM. As in the case of the TTM, MI was initially developed to assist therapists to work with alcohol- and drug-dependent individuals who were often resistant to more traditional methods of counseling developed for purely voluntary and self-motivated clientele.

The overall focus of MI was to engage alcohol- and drug-abusing clients, commonly referred as a result of complaints by family members and/or violations of the law. Specific interviewing methods are employed that are designed to mobilize intrinsic motivation within the client's circumstance by developing cognitive and behavioral discrepancies and by exploring and resolving the sources of ambivalence that inhibit change. As in the case of the TTM, there are similarities between the motivational dynamics of the substance-abusing and the partner-abusing client, who is also doing harm to family members and violating the law through acts of domestic violence. These similarities have made the use of MI strategies well worth investigating for their potential utility in cases of intimate partner violence.

Motivational interviewing attempts to establish a therapeutic alliance with the client by using a high level of empathic listening, affirming the client's autonomy and choice, and matching interventions to the client's stage of change. As such, it is intended to create a nonjudgmental, nonconfrontational, and nonadversarial climate in which the client is "accepted" despite the presence of "unacceptable behavior." The approach attempts to increase the client's awareness of the potential problems caused, consequences experienced, and risks faced as a result of the unhealthy behavior in question. Therapists help clients realize the benefits of change and help them become motivated and committed to achieve it.

Motivational interviewing is based on four basic therapeutic principles.

1. Assessment of the client's stage of change and perspective to allow the therapist to communicate understanding, empathy, and congruence with the client's perspective.

2. Development of cognitive and attitudinal discrepancies to help clients appreciate the value and potential benefits of change by exploring the difference between how clients want their lives to be versus how they currently are functioning, thinking, and behaving.
3. Acceptance of resistance by defining the client's defenses and reluctance to change as a process and phase rather than a pathological sign of character flaw and failure.
4. Support self-efficacy by embracing the client's autonomy and power to change, or not to change, to facilitate movement toward active decision making and action.

The chapters in this book represent important applications of the TTM and MI strategies to intimate partner violence (IPV) and abuse. These studies include descriptive longitudinal research on both victims and perpetrators of abuse, measurement issues in assessing stages of change, and applications of motivational interviewing methods for facilitating change. Many of the contributions have been drawn from recently published issues of the journal *Violence and Victims* (vol. 23, numbers 4 and 5). Other chapters have been modified or added to the present book version to allow for a more expanded and updated treatment of these topics.

Stages of Change in Perpetrators of Domestic Violence and Abuse

Five chapters in this book focus on application of the TTM to male perpetrators of IPV. Begun and colleagues (chapter 9) provide a nice example of the psychometric sophistication of recent efforts to develop and validate measures of the stages of change for this population. They have put considerable effort into developing items that reflect the distinct stages of change for abusive individuals. Their chapter describes the factor structure of the revised measure, including detailed information to support the addition of a maintenance factor. It also discusses some of the prior data on the validity of this instrument.

Levesque, Driskell, Prochaska, and Prochaska (chapter 3) describe the TTM's stages and examine the acceptability of a computer-administered multimedia stage-matched expert system intervention among 58 men who have battered. Thirty-three of the men were recruited at program intake and 25 from ongoing groups. The expert system assessed the stage of change, decisional balance, processes of change, self-efficacy, and strategies used to progress to ending violence. The participants were provided immediate individualized feedback during their intervention. Overall, the vast majority (87%) of these men reported that the program was easy to use, and most (98%) felt that the system could "probably" or "definitely" help change their attitudes or behaviors.

In applying the stage-of-change model to partner-violent men, three of these studies uncovered interesting similarities and differences. Alexander and Morris (chapter 6) identified two distinct stages-of-change clusters, one reflecting a classic precontemplation/immotive profile and the other reflecting a contemplation/preparation profile with greater readiness to attempt personal change. In identifying four clusters, Eckhardt, Holtzworth-Munroe, Norlander, Sibley, and Cahill (chapter 5) appear to have divided those who were relatively unprepared for change into a "reluctant" cluster, who deny any problem with abuse or any need for change, and a "preparticipation" cluster, who have a "flat" profile reflecting some acknowledgment of problems and the need for change but no clear commitment to the change process. In addition, their analysis identified an "unprepared" action cluster of men who are relatively high on the active change scale but low on scales reflecting cognitive preparation to change and awareness of relapse potential. Brodeur, Rondeau, Brochu, Lindsay, and Phelps (chapter 7) uncovered five clusters. Similar to Eckhardt and colleagues (chapter 5), they found several early-stage groups, labeled reluctant, immotive, and preparticipation. In addition, they found two action clusters distinguished by whether they also reported high fear of relapse.

The differences between these three studies reflect an inherent limitation in cluster and profile analysis, namely, that there is no universally accepted way nor any hard-and-fast statistical criterion to rely on in choosing the number of clusters. Greater parsimony and simplicity may result from fewer clusters, yet important subgroup distinctions may be uncovered from having more clusters. Given the inherently descriptive nature of cluster-analytic techniques, newer approaches such as latent class analysis, mixture modeling, and taxometric analysis may provide some advantages for determining whether observed data conform to a predicted categorical structure or whether continuous variable indicators, such as observed scores on stage-of-change scales, appear to result from an underlying categorical causal process. To date, applications of the TTM stage concept have likewise relied almost exclusively on cluster analysis, and therefore the hypothesized stage categories have not been systematically subjected to confirmatory tests.

In addition, readers must be mindful of the fact that cluster analysis creates profiles based on *relative* rather than *absolute* scale scores. Thus, these clusters should be conceptualized as prepared or unprepared for change *relative to their sample counterparts* and not necessarily as prepared or unprepared for change in an absolute sense. This scoring and assignment method places limitations on the clinical use of these findings in the individual case.

It is also important to note that Alexander and Morris (chapter 6) sampled individuals who presented for an initial counseling intake at a suburban, community-based domestic violence agency, whereas Brodeur and colleagues (chapter 7) sampled men presenting at urban counseling programs who were willing to participate in a research study, whereas Eckhardt and colleagues (chapter 5) sampled directly from the court in an urban area. The court sample included a large number of cases who never attended intake orientation at a domestic violence program and was characterized by a very high rate of probation violation. Thus, it is likely that this sample contained a greater proportion of individuals who were unwilling to acknowledge problems with abusive behavior or the need for change. Sample variations in ethnic, cultural, and linguistic backgrounds may also influence how individuals respond to assessment measures in ways not yet studied and known.

Despite important differences in sampling and data analysis, two of the three studies revealed significant differences among those in different stage of change clusters. Those who appear relatively more ready to change self-reported more abusive behavior than those who appear relatively less ready to change. However, the Alexander and Morris (chapter 6) study found that abuse reports from victim partners were more similar across clusters, suggesting that the self-report results may reflect the willingness to disclose abusive behavior rather than actual subgroup differences in perpetration of abuse. Along similar lines, in the study by Eckhardt and colleagues (chapter 5), those in the decision-making cluster who appeared most ready to change also acknowledged the greatest level of problems with hostile thinking and anger. Likewise, Alexander and Morris (chapter 6) found that those in the prepared cluster self-reported more anger as well as greater anxiety and depression than those in the immotive cluster. Interestingly, they also found that the prepared cluster showed greater reductions in self-reported anxiety and depression and greater increases in self-reported anger control after treatment. These findings underscore the importance of assessing anger in men who are violent and abusive toward intimate partners (cf. Maiuro &

Eberle, 2008). The present results specifically suggest that anger and hostility may not only be an important focus of treatment for many abusive men but also may provide a diagnostic marker of emotional awareness or "mindfulness" associated with readiness to change.

In all three of these studies, stage-of-change cluster was not predictive of treatment completion. Likewise, in the intervention study by Musser and colleagues (chapter 4), motivational interviewing affected positive group behavior, homework compliance, and the working alliance but did not affect treatment session attendance. It appears that session attendance is influenced by factors other than self-reported motivational or readiness to change among partner-abusive men. For example, given that the samples were predominantly or exclusively court ordered to treatment, session attendance may reflect participant's fear of legal reprisals for noncompliance. Practical barriers, such as transportation, work schedules, and child care, may also limit compliance for those who are otherwise motivated to attend. Conversely, these findings may reflect complications in measuring readiness to change, wherein self-reports are influenced both by genuine attitudes and by impression management, watering down the prediction of treatment compliance.

Finally, in two of the three investigations, although the results should be considered preliminary because of limited availability of follow-up data, the tendency to score high on the precontemplation scale was predictive of continuing problems with abuse. Thus, stage-of-change clustering may be less useful in predicting abuse recidivism relative to continuous variable measurement of precontemplation, which indicates denial of a need for change.

The study by Eckhardt and colleagues (chapter 5) provides additional interesting findings with respect to the prominent typology model proposed by Holtzworth-Munroe and Stuart (1994) and Holtzworth-Munroe, Meehan, Herron, Rehman, and Stuart (2000). In addition to replicating a number of correlational findings for the typology, the results showed associations with stage-of-change clusters that were somewhat inconsistent with the hypotheses. Most notably, the least severely abusive and least pathological subgroup (family only) were overrepresented in the reluctant (precontemplation) cluster, whereas the more pathological and severe types of abusers (borderline/dysphoric and generally violent/antisocial) were overrepresented in the decision-making or unprepared action clusters, demonstrating greater perceived need for change and/or self-reported efforts to change. These findings suggest a possible need to correct for "test taking attitude" differences that may exist between subtypes of abusers when assessing readiness to change. The fact that abuser subtype was significantly associated with program completion and criminal recidivism, whereas stage cluster was not, also speaks to the possible greater power of abuser subtype as an initial predictor of outcome.

Stage-of-Change Profiles for Victims of Intimate Partner Abuse

Chapter 12 by Burkitt and Larkin is unique in several respects, most notably in using a prospective design with a sample of IPV victims obtained from a level I trauma center. The emergency medicine and public health perspective on change in abused women is very important, as those who present for medical services may reflect a broader cross-section of abused women in comparison to those who seek counseling or shelter services at domestic violence programs. Thus, stage-of-change and related phenomena can be studied in this population separately from the dynamics of help seeking for self-identified abuse victimization. In addition, the sample was rather severely affected by IPV, with more than four-fifths reporting injuries and more than two-thirds having obtained medical care for IPV.

The study sample exhibited an interesting pattern of movement through the stages of change over time, with a sizable number of women shifting toward action and the general trend being progression of a cluster of behavioral tendencies over the course of the study. Interestingly, those who progressed further on the stage-of-change measure were considerably more likely to end their relationships by the follow-up assessment. Burkitt and Larkin (chapter 12) also identified a number of important factors that differ across stage-of-change clusters, including decisional balance regarding the pros and cons of leaving the relationship, temptation to remain in or return to the abusive relationship, the use of community resources, and the presence of children. Thus, this chapter highlights the utility of the TTM in understanding both the emotional and the practical barriers to change as well as the general tendency for seriously abused women in the community to eventually leave the abusive partner.

Burke, Mahoney, Gielen, McDonnell, and O'Campo (chapter 11) also examine women's experience of interpersonal victimization (mainly severe physical abuse) by comparing stage assignment (precontemplation, contemplation, preparation, action, and maintenance) with safety behaviors, stage of leaving the relationship, and desired services. They develop a novel approach for assigning women to stages of change based on prior in-depth qualitative interviews and the use of logic similar to that employed with addictive and health promotion behaviors. The majority of their sample (65%) of 96 abused, urban women (primarily African American and low income) from six health care settings were in the action stage, reporting that they had been exposed to abuse and had taken action to keep themselves safe from abuse within the past 6 months. Burke and colleagues found interesting and complex links between stage of change and use of safety behaviors, with most extensive use in the pre-action stage. This result may have been due in part to the nonlinear and variable rates of progression between safe and unsafe situations inherent to the lives of battered women (Chang et al., 2006). This study provides unique insight into the relationships between stages of change and clinically important behavioral variables, including safety behaviors and perceived need for services.

Readiness to Change in a Sample of Women Batterers Compared to a Comparison Group of Men Charged With Abuse

The study conducted by Simmons, Lehmann, and Cobb (chapter 10) is unique in offering data on a group of women charged with domestic violence, using a comparison sample of men charged with similar behavior. The groups were compared on a variety of risk factors, attitudes toward the use of violence in their intimate relationships, as well as their self-report stage of change as measured by the University of Rhode Island Change Assessment for Domestic Violence (URICA-DV; Levesque, Gelles, & Velicer, 2000). Most women were found to be in the action stage of change at the point of pretreatment. No differences were found between women and men on precontemplation, contemplation, and action indices. Interestingly, the only difference in readiness to change that emerged was a relatively small one with regard to maintenance of non-violence with one's partner, with men scoring higher than women on this subscale. Although such results appear counterintuitive given the fact that men are often presumed to have more ingrained traits related to aggression, the authors argue that these differences may stem from the women's tendency to perceive their own violence to be more justifiable than men's violence. It would be of interest to see if these gender differences continued to be present when the offender samples were refined by limiting the men and women selected to "primary aggressors." Such results support the importance of using contextual and gender-sensitive frames of reference when interpreting stage-of-change data, and the need to further explore attitudes that may moderate the associations between readiness to change and successful cessation of violent behavior.

Motivational Interviewing With Abuse Perpetrators

Chapters 2, 4, and 8 provide encouraging findings from experimental tests of motivational interviewing (MI) for partner-abusive men. Chapter 8 presents findings from a novel application of MI to a nonadjudicated community sample of men. Using an approach modeled after the "Drinker Check-up," an early application of MI to individuals with concerns about their drinking, the study solicited participants with personal concerns about their abusive behavior through community announcements and advertisements. The investigators targeted a subgroup of respondents who had children. They found that participants who received a brief telephone MI intervention with personalized assessment feedback had lower levels of abusive behavior over the subsequent 30-day interval than those in the control group. Although readiness to change, formal treatment seeking, and willingness to participate in an optional in-person session after the initial phone consultation were not significantly higher among those who received MI, the results for at least temporary decreases in abusive behavior subsequent to the brief MI intervention provide encouragement for continued examination of motivational therapy with abusive men.

The studies presented in chapters 2 and 4 provided two sessions of MI to partner-abusive men prior to their assignment to standard group counseling. In the Kistenmacher and Weiss (chapter 2) study, the control group was randomly assigned to receive no pregroup intervention. In the study by Musser and colleagues (chapter 4), the control group was constructed on a quasi-random basis in which cohorts of consecutive intakes were assigned to receive a structured intake with no MI versus the MI intervention.

The findings by Kistenmacher and Weiss (chapter 2) focus on readiness to change and the tendency to externalize blame for abusive behavior. The MI group showed increases in contemplation and action and increases in responsibility assumption for their abusive behavior, suggesting progression through the stages of change associated with the MI intervention. Interestingly, the outcome measures were taken immediately after the second MI session and were therefore likely sensitive to the short-term effects of this counseling style.

The study by Musser and colleagues (chapter 4) likewise found evidence for increased personal responsibility assumption for abusive behavior associated with MI but in a very different mode of assessment, namely, coded verbalizations during early group treatment sessions. In addition, those who received MI in this study expressed greater belief in the value of treatment, completed considerably more structured home assignments in the cognitive-behavioral therapy (CBT) program, and ended up with higher therapist ratings of the working alliance late in treatment. They also engaged in more help seeking outside the CBT program than those in the control group. Interestingly, no differences emerged on the stages-of-change measure in this latter study, perhaps because this outcome was assessed during the first group treatment session, possibly also due to variable time durations from the initial completion of intake (due to the lag in constructing treatment groups). Finally, it is interesting to note that some of the factors influenced by the MI intervention in the Musser and colleagues study (chapter 4), specifically therapist ratings of the alliance and homework compliance, have been shown to predict lower postintervention abuse (Taft, Murphy, King, Musser, & DeDeyn, 2003).

CONCEPTUAL AND EMPIRICAL CHALLENGES

The Influence of Relationship Context

The individual level of analysis inherent in most applications of the TTM may be complicated by problems that are significantly influenced by interactional, multiperson processes. In application to abuse perpetrators, for example, some individuals may be violent in the presence of specific relationship and life conditions. A response to physical attacks by the partner is perhaps the most obvious example. The discovery of a partner's infidelity, imminent separation, child custody disputes, or other acute relationship stressors may likewise enhance the risk for interpersonal conflict to escalate to physical assault. For victims, factors such as the abusive partner's involvement in counseling, with the attending hope for change, may substantially influence decisions to leave the abusive relationship (Gondolf, 1988). In brief, relationship circumstances and the other intimate partner's behaviors and attitudes may play a substantial interactive role in readiness to change in an abusive relationship.

The Complexity of the Target Behavior

To date, most of the applications of the TTM focus on relatively simple and quantifiable target behaviors, such as smoking, use of alcohol and drugs, or physical exercise. Although aspects of physical assault (e.g., pushing, hitting, and so on) can be operationalized in a relatively straightforward way, other aspects of partner abuse problems, including the many forms of coercion and emotional abuse, are more idiosyncratic and complex. The target behavior for change is particularly complex with regard to victims of partner violence, as it may involve altering their own relationship or help-seeking behaviors, influencing the partner to get help, and/or leaving the abusive relationship. Likewise, those in abusive relationships may define their problem(s) in a number of distinct ways. For some, the problem is perceived as "having gotten in trouble with the law." For others, it may involve attributions about drinking or drug abuse. Some individuals may define the problem as belonging entirely to the partner rather than oneself. Some conceptualize the problem as a bad temper, others as a bad relationship. Similarly, some victims want the abuse to end but not the relationship, and may then be willing to engage in some action steps but not others. Such variables may influence assessment of readiness to change in complex ways, depending in part on the manner in which the questions are asked and the context in which the assessment takes place.

These caveats are illustrated in the present text as several different strategies to measure stages of change in abusive individuals are represented, using different means to identify the problem behavior. For example, the URICA-DV developed by Levesque and colleagues (2000) and used by Eckhardt and colleagues (chapter 5) and Brodeur and colleagues (chapter 7) explicitly mentions partner violence in the scale items. The adapted URICA used by Alexander and Morris (chapter 6) also has a general introduction that orients the participant to domestic violence. However, the item wordings refer to "the problem" without explicit reference to violence or abuse. Finally, the Safe-at-Home measure developed by Begun and colleagues (chapter 9; 2003) uses a variety of different terms and phrasings to identify the problems and attitudes about change, wordings that arose in focus groups with treatment providers. Thus, differences in findings may in part reflect divergence in abusive individuals' reactions to the way that their problems are described or worded in the various measures.

Disclosure and Response Bias

Perhaps the greatest challenge in assessing readiness to change and its implications for partner violence arises from individual differences in honesty and self-disclosure, which are likely influenced by perceived costs and benefits of responding in a socially desirable fashion to the assessments. Such influences are readily apparent in several studies to date. For example, the unexpected findings of Eckhardt and colleagues (chapter 5) regarding stage-of-change cluster and violence subtype are very interesting. In their data, those with fewer or less objective indications of an abuse problem were also very unlikely to acknowledge the need for change. It may be that at some level of abusive behavior perpetration, denial breaks down, making it very difficult not to acknowledge having some type of problem.

A multisite study in Maryland using the URICA with clinical male partner-violent offenders revealed two distinct clusters of individuals with relatively high readiness to change scores (Murphy, Alexander, Black, & Morris, 2005). One cluster had the classic profile of a prepared or committed group with low precontemplation scores and relatively high scores on the contemplation, action, and maintenance scales. A second cluster had very high precontemplation scores, average contemplation scores, and high action and maintenance and were labeled the false maintenance cluster. At baseline, the prepared group had considerably lower scores on a measure of impression management and higher self-reports of abusive behavior than the false maintenance cluster, yet their collateral partner reports of abuse were quite similar (with the false maintenance cluster having somewhat higher levels of sexual coercion). At a collateral partner follow-up 6 months later, the prepared cluster had low prevalence rates of partner violence, whereas the false maintenance cluster had very high rates. These data suggest that some individuals who appear motivated on overall readiness-to-change scores are expressing a belief that they have already solved the problem with abuse without having gone through the efforts normally needed to make lasting behavior change.

FUTURE PROSPECTS

Clinical Applications

Intervention work with partner-violent individuals would greatly benefit from accurate preintervention screening to detect cases at very high risk for severe and repetitive violence recidivism (Gondolf, 2002). To date, traditional risk-screening strategies adopted from criminal justice interventions, most notably those assessing psychopathic personality traits and related risk indicators, have afforded modest and inconsistent prediction of abuse recidivism in samples of clinical partner-violent men (Dutton, Bonarchuk, Kropp, Hart, & Ogloff, 1997; Gondolf & White, 2001; Kropp & Hart, 2000; Remington & Murphy, 2001). Several other risk assessment or prognostic instruments suggest that the major recidivism predictors relate to the level, severity, and extent of previous partner violence (Hilton et al., 2004; Kropp & Hart, 2000; Murphy, Morrel, Elliott, & Neavins, 2003) or victim predictions of risk for future violence (Weisz, Tolman, & Saunders, 2000).

Considerable optimism accompanied initial applications of the TTM to abusive clients in counseling, reflecting the hope that the stage of change construct might provide sound prediction of treatment response and/or a mechanism for assignment to different interventions. As with many new applications, reality appears to be more complex than initial expectations, as the predictive findings have not always turned out as expected despite evidence that the measures have sound psychometric properties. Thus, as yet, measures of readiness to change have not afforded strong prediction of intervention response despite having provided conceptually interesting findings. Conversely, the research presented by Burkitt and Larkin (chapter 12) suggests that change in relationship status over time may be a more predictable outcome from TTM variables for victims than is violence cessation for offenders.

Motivational interviewing, an intervention approach that relies in part on the stage-of-change concept, looks promising as an early intervention for partner-violent men in initial clinical trials. The significant impact of MI has been demonstrated in reducing initial resistance to treatment and enhancing treatment engagement. These findings need to be considered in light of two important known facts about partner-violent individuals. First, many of them are resistant to treatment. Second, to date, no specific intervention approach has been shown to be significantly more helpful than any other for this population (Babcock,

Green, & Robie, 2004). Thus, the mere fact that two trials have shown initial evidence of the utility of a specific intervention approach with this population is very encouraging, even though the outcomes are relatively modest in scope.

The present findings help bolster the conclusion emerging from other recent research on partner-abusive men, namely, that introductory supportive, empathic, alliance-building clinical strategies may improve intervention outcomes for this population. First, the collaborative working alliance between therapist and client has been associated with lower posttreatment abuse in two separate studies with distinct intervention formats (Brown & O'Leary, 2000; Taft et al., 2003). Likewise, supportive communication about treatment attendance after missed sessions, which included a personalized handwritten note and a phone call to express concern and encourage attendance, was associated with increased session attendance and lower dropout for this population (Taft, Murphy, Elliott, & Morrel, 2001). The presently reported studies offer firm support that MI can effect the client's report of active change efforts, positive verbalizations during treatment sessions, and compliance with structured treatment task.

Research Directions

Several potentially important research directions are suggested throughout this publication. First, better strategies are needed for taking response biases into account in assessing readiness to change. It may be helpful to develop methods that do not rely on self-report and to use techniques such as cluster analysis and mixture modeling to separate out groups who are genuinely motivated to change from those who may be endeavoring to fake good on self-report assessments. Such statistical methods may need to use measures of response tendencies in addition to the transtheoretical measures to achieve these goals, as simple statistical control for social desirability may not be sufficient to detect complex response patterns. Second, as noted by Kropp, one of the developers of the Spouse Assault Risk Assessment Guide, the goal is not simply to predict poor intervention response or recidivism but rather to use risk information in order to prevent future violence from occurring (Douglas & Kropp, 2002; Kropp, 2004). Thus, future studies may profitably focus on readiness to change as part of a more comprehensive risk-management and violence-prevention strategy. Matching clients to treatments on the basis of readiness to change is one potential direction for this work, but there are others as well, such as increased monitoring and safety planning for high-risk cases and the use of more extensive pretreatment preparation strategies to overcome initial resistance to change.

Another interesting direction involves the integration of motivational interviewing with other treatment techniques. As a general counseling approach, MI is quite distinct from behavioral and cognitive approaches and a number of other interventions, including pure-form client-centered therapy (Miller & Rollnick, 2002). Thus, there may be a challenge in shifting from MI to the more directive types of treatment strategies that are predominant in work with abusive clients. In fact, in a randomized trial of methods to help clinicians learn motivational interviewing for use with substance-abusing clientele, Miller, Yahne, Moyers, Martinez, and Pirritano (2004) found that the main changes observed were with regard to a decrease in therapist behaviors that *were inconsistent rather than consistent* with the principles of MI. Each approach may have its advantages, with MI primarily used to address ambivalence and reluctance to change during early stages of change, whereas more directive interventions may be more helpful and appropriate at later stages. Further treatment development is needed to address the best ways to integrate such approaches (cf., Murphy & Eckhardt, 2005).

A third direction involves new intervention or assessment approaches that are based on or related to a stage-of-change model. Two general strategies for intervention that have developed in other areas of behavior change may apply here. One approach involves the use of multiple doses of relatively brief, targeted feedback and guidance that is specifically tailored to the individual's stage of change (e.g., Brug & van Assema, 2000; Dijkstra, De Vries, Roijackers, & van Breukelen, 1998), such as using automated protocols for delivering targeted feedback. The second approach involves developing a general sequential treatment process that is derived from a stage-of-change model (Morris & Alexander, 2005; Valesquez, Maurer, Crouch, & DiClemente, 2001).

From an assessment perspective, we now have a number of different methods and instruments for assessing stages of change. In a recent study, some of the same investigators featured in the current volume (Levesque, Velicer, Castle, & Greene, 2008) have developed a measure of "therapeutic resistance" to assess mind-sets and attitudes that might stand in the way of or discourage change. This new research represents a significant advance in the conceptualization of client resistance beyond the often mentioned denial and victim blaming to include system blaming, ongoing problems with the partner, problems in the treatment relationship or alliance, social justification, hopelessness, isolation, as well as countercontrolling reactance of an active or passive nature.

A fourth direction for future research involves more detailed application of specific components of the TTM, such as the processes of change, levels of change, decisional balance, and self-efficacy. Initial efforts have been made to address some of these constructs, such as victim changes over time in the study by Burkitt and Larkin (chapter 12) and treatment attendance and compliance in the study of Brodeur and colleagues (chapter 7). However, any attempt at component analysis remains in its infancy, in part because of a lack of assessment methods, when compared to the basic stage-of-change construct.

GENERAL SUMMARY

This book provides a sound and promising basis for applying TTM and MI concepts to facilitate change in both victims and perpetrators of intimate partner abuse. These studies also illustrate both the benefits and the challenges inherent in assessing and applying the concepts of readiness and motivation to change in this area. Despite many conceptual and measurement challenges, their results indicate that greater attention to stages of change and motivation to change in interventions for both perpetrators and victims of intimate partner abuse may have considerable payoff in refining our intervention methods for domestic violence and abuse. We hope this collection of studies will be useful not only as a summary and discussion of our present understanding but also as a stimulus for future development of the field.

REFERENCES

Babcock, J. C., Green, C. E., & Robie, C. (2004). Does batterers' treatment work? A meta-analytic review of domestic violence treatment. *Clinical Psychology Review, 23*, 1023–1053.

Begun, A. L., Murphy, C. M., Bolt, D., Weinstein, B., Strodthoff, T., Short, L., et al. (2003). Characteristics of the safe at home instrument for assessing readiness to change intimate partner violence. *Research on Social Work Practice, 13*, 80–107.

Brown, J. (1997). Working toward freedom from violence. *Violence Against Women, 3*, 5–26.

Brown, P. D., & O'Leary, K. D. (2000). Therapeutic alliance: Predicting continuance and success in group treatment for spouse abuse. *Journal of Consulting and Clinical Psychology, 68*, 340–345.

Brug, J., & van Assema, P. (2000). Differences in use and impact of computer-tailored dietary fat-feedback according to stage of change and education. *Appetite, 34,* 285–293.

Chang, J. C., Dado, D., Ashton, S., Hawker, L., Cluss, P. A., Buranosky, R., et al. (2006). Understanding behavior change for women experiencing intimate partner violence: Mapping the ups and downs using the stages of change. *Patient Education and Counseling, 62,* 330–339.

Daniels, J. W., & Murphy, C. M. (1997). Stages and processes of change in batterers' treatment. *Cognitive and Behavioral Practice, 4,* 123–145.

Dijkstra, A., De Vries, H., Roijackers, J., & van Breukelen, G. (1998). Tailored interventions to communicate stage-matched information to smokers in different motivational stages. *Journal of Consulting and Clinical Psychology, 66,* 549–557.

Douglas, K. S., & Kropp, P. R. (2002). A prevention-based paradigm for violence risk assessment: Clinical and research applications. *Criminal Justice and Behavior, 29,* 617–658.

Dutton, D. G. (1995). *The domestic assault of women: Psychological and criminal justice perspectives* (Rev. ed.). Vancouver: University of British Columbia Press.

Dutton, D. G., Bonarchuk, M., Kropp, R., Hart, S. D., & Ogloff, J. P. (1997). Client personality disorders affecting wife assault post-treatment recidivism. *Violence and Victims, 12,* 37–50.

Gondolf, E. W. (1988). The effect of batterer counseling on shelter outcome. *Journal of Interpersonal Violence, 3,* 275–289.

Gondolf, E. W. (2002). *Batterer intervention systems: Issues, outcomes, and recommendations.* Thousand Oaks, CA: Sage.

Gondolf, E. W., & White, R. J. (2001). Batterer program participants who repeatedly reassault: Psychopathic tendencies and other disorders. *Journal of Interpersonal Violence, 16,* 361–380.

Hilton, Z. N., Harris, G. T., Rice, M. E., Lang, C., Cormier, C. A., & Lines, K. J. (2004). A brief actuarial assessment for the prediction of wife assault recidivism: The Ontario Domestic Assault Risk Assessment. *Psychological Assessment, 16,* 267–275.

Holtzworth-Munroe, A., Meehan, J. C., Herron, K., Rehman, U., & Stuart, G. L. (2000). Testing the Holtzworth–Munroe and Stuart (1994) batterer typology. *Journal of Consulting and Clinical Psychology, 68,* 1000–1019.

Holtzworth-Munroe, A., & Stuart, G. L. (1994). Typologies of male batterers: Three subtypes and the differences among them. *Psychological Bulletin, 116,* 476–497.

Kropp, P. R. (2004). Some questions regarding spousal assault risk assessment. *Violence Against Women, 10,* 676–697.

Kropp, P. R., & Hart, S. D. (2000). The spousal assault risk assessment (SARA) guide: Reliability and validity in adult male offenders. *Law and Human Behavior, 24,* 101–118.

Levesque, D. A., Gelles, R. J., & Velicer, W. F. (2000). Development and validation of a stages of change measure for men in batterer treatment. *Cognitive Therapy and Research, 24,* 175–199.

Levesque, D. A., Velicer, W. F., Castle, P. H., & Greene, R. N. (2008). Resistance among domestic violence offenders. *Violence Against Women, 14,* 158–184.

Maiuro, R. D., & Eberle, J. A. (2008). State standards for domestic violence perpetrator treatment: Current status, trends, and recommendations. *Violence and Victims, 23,* 133–155.

Miller, W. R., & Rollnick, S. (2002). *Motivational interviewing: Preparing people to change addictive behavior* (2nd ed.). New York: Guilford Press.

Miller, W. R., Yahne, C. E., Moyers, T. B., Martinez, J., & Pirritano, M. (2004). A randomized trial of methods to help clinicians learn motivational interviewing. *Journal of Consulting and Clinical Psychology, 72,* 1050–1062.

Morris, E. S., & Alexander, P. C. (2005, July). *Stages of change and the group treatment of batterers.* Paper presented at the Ninth International Family Violence Research Conference, Portsmouth, NH.

Murphy, C. M., Alexander, P. C., Black, D. A., & Morris, E. S. (2005, July). *Different perspectives on readiness to change of batterers.* Paper presented at the Ninth International Family Violence Research Conference, Portsmouth, NH.

Murphy, C. M., & Eckhardt, C. I. (2005). *Treating the abusive partner: An individualized, cognitive-behavioral approach.* New York: Guilford Press.

Murphy, C. M., Morrel, T. M., Elliott, J. D., & Neavins, T. M. (2003). A prognostic indicator scale for the treatment of domestic abuse perpetrators. *Journal of Interpersonal Violence, 18,* 1087–1105.

Prochaska, J. O., & DiClemente, C. C. (1984). *The transtheoretical approach: Crossing the traditional boundaries of therapy.* Homewood, IL: Dow Jones-Irwin.

Prochaska, J. O., & DiClemente, C. C. (2005). The transtheoretical approach. In J. C. Norcross & M. R. Goldfried (Eds.), *Handbook of psychotherapy integration* (2nd ed., pp. 147–171). London: Oxford University Press.

Prochaska, J. O., DiClemente, C. C., & Norcross, J. C. (1992). In search of how people change: Applications to addictive behaviors. *American Psychologist, 47,* 1102–1114.

Prochaska, J. O., Johnson, S., & Lee, P. (1998). The transtheoretical model of behavior change. In S. A. Shumaker, E. B. Schron, & J. K. Ockene (Eds.), *Handbook of health behavior change* (2nd ed., pp. 59–84). New York: Springer.

Prochaska, J.O., & Velicer, W. F. (1997). The transtheoretical model of health behavior change. *American Journal of Health Promotion, 12,* 38–48.

Remington, N., & Murphy, C. (2001, November). *Treatment outcomes of partner violence perpetrators with psychopathic and borderline personality characteristics.* Paper presented at the annual meeting of the Association for the Advancement of Behavior Therapy, Philadelphia.

Taft, C. T., Murphy, C. M., Elliott, J. D., & Morrel, T. M. (2001). Attendance enhancing procedures in group counseling for domestic abusers. *Journal of Counseling Psychology, 48,* 51–60.

Taft, C. T., Murphy, C. M., King, D. W., Musser, P. H., & DeDeyn, J. M. (2003). Process and treatment adherence factors in group cognitive-behavioral therapy for partner violent men. *Journal of Consulting and Clinical Psychology, 71,* 812–820.

Valesquez, M. M., Maurer, G. G., Crouch, C., & DiClemente, C. C. (2001). *Group treatment for substance abuse: A stages-of-change therapy manual.* New York: Guilford Press.

Weisz, A. N., Tolman, R. M., & Saunders, D. G. (2000). Assessing the risk of severe domestic violence: The importance of survivors' predictions. *Journal of Interpersonal Violence, 15,* 75–90.

Working With Perpetrators

2

Motivational Interviewing as a Mechanism for Change in Men Who Batter: A Randomized Controlled Trial

BARBARA R. KISTENMACHER AND ROBERT L. WEISS

During the last three decades, domestic violence has received increased attention in the clinical literature. The enactment of mandatory arrest laws for domestic violence in the late 1970s brought about a dramatic increase in the use of court-mandated treatment for men who batter. Since then, researchers have been grappling with the question of whether batterers' treatment is effective in reducing or ceasing abusive behavior. A recent review of methodologically sound outcome studies conducted over the past decade concluded that, at best, batterers' treatment can produce modest reductions in violence for certain types of men (Babcock & LaTaillade, 2000). Regardless of the model used, batterers' treatment is more likely to work when delivered in the context of a coordinated community response (Babcock & LaTaillade, 2000; Babcock & Steiner, 1999; Murphy, Musser, & Maton, 1998). Unfortunately, implementation of this approach is hampered by the lack of community follow through with legal sanctions for noncompliance (Babcock & Steiner, 1999). Further, a one-size-fits-all approach is no longer deemed effective, as treatment matching seems to be crucial to achieving successful outcomes (Levesque, Gelles, & Velicer, 2000). In sum, small effect sizes, the paucity of effectively coordinated community programs, and the lack of attention paid to treatment matching have left researchers and clinicians feeling less than optimistic about the effectiveness of any particular model of batterers' treatment.

In addition to program effectiveness, batterers' motivation to change remains central to the discussion of whether treatment is an appropriate vehicle through which to reduce or end domestic violence. Most battering men are motivated to enter treatment by external pressure rather than by the type of internal motivation that is usually connected with treatment success. Daniels and Murphy (1997) assert that the apparent lack of treatment benefit reflected by small effect sizes is related to treatment programs' failure to address directly this lack of motivation. The current study tests the potential utility of an intervention, motivational interviewing (MI), that matches counselor approach to batterer motivation.

THE TRANSTHEORETICAL MODEL AND BATTERERS' TREATMENT

For over a decade, researchers have been considering the utility of the transtheoretical model of change (Prochaska & DiClemente, 1982) as an adjunct to existing batterers' treatment models (Begun, Strodhoff, Weinstein, Shelley, & Short, 1997; Daniels & Murphy, 1997; Levesque, Gelles, & Velicer, 1997; Murphy & Baxter, 1997). Interest in this model has piqued given that the two major approaches to batterers' treatment (cognitive behavioral and feminist psychoeducational) have been criticized for operating under simplistic assumptions about the process of change. The cognitive behavioral approach assumes the batterer is in the action stage and is therefore ready to learn new skills. On the other hand, the feminist psychoeducational approach assumes the batterer is in the precontemplation stage and therefore is not motivated to change his behavior. Further, feminist models often assume that the "content to be changed" (i.e., gender role socialization) is the same for every batterer. A central tenant of the transtheoretical model is that clients vary in their readiness for change and that therapeutic outcome depends on how well a therapist adjusts his/her strategy accordingly (Prochaska & DiClemente, 1992).

Work conducted by Levesque and colleagues (2000) indicated that domestic abusers who were in the more advanced stages of change were more likely to try to end their violence, blame their partners less, value the pros of changing more than the cons, make the greatest rates of positive change, and more likely to remain in treatment than those in the less advanced stages. An intervention that is tailored to a batterer's level of motivation while, at the same time, focused on propelling him to a more advanced stage of change is worthy of investigation.

MOTIVATIONAL INTERVIEWING AND BATTERERS' TREATMENT

Developed in the spirit of the transtheoretical model, MI (see Miller & Rollnick, 1991) was designed to facilitate movement through the stages of change. Outcome studies indicate that MI not only has been successful with highly resistant alcoholics, but has also been instrumental in helping other groups make significant changes in their behavior (Bien, Miller, & Boroughs, 1993; Brown & Miller, 1993; Miller, Benefield, & Tonigan, 1993). Given that lack of motivation is the greatest obstacle to treating battering men (Daniels & Murphy, 1997; Ganley, 1987), combined with the documented success rates of MI with other populations, the application of MI to batterers' treatment is a logical next step (Murphy & Baxter, 1997).

Motivational interviewing may be a useful model for addressing battering men's denial because the goal is for them to become confronted with a discrepancy between what they believe or want and how they behave. Most battering men do not believe in hitting women, yet their behavior suggests otherwise. The means by which denial is addressed by MI, however, is not one of direct confrontation, which is heavily relied upon by many batterers' treatment programs. Rather, the client is invited to make the arguments for change; the therapist simply provides the direction (via the use of open-ended questions that invite change talk) and the atmosphere (i.e., one of unconditional positive regard) in which this can happen. Further, MI may work in conjunction with men's tendency to solve problems independently (Ganley, 1987) because this approach emphasizes autonomy over one's decisions and behavior.

HYPOTHESES

The purpose of the present investigation is to test whether the documented success of MI can be extended to a population of battering men who have been court mandated to a batterer's treatment program. Before attending their mandated treatment program, battering men were randomized to either two sessions of MI or a no-treatment control condition. Hypotheses include these: (a) the MI group will demonstrate a significantly greater pre-to-post increase in their readiness for changing violent behavior compared to the control group; more specifically, readiness for change will be demonstrated by a greater decrease in precontemplation, and a greater increase in contemplation and action; and (b) the MI group will demonstrate a significantly greater pre-to-post decrease in self-reported external attributions for their violence compared to the control group.

METHOD

Participants

A total of 123 men from Lane County, Oregon, were arrested for domestic violence and mandated to batterers' treatment during the 1-year period the study was conducted. Of these men, 33 (27%) participated in the current study. Also, 90 (73%) men did not participate because they refused the offer, had already begun the treatment program, had been sent back to jail, or were never offered participation. No one refused research consent once they agreed to participate and attended the first visit.

Participants were recruited from one of three potential entry points into the Lane County batterers' treatment system. In all, 64% (n = 21) were recruited from the local parole and probation office, 30% (n = 10) were recruited from a local mental health treatment program that was responsible for screening and referring mandated populations to treatment, and 6% (n = 2) were recruited from a local batterers' treatment program that offered services to mandated clients. All participants, regardless of recruitment source, were recruited in a private space or over the telephone. Those directly or indirectly involved in the batterers' court cases (i.e., parole officers, counselors from the treatment program to which they were mandated, etc.) were not informed of their decision to participate or decline. To reduce the potential that behavior would be motivated by the desire to perform in a socially desirable manner, participants were informed that their participation would not be communicated to anyone involved in their case, even if they requested for this to happen.

A total of 48% (n = 16) of the participants endorsed committing at least one severe act of partner violence over the past year on the Conflict Tactics Scale (CTS; Straus, 1979). Participants also had a noteworthy arrest history with an average of 6.94 arrests (SD = 10.97) for any crime. Finally, 64% of the men had been referred to drug and/or alcohol treatment at one point in their lives. Demographic information on the sample is provided in Table 2.1.

Table 2.1

PARTICIPANT DEMOGRAPHIC INFORMATION BY GROUP

VARIABLE	TREATMENT	CONTROL	FULL SAMPLE
Mean age (years)	35.1 (9.3)	39.4 (12.1)	37.3 (10.9)
Mean monthly income ($)	$1,102 ($884)	$1,626 ($1,310)	$1,381 ($1,144)
Highest education completed (years)	11.2 (2.6)	11.2 (3.3)	11.2 (2.9)
Ethnicity			
% Euro-American	75	94	8
% Native-American	13	6	9
% African American	6	6	3
% Asian	6	6	3
Mean number of times married	1.0 (1.0)	1.0 (.9)	1.0 (1.0)
Mean number of times divorced	.8 (.9)	.7 (.9)	.7 (.9)
Mean number of children	1.4 (1.1)	2.4 (2.1)	1.9 (1.8)

Note. Standard deviations are in parentheses. There were no significant differences between treatment and control groups on all variables.

Men who were arrested for partner violence, mandated to batterers' treatment, and who had not yet attended the first mandated group were eligible for the study. Participants were randomly assigned to either receive MI ($n = 16$) or no intervention ($n = 17$). They were paid $15 for completing baseline assessments (both groups) and participating in the first MI session (experimental group), and an additional $25 for completing the posttest assessments (both groups) and participating in the second MI session (experimental group).

Materials

Conflict Tactics Scale Form N (CTS)

The CTS (Straus, 1979) is a 36-item self-report questionnaire that measures the extent to which partners use certain tactics to handle relationship conflict. In the present study, all three subscales were used to provide participants with feedback as a part of the MI intervention, and the physical violence subscale was used to assess participants' level of relationship violence for descriptive purposes. For husband-to-wife conflict, internal consistency reliability is low (α = .50) for the reasoning subscale and high (α = .80 and .83) for the verbal aggression and violence subscales, respectively (Straus, 1979). When college students' reports of husband-to-wife CTS scores were compared to their parents' reports, correlations were .19, .51, and .64 for the reasoning, verbal aggression, and violence subscales, respectively (Bulcroft & Straus, 1975). These correlations indicate a low level of concurrent validity for reasoning and a high level of concurrent validity for the verbal aggression and violence subscales (Straus, 1979).

Revised Gudjonsson Blame Attribution Inventory (BAI-R)

The BAI-R (Gudjonsson & Singh, 1989) is a 42-item, forced-choice, self-report measure of an individual's attributions for a particular crime. Participants respond to each item by circling true or false. Only the 15-item external attribution subscale was used in the present study. External attributions are defined by the extent to which subjects blame the victim and society for their behavior and report certain justifications for their crime. Sample items include: (a) "What I did was beyond my control"; and (b) "I am entirely to blame for my crime" (reverse scored). The external attribution subscale is scored by adding the number of subscale-consistent responses (true or false). The 2-month test–retest reliability for the external attribution subscale is .85 (Gudjonsson, 1984). Construct validity for the external attribution subscale is suggested by low, but significant, correlations with Rotter's External Locus of Control Scale (r = .24), the Hostility and Direction of Hostility Questionnaire (r = .21), and the Eysenck Personality Questionnaire Psychotocism subscale (r = .21) (Gudjonsson & Singh, 1989).

Stages of Change Questionnaire (SOCQ)

The SOCQ (McConnaughy, Prochaska, & Velicer, 1983) is a 32-item self-report measure of an individual's readiness for changing a problem behavior. For the present study, the wording of all 32 items was revised to specify violence as the problem. For example, the SOCQ precontemplation item, "As far as I'm concerned, I don't have any problems that need changing," was changed to, "As far as I'm concerned, I don't have any problems with violence that need changing." This strategy is consistent with that used by substance abuse researchers to increase the specificity of SOCQ items (Rollnick, Heather, Gold, & Hall, 1992). The SOCQ is composed of four 8-item subscales that measure each of the stages of change (precontemplation, contemplation, action, and maintenance) specified by Prochaska and DiClemente (1992). Each item is rated on a Likert scale ranging from 1 (strongly disagree) to 5 (strongly agree). Each subscale is scored by computing a mean of the Likert responses for each item.

The SOCQ was also used during the MI intervention to provide feedback regarding participants' readiness for change. Based on a profile of the four subscale scores, each participant was classified into 1 of 10 clusters that define his readiness for change (McConnaughy, DiClemente, Prochaska, & Velicer, 1989; McConnaughy et al., 1983). The SOCQ has high internal consistency with subscale alpha coefficients ranging from .88 to .89 in one study (McConnaughy et al., 1983) and ranging from .79 to .84 in a second study (McConnaughy et al., 1989).

Therapist Training

Two male and three female therapists were trained over the course of 4 months on MI strategies (Miller & Rollnick, 1991). Of these, four were third-year doctoral students in clinical or counseling psychology, and one of the therapists was an undergraduate student with past clinical experience working with alcohol abusers. Therapist training included weekly 2-hour training sessions, supplemented by instructional videotapes and reading assignments (Miller & Rollnick, 1991). The first 2 months of the weekly training sessions included a discussion of strategies and role plays of various techniques. During the last month of training, therapists participated in four 50-minute role plays with either an undergraduate male actor or a former batterer who had completed a domestic violence treatment program. The principal investigator provided each therapist with 1 hour of supervision for each role play and randomly selected role plays were critiqued in peer supervision. Therapists also became familiar with the battering population by attending at least one 3-hour feminist psychoeducational batterers' treatment group at a local counseling agency.

Each therapist's final role play was rated by the principal investigator and another experienced doctoral level MI researcher on adherence to MI. Ratings were based on the first pass global ratings of the Motivational

Interviewing Skill Code (Miller, 1998). The raters also made a global forced choice (yes/no) judgment about whether the therapist adhered to MI. Finally, the first and last 10 minutes of each role play were coded for whether the therapists' behavior was MI Consistent, MI Inconsistent, or Other. To be qualified for the study, therapists had to meet the following criteria: (a) the average of the raters' ratings of the six therapist behavior dimensions of the first pass MI Skill Code had to be at least 5 on a 7-point scale; (b) both raters (PI and doctoral level researcher) had to answer "yes" to the question about whether the therapist adhered to MI; and (c) the average percentage of the two raters' ratings of MI consistency had to be at least 70%. All but one male therapist met the criteria, resulting in four trained therapists (three female and one male) for the study. On average, the four trained therapists were 77% MI consistent at the beginning of the study. The average rating for adherence to MI based on the six therapist behavior dimensions was 6 on a scale of 1–7.

Adherence to the MI Model

To determine fidelity to the MI model, therapist speech was coded by four undergraduate research assistants. They were trained over the course of 6 months on the Second Pass Behavior Counts of the Motivational Interviewing Skill Code (Miller, 1998). During the first 2 months of training, coders watched instructional videotapes (Miller, Rollnick, & Moyers, 1998), read the MI manual (Miller & Rollnick, 1991), and participated in weekly 1-hour meetings. During the next 4 months, they learned the MI Skill Code and achieved a standard of reliability. The MI Skill Code involves having coders classify every therapist utterance into 1 of 20 categories, some of which are consistent, some of which are inconsistent, and one of which is neither consistent nor inconsistent with MI strategies. Weekly 2-hour meetings were used to discuss weekly coding assignments and discrepancies among coders. Coders were considered reliable when the mean of every possible correlation between coders was at least .75 for each of the 20 codes.

All MI sessions were videotaped. After coders were fully trained, each therapist utterance was coded by two of four trained undergraduate research assistants. Sessions were randomly assigned to coders so that every possible combination of two coders was used equally and so that coders coded an equal number of first and second MI sessions. In all, 25% ($n = 7$) of the MI sessions were coded by all four coders for the purpose of determining reliability.

For these sessions, separate alpha coefficients were computed for each of the 10 MI behavior codes that occurred with sufficient frequency (at least once according to each coder). Alphas ranged from .63 to .97, with a mean alpha of .87 across the following 10 codes: Inform–General Information, Closed-ended Question, Open-ended Question, Reflect, Structure, Support, Affirm, Facilitate, Filler, and Inform–Personal Feedback. For the remaining 10 codes, alpha coefficients could not be computed because there were too many behavior counts of zero. Five of these 10 codes (Reframe, Direct, Warn, Raise Concern With Permission, and Raise Concern Without Permission) received counts of zero from every rater across all sessions, thus indicating good reliability, in that coders saw no behavior. The remaining five codes (Advise With Permission, Inform–Self-Disclosure, Advise Without Permission, Confront, and Emphasize Control) received mostly zeros with a few scattered counts of one or two, thus indicating good reliability.

To test the extent to which the therapists delivered the experimental intervention, therapist behavior counts from the Motivational Interviewing Skill Code were tallied for each coded session. For each of the 20 possible codes/behaviors, an average was computed across all (either two or four) coders, and then a total was computed for all MI sessions. Each of the 20 codes was categorized as either (a) MI Consistent, (b) MI Inconsistent, or (c) Other. The percentage of MI-consistent therapist behaviors was calculated by dividing the total number of MI-consistent utterances by the total number of utterances for all sessions (averaged across coders). The same procedure was followed for computing the percentage of MI Inconsistent and Other therapist behaviors.

Procedure

Assignment to either the experimental or control condition was randomly made before participants agreed to be in the study. During the first (time 1) visit, both experimental and control participants completed a battery of self-report questionnaires. Participants assigned to the experimental group then met with one of four trained therapists for 50–60 minutes; the therapist provided objective feedback on the results of the CTS and the SOCQ using MI strategies (Miller & Rollnick, 1991). Control participants received nothing.

Approximately 2 weeks after their first visit, participants presented to the University of Oregon a second time (time 2). Individuals in the experimental group first met with the same therapist as in time 1 for 50–60 minutes. During the session, the therapist used MI strategies to engage the participant in a discussion about his battering behavior and required entry into treatment. The session focused on unearthing the client's ambivalence about his battering behavior, using OARS techniques (i.e., open-ended questions, affirmations, reflections, and summaries), strategies for handling resistance (e.g., reflection), and strategies for eliciting change talk (e.g., evocative open-ended questions, inviting elaboration of change talk, looking forward, exploring goals and values, etc.). The goal of the session was to provide a collaborative, nonjudgmental environment in which the therapist could invite the client to make his own arguments for change and ultimately experience increased motivation for reducing or ending battering behavior. Finally, at the end of the second visit, experimental and control participants completed the same battery of questionnaires.

RESULTS

Participant Attrition

Of the original 33 participants, 28 (85%) men completed both phases of the study. More specifically, 16 of the original 17 (94%) control participants and 12 of the original 16 (75%) MI participants completed time 1 and time 2. Fisher's exact test indicated that the difference in dropout rates between the two groups was not statistically significant, $p = .18$.

Tests of Experimental Integrity

Sample Integrity

To test whether participants differed from nonparticipants (i.e., those who refused the offer to participate), a series of independent samples t tests and chi-square tests were conducted on demographic variables.[1] To meet the chi-square requirement that cells have a minimum frequency count of 5, the education and ethnicity variables were collapsed into two levels (high school diploma or less vs. more than high school diploma; and White vs. other). There were no significant differences between participants and nonparticipants on a variety of demographic attributes, including age, monthly income, number of times married and divorced, number of children, education, and ethnicity. Further, these two groups did not differ on number of arrests for any crime, number of arrests for domestic violence, participation in past domestic violence treatment, and past referral to drug or alcohol treatment. Participants did spend significantly more days in jail for a domestic violence charge than non-participants, $t(88) = 2.56$, $p < .05$. This difference, however, seemed to be more a function of outliers and was not statistically significant when the outliers were removed, $t(83) = 2.13$, $p = .11$.

Pretreatment Equivalence of Groups

Participants assigned to the MI group were compared to those assigned to the control group on demographic variables and time 1 dependent variables. A series of independent samples t tests, chi-square tests, and Fisher's exact tests indicated that MI participants did not significantly differ from control participants on age, monthly income, number of times married and divorced, number of children, education, and ethnicity. Further, the two groups did not significantly differ on domestic violence—specific variables, including number of arrests for any crime, number of arrests for domestic violence, number of months spent in jail for a domestic violence charge, past participation in domestic violence treatment, and past referral to drug or alcohol treatment. Finally, the two groups did not significantly differ on all time 1 dependent variables.

Dropouts Versus Completers

Participants who completed time 1 and time 2 were compared to those who dropped out on all demographic variables. A series of independent samples t tests, chi-square tests, and Fisher's exact tests indicated that completers did not significantly differ from dropouts on age, monthly income, number of times married and divorced, number of children, education, and ethnicity. In addition, the two groups did not significantly differ on number of arrests for any crime, number of arrests for domestic violence, number of months spent in jail for domestic violence, past participation domestic violence treatment, and past referral to drug or alcohol treatment.

Intervention Integrity

A total of 91% of the therapist utterances were MI Consistent (range = 85%–94.5%), 8% were MI Inconsistent (range = 5%–14%), and 1% were Other (range = .5%–2%). Therefore, therapists demonstrated substantial fidelity to the MI manual.

Data Manipulation

For all dependent variables, difference scores were calculated by subtracting the score that was expected to be smaller from the score that was expected to be larger, according to the hypotheses. For example, if an increase in a particular variable was expected, the formula for the difference score would be: (T2–T1). Conversely, if a decrease in a particular variable was expected, the formula for the difference score would be: (T1–T2). For each group (MI and control), time 1, time 2, and difference score data were examined for missing values, normality, and univariate outliers. Difference score data were missing for all variables for one control and four MI participants as a result of attrition from time 1 to time 2. Means and standard deviations for all dependent variables, after outliers were removed, are displayed in Table 2.2.

Data Analyses

A one-way, between-subjects, multivariate analysis of variance (MANOVA) was conducted to test whether the MI group, relative to the

Table 2.2

MEANS AND STANDARD DEVIATIONS FOR ALL DEPENDENT VARIABLES

| VARIABLE | MI | | | CONTROL | | |
	T1	T2	DIFFERENCE SCORE	T1	T2	DIFFERENCE SCORE
Precontemplation	2.11 (.15)	2.17 (.20)	−.13 (.13)	2.40 (.21)	2.35 (.19)	.05 (.11)
Contemplation	3.85 (.16)	3.93 (.18)	.01 (.09)	3.76 (.18)	3.56 (.25)	−.29 (.14)
Action	3.61 (.16)	3.76 (.12)	.17 (.16)	3.74 (.20)	3.51 (.24)	−.24 (.12)
External Attributions	5.06 (3.44)	4.10 (2.18)	1.40 (2.32)	4.76 (2.95)	4.69 (3.03)	−.06 (1.12)

Note. T1 = Time 1; T2 = Time 2. See text for explanation of how difference scores were computed for each variable. Sample size varies according to variable owing to missing data and removal of outliers; see text for explanation of sample size. Standard deviations are in parentheses.

control group, demonstrated a significantly greater pre-to-post increase in their readiness for change. Precontemplation, contemplation, and action difference scores from the SOCQ served as the dependent variables. Two outlying contemplation difference scores were removed from the analysis based on the following criteria: (a) they had to appear as outlying values in the box and whiskers plot, and (b) they had to be greater than two standard deviations from the mean. Group (MI vs. control) served as a two-level between-subjects independent variable. The group main effect was statistically significant, Wilks's $\lambda = .70$, $F(3, 22) = 3.3$, $p = .04$.[2] Follow-up univariate analyses revealed that action was the variable that maximized group differences. This was consistent with predictions, as the MI group demonstrated a pre-to-post increase in action, and the control group showed a decrease in action. Similarly, the MI group demonstrated a pre-to-post increase in contemplation, and the control group showed a pre-to-post decrease in contemplation. This difference was not statistically significant, although a trend was present, $p = .11$. Contrary to predictions, the control group demonstrated a pre-to-post decrease (trend) in precontemplation, and the MI showed a slight increase in precontemplation, $p = .06$. The strength of association between the independent variable (Group) and the linear combination of dependent variables was $\eta^2 = .31$, indicating that 31% of the variance in the dependent variables is attributable to group differences.

An unequal variance independent samples t test was conducted to determine whether the MI group, relative to the control group, demonstrated a significantly greater pre-to-post decrease in external attributions. The dependent variable was the external attributions difference score (T1–T2). Group (MI vs. control) served as the two level between subjects independent variable. Two outlying time 2 external attribution scores were removed from the analysis based on the aforementioned criteria for removing outliers (see stages of change analyses). The predicted effect for Group was significant at the one-tailed level, $t(11.68) = -1.9$, $p = .04$.[3] Table 2.3 provides a summary of data analyses outcomes.

DISCUSSION

The goal of the present study was to determine whether motivational interviewing (MI) is an effective strategy for increasing readiness to change violent behavior and decreasing external blame in battering men. Partial support was found for the hypotheses under investigation. Consistent with predictions, the MI group demonstrated a significantly

Table 2.3

TEST STATISTICS AND CORRESPONDING *p*-VALUES FOR DEPENDENT VARIABLES

VARIABLE	df	TEST STATISTIC	p
Precontemplation	1, 24	3.91	.06
Contemplation	1, 24	2.71	.11
Action	1, 24	5.44	.03*
External Attributions	11.68	−1.86	.04*

Note. The test statistic for the Precontemplation, Contemplation, and Action variables is *F.* The test statistic for the External Attributions variable is *t.*
*p < .05.

greater overall improvement on stages of change subscales. More specifically, the MI group demonstrated a significant pre-to-post increase in self-reported action toward changing their violent behavior; the control group reported taking less action over time. Consistent with this finding, the MI group also demonstrated a pre-to-post increase (trend) in contemplation about changing their violent behavior, but the control group contemplated change less over time. Contrary to predictions, the control group demonstrated a pre-to-post decrease (trend) in precontemplation scores, and the MI group demonstrated a slight increase in precontemplation over time. Consistent with predictions, the MI group placed less blame on their victim, society, and other external factors as a function of the intervention.

At first glance, it might be tempting to interpret the precontemplation findings as MI contributing to resistance. The greater precontemplation difference score for the control group, however, was largely due to a decrease in precontemplation scores from time 1 to time 2 for the control group as opposed to an increase in these scores for the MI group. Further, the idea that MI contributes to resistance is not supported by the action and contemplation findings. More likely, the individual stages of change subscales should not be interpreted in isolation of one another. A profile analysis that examines the relative position of each subscale may provide a more comprehensive story. In fact, this is the method recommended by Prochaska and DiClemente (1992). Simultaneous examination of the three subscale difference scores paints a picture of decreased resistance combined with a decrease in contemplation and action for the control group, and little change in resistance combined with increased contemplation and action for the MI group. Based on these findings, it is possible that MI facilitates motivation via increasing thoughts of readiness for change rather than decreasing thoughts related to resistance about change. This hypothesis is consistent with recent research that indicates the mechanism of action for MI lies in increased commitment statements, driven by change talk. Given a larger sample, it would be fruitful to conduct a profile analysis of SOCQ subscale scores to see whether MI produced an overall improvement in stages of change clusters.

Men who received the MI intervention were able to take more responsibility for their behavior than those who did not receive MI. This finding is promising in light of the attribution literature indicating that battering men rarely attribute the cause of their violent behavior to themselves (Bograd, 1988; Dutton, 1986; Shields & Hanneke, 1983). This finding, combined with the SOCQ findings, is consistent with other data that indicate batterers in the most advanced stage of change clusters engage in less partner blame (Levesque et al., 2000).

These data beg the question: Does increased motivation and decreased external attributions set the stage for violence reduction? In other words, can thoughts about violence predict violent behavior and, if so, should therapeutic intervention focus on altering batterer's thoughts, perceptions, or cognitions? Recent research suggests a connection between beliefs about aggression and actual performed acts of aggression (Archer & Graham-Kevan, 2003), although the direction of this connection is unclear owing to the lack of a randomized controlled design. Archer and Kevan found that instrumental beliefs about violence (i.e., that violence is sometimes necessary to get something accomplished) are predictive of violent behavior toward an intimate partner. Interestingly, the scale items that are used to measure instrumental beliefs (EXPAGG items) and external attributions (BAI-R items) are similar. Questions worth exploring in future studies include the following: (a) Are external attributions predictive of violent behavior in a similar way that instrumental beliefs are? (b) What is the directional relationship between beliefs about violence and violent behavior? Answers to these questions would get us one step closer to determining whether therapeutic efforts should focus on changing perceptions about violence.

Future studies should consider the following methodological improvements. First, a larger sample size is mandatory. Although group differences were found with a small sample size, more participants are needed to statistically compare dropouts and completers in order to conduct more sophisticated analyses (i.e., profile analyses) and to see whether trends identified in the current study would evolve into stronger findings. Second, an equivalent control condition should be created to equalize the amount of effort required to participate across the two conditions and to test whether MI is responsible for changes as opposed to the experience of receiving attention from a therapist. Third, it is important to keep in mind the brevity of the MI intervention. The modest findings may be related to the fact that the difference in the two levels of the independent variable was not very strong. The impact of a higher "dosage" of MI on readiness to change and external blame should be explored in future studies.

Finally, the effectiveness of MI in reducing domestic violence behavior should be examined. For this to be accomplished, MI should be paired with a particular treatment protocol, and behaviors such as treatment compliance and violent behavior should be measured. Motivational interviewing is not necessarily a strategy that can be used alone to change violent behavior, but rather one that could be used in conjunction with existing models (e.g., CBT, mindfulness, etc.) to improve outcomes. Perhaps variables such as readiness for change and external attributions mediate the relationship between MI and more concrete behavior.

The current study represents one of the first empirical attempts to measure the effectiveness of MI with battering men. Study findings indicated that MI was useful in moving participants toward greater action about changing their violent behavior. Participants receiving MI, compared to those who did not, also tended to blame external factors for their violence less. In summary, MI shows promise as a potential strategy for increasing readiness for change in battering men.

ACKNOWLEDGMENTS

The authors express sincere appreciation to David Boyer, Anne DePrince, Heidi Ellis, and Krista Gragg, for giving their time to serve as MI therapists. We also thank Bill Miller for providing expertise and support in training the principal investigator on MI techniques. Appreciation also goes to Ruth Golar for coordinating a team of 15 research assistants. We also thank the Lane County Corrections Parole and Probation Unit and Lane County Mental Health in Eugene, Oregon, for assisting in the recruitment of study participants. Finally, special thanks goes to study participants for making themselves vulnerable enough for us to learn from them.

NOTES

1. Agency staff collected demographic data for every man who was eligible to participate. These data were later sorted by the principal investigator and classified as participant or nonparticipant data.
2. A trend ($p = .11$) was demonstrated when outliers were retained.
3. The effect of group was not significant when outlying values were retained.

REFERENCES

Archer, J., & Graham-Kevan, N. (2003). Do beliefs about aggression predict physical aggression to partners? *Aggressive Behavior, 29,* 41–54.

Babcock, J. C., & LaTaillade, J. (2000). Evaluating interventions for men who batter. In J. Vincent & E. Jouriles (Eds.), *Domestic violence: Guidelines for research-informed practice* (pp. 37–77). Philadelphia: Jessica Kingsley Publishers.

Babcock, J. C., & Steiner, R. (1999). The relationship between treatment, incarceration, and recidivism of battering: A program evaluation of Seattle's coordinated community response to domestic violence. *Journal of Family Psychology, 13,* 46–59.

Begun, A., Strodhoff, T., Weinstein, B., Shelley, G., & Short, L. (1997, June). *Development of an instrument to assess readiness to change battering behavior: Preliminary results.* Paper presented at the 5th International Family Violence Research Conference, Durham, NH.

Bien, T. H., Miller, W. R., & Boroughs, J. M. (1993). Motivational interviewing with alcohol outpatients. *Behavioural and Cognitive Psychotherapy, 21,* 347–356.

Bograd, M. (1988). How battered women and abusive men account for domestic violence: Excuses, justifications, or explanations? In G. T. Hotaling, D. Finkelhor, J. T. Kirkpatrick, & M. A. Straus (Eds.), *Coping with family violence: Research and policy perspectives* (pp. 60–70). Newbury Park, CA: Sage.

Brown, J. M., & Miller, W. R. (1993). Impact of motivational interviewing on participation and outcome in residential alcoholism treatment. *Psychology of Addictive Behaviors, 7,* 211–218.

Bulcroft, R., & Straus, M. (1975). *Validity of husband, wife, and child reports of intra-family violence and power.* University of New Hampshire, Family Violence Research Program, mimeographed paper V16.

Daniels, J. W., & Murphy, C. M. (1997). Stages and processes of change in batterer's treatment. *Cognitive Behavioral Practice, 4,* 123–145.

Dutton, D. G. (1986). Wife assaulters' explanations for assault: The neutralization of self-punishment. *Canadian Journal of Behavioral Science, 18,* 381–390.

Ganley, A. L. (1987). Perpetrators of domestic violence: An overview of counseling the court-mandated client. In D. J. Sonkin (Ed.), *Domestic violence on trial: Psychological and legal dimensions of family violence* (pp. 155–174). New York: Springer.

Gudjonsson, G. H. (1984). Attribution of blame for criminal acts and its relationship with personality. *Personality and Individual Differences, 5,* 53–58.

Gudjonsson, G. H., & Singh, K. K. (1989). The revised Gudjonsson blame attribution inventory. *Personality and Individual Differences, 10,* 67–70.

Levesque, D. A., Gelles, R. J., & Velicer, W. F. (2000). Development and validation of a stages of change measure for men in batterer treatment. *Cognitive Therapy and Research, 24,* 175–199.

McConnaughy, E. A., DiClemente, C. C., Prochaska, J. O., & Velicer, W. F. (1989). Stages of change in psychotherapy: A follow-up report. *Psychotherapy, 26,* 494–503.

McConnaughy, E. A., Prochaska, J. O., & Velicer, W. F. (1983). Stages of change in psychotherapy: Measurement and sample profiles. *Psychotherapy: Theory, Research, and Practice, 20,* 368–375.

Miller, W. R. (1998). *Motivational interviewing skill code.* Unpublished manuscript.

Miller, W. R., Benefield, G., & Tonigan, J. S. (1993). Enhancing motivation for change in problem drinking: A controlled comparison of two therapist styles. *Journal of Consulting and Clinical Psychology, 61,* 455–461.

Miller, W. R., & Rollnick, S. (Eds.). (1991). *Motivational interviewing: Preparing people to change addictive behaviors.* New York: Guilford Press.

Miller, W. R., Rollnick, S., & Moyers, T. (1998). *Motivational interviewing: Professional training videotape series* [Videotape Series]. (Available from The University of New Mexico, Albuquerque, New Mexico.)

Murphy, C. M., & Baxter, V. A. (1997). Motivating batterers to change in the treatment context. *Journal of Interpersonal Violence, 12,* 607–619.

Murphy, C. M., Musser, P. H., & Maton, K. (1998). Coordinated community intervention for domestic abusers: Intervention system involvement and criminal recidivism. *Journal of Family Violence, 13,* 263–284.

Prochaska, J. O., & DiClemente, C. C. (1982). Transtheoretical therapy: Toward a more integrative model of change. *Psychotherapy: Theory, Research, and Practice, 19,* 276–288.

Prochaska, J. O., & DiClemente, C. C. (1992). Stages of change in the modification of problem behaviors. In R. M. Eisler, M. Hersen, & P. M. Miller (Eds.), *Progress in behavior modification* (pp. 184–218). Sycamore, IL: Sycamore.

Rollnick, S., Heather, N., Gold, R., & Hall, W. (1992). Development of a short 'readiness to change' questionnaire for use in brief, opportunistic interventions among excessive drinkers. *British Journal of Addiction, 87,* 743–754.

Shields, N. M., & Hanneke, C. R. (1983). Attribution processes in violent relationships: Perceptions of violent husbands and their wives. *Journal of Applied Social Psychology, 13,* 515–527.

Straus, M. A. (1979). Measuring intrafamily conflict and violence: The conflict tactics (CT) scales. *Journal of Marriage and the Family, 41,* 75–88.

Acceptability of a Stage-Matched Expert System Intervention for Domestic Violence Offenders

DEBORAH A. LEVESQUE, MARY-MARGARET DRISKELL,
JANICE M. PROCHASKA, AND JAMES O. PROCHASKA

In 1984, the U.S. Attorney General's Task Force on Family Violence wrote that arrest followed by court-ordered psychotherapeutic treatment offers "great hope and potential for breaking the destructive cycle of violence" in intimate relationships (U.S. Attorney General's Task Force, 1984, p. 48). Court-mandated treatment has since emerged as society's intervention of choice for men who assault their wives and partners. However, research examining the efficacy of batterer intervention programs has yielded inconsistent and disappointing results. One meta-analysis of published and unpublished outcome studies found no overall effect for batterer treatment across seven studies relying on partner reports of recidivism, with mean weighted recidivism rates of 31.9% for treatment and 34.2% for comparison groups (Cohen's h = .06, ns). A fairly small effect was found across 11 studies relying on police reports and court records, where mean weighted recidivism rates were 14.3% for treatment and 21.8% for comparison groups (Cohen's h = .19, $p < .01$) (Levesque & Gelles, 1998). Another meta-analysis of 22 outcome studies found effect sizes of d = .09 and d = .12 for studies relying on partner reports of recidivism and criminal justice records, respectively (Babcock, Green, & Robie, 2004). To provide perspective, the authors compared effect sizes they found to those reported for psychotherapy (d = .85) and corrections treatment with adult prisoners (d = .25) and concluded that our interventions for men who batter "have a minimal impact on reducing recidivism beyond the effect of being arrested."

Outcome studies may underestimate the overall impact of treatment on the problem of male-to-female violence because a significant portion of the target group does not receive the full "dose" of treatment. In a nationwide survey of batterer treatment programs, Pirog-Good and Stets (1986) found that estimates of program attrition averaged 40% across programs. A similar rate of 36% was found across studies in a meta-analysis of 21 treatment outcome studies reporting on treatment dropout (Levesque, 1998). Cadsky, Hanson, Crawford, and Lalonde (1996) note that variables predicting dropout from other forms of treatment tend to fall into one of two categories: those representing lifestyle instability and those representing client–treatment incongruence (Baekeland & Lundwall, 1975; Wierzbicki & Pekarik, 1993). Factors representing lifestyle stability, such as education, employment, and marital status have been measured repeatedly in studies of batterer treatment attrition and completion and have been found to predict completion more often than not (e.g., Daly & Pelowski, 2000; Daly, Power, & Gondolf, 2001; DeMaris, 1989; Petrik, Gildersleeve-High, McEllistrem, & Subotnik, 1994; Rondeau, Brodeur, Brochu, & Lemire, 2001; Saunders & Parker, 1989).

Cadsky and colleagues (1996) conceptualized client–treatment congruence as the degree of match between clients' perceptions of their problems and the benefits of treatment and suggested that we focus on congruence since it is easier to modify than lifestyle instability. A number of studies have found a relationship between treatment completion and variables that seem to tap client–treatment congruence, including self-admitted problems with intimate violence (Cadsky et al., 1996), higher level of agreement with therapists (Rondeau et al., 2001), and motivation for treatment (Daly & Pelowski, 2000).

The transtheoretical model of behavior change (TTM; Prochaska, DiClemente, & Norcross, 1992) offers a promising approach to increasing client–treatment congruence, decreasing resistance, and increasing domestic violence offenders' motivation to participate in and benefit from treatment (Begun, Shelley, Strodthoff, & Short, 2002; Daly & Pelowski, 2000; Daniels & Murphy, 1997; Dutton, Bodnarchuk, Kropp, Hart, & Ogloff, 1997; Levesque, Gelles, & Velicer, 2000; Murphy & Baxter, 1997). Briefly, the TTM understands change as progress, over time, through a series of stages: precontemplation, contemplation, preparation, action, and maintenance. Stage of change is a good predictor of dropout from batterer treatment (Levesque & Chell, 1999), psychotherapy (Brogan,

Prochaska, & Prochaska, 1999), and of outcome among patients receiving pharmacological treatment for panic disorder (Beitman et al., 1994). Most interventions for batterers are action oriented and designed for the minority of individuals who are in the later stages of change and prepared to end the violence. Research conducted over 25 years on a variety of health behaviors has identified the principles and processes of change that work best in each stage to facilitate progress through the stages and minimize resistance. Research on domestic violence offenders in treatment supports the validity of the model's theoretical constructs and the hypothesized relationships between them (Begun et al., 2002; Eckhardt, 2001; Levesque, Driskell, & Prochaska, 2001; Levesque et al., 2000) and provides a foundation on which to build empirically based stage-matched interventions for partner violence cessation.

This article reports on the acceptability of an innovative computer-administered expert system intervention based on the TTM. The intervention maximizes client–treatment congruence by providing individualized feedback tailored to individual readiness to change. The intervention is designed as an adjunct to traditional one-size-fits-all batterer treatment delivered in a group format.

THE TTM

The TTM is an intuitively appealing model of behavior change that has been shown to be remarkably robust in its ability to explain and facilitate the change process across a broad range of behaviors, including smoking cessation (Velicer, Prochaska, Fava, Laforge, & Rossi, 1999), exercise adoption (Marcus et al., 1998), dietary change (Greene et al., 1999), psychotherapy (Prochaska & DiClemente, 1982), and alcohol treatment (DiClemente & Hughes, 1990). The TTM systematically integrates a number of theoretical constructs central to change: stages of change, decisional balance (Janis & Mann, 1977), self-efficacy (Bandura, 1977), and processes of change (Prochaska, Velicer, DiClemente, & Fava, 1988). The following is a description of the core constructs of the TTM.

Stage of Change

Stage of change, the central organizing construct of the TTM, represents the temporal and motivational dimension of the change process. In the first stage of change, the precontemplation stage, individuals deny that they have a problem and thus are resistant to change, are unaware of the negative consequences of their behavior, believe that the consequences are insignificant, or have given up the thought of changing because they are demoralized. Individuals in the contemplation stage are more likely to recognize the benefits of changing. However, they continue to overestimate the costs and, therefore, are ambivalent and not quite ready to change. Individuals in the preparation stage have decided to make a change in the near future and have already begun to take small steps toward that goal. Individuals in the action stage are overtly engaged in modifying their problem behaviors or acquiring new, healthy behaviors. Research on domestic violence offenders has identified two types of batterers in action: those with high temptation to relapse (action/high relapse) and those with low temptation (action/low relapse). While both groups are judged by intake staff to be relatively motivated for treatment, batterers in the action/high relapse group are about twice as likely to drop out of treatment as individuals in the action/low relapse group (Levesque & Chell, 1999). Individuals in the maintenance stage have been able to sustain change for a while and are actively striving to prevent relapse. For most people, the change process is not linear but spiral with several relapses to earlier stages before attaining permanent behavior change (Prochaska & DiClemente, 1986).

Transtheoretical model of behavior change research on men who batter finds that only 21% to 36% of men attending domestic violence treatment are in the preparation or action stages for partner violence cessation (Levesque & Chell, 1999; Levesque et al., 2001). These data suggest that if we offer action-oriented interventions to all battering men in treatment, we are misserving the majority who are not prepared to change.

Decisional Balance

The Decisional Balance Inventory (Velicer, DiClemente, Prochaska, & Brandenburg, 1985) consists of two scales: the *pros* of change and the *cons* of change. Longitudinal studies have found these measures to be among the best available predictors of future change (e.g., Velicer et al., 1985). In an integrative report of 12 studies, Prochaska and colleagues (1994) found that the balance of pros and cons was systematically related to stage of change in all 12 behaviors examined. The cons of changing to a health-promoting behavior outweighed the pros in the precontemplation stage, the pros surpassed the cons in the middle stages, and the pros outweighed the cons in the action stage. From these 12 studies, Prochaska (1994) discovered the degree of change in pros and cons needed to progress across the stages of change. Progression from precontemplation to action involved approximately a one-standard-deviation increase in the pros of making the healthy behavior change and a one-half-standard-deviation decrease in the cons. These same patterns were found among men involved in domestic violence treatment (Levesque et al., 2000). Increasing the salience and enhancing the decisional weight of the pros of ending the violence (e.g., "Children in a violent home live in fear," "If I ended the violence I'd receive more love and kindness from my partner") and decreasing the cons (e.g., "If I ended my violent behavior, I would lose my sense of control in my relationship") can help increase offenders' readiness to end the violence and participate in formal and informal behavior change activities.

Processes of Change

In a comparative analysis of 24 major systems of psychotherapy, Prochaska (1984) distilled a set of 10 fundamental processes by which people change. The set was refined following further theoretical analyses (Prochaska & DiClemente, 1984) and empirical studies (Prochaska & DiClemente, 1985, 1986). These processes describe the basic activities therapists try to encourage or elicit to help clients change problem behaviors, affects, cognitions, or interpersonal relationships. Our research on domestic violence offenders has identified the 12 processes of change for partner violence cessation (Levesque & Driskell, unpublished data). The following nine processes are included in the expert system intervention and stage-matched manual:

1. *Consciousness raising.* Considering information about domestic violence and strategies for change
2. *Environmental reevaluation.* Experiencing negative emotions about domestic violence or its consequences, especially the consequences for children and partners
3. *Self-reevaluation.* Thinking about the kind of man one wants to be and experiencing emotions that go along with that image
4. *Self-liberation.* Realizing one's ability to choose to be nonviolent and making a commitment to change
5. *Helping relationships.* Seeking and using social support to make and sustain changes

6. *Contingency management.* Increasing the rewards to oneself for nonviolence
7. *Stimulus control.* Removing cues to engage in violence against a partner and adding cues to engage in healthier behavior
8. *Counterconditioning.* Substituting violence with healthier behaviors and cognitions (e.g., assertive communication, exercise, time-out)
9. *Partner collaboration.* Seeking and using support and encouragement from one's partner to make and sustain changes; involving the partner by sharing information

Research determined the set of processes most important in each stage to facilitate progress among domestic violence offenders.

Self-Efficacy

Self-efficacy, or the degree to which an individual believes he or she has the capacity to attain a desired goal, can influence motivation and persistence (Bandura, 1977). Self-efficacy has two distinct but related components: *confidence* to make and sustain changes and *temptation* to relapse. Like decisional balance, levels of self-efficacy differ systematically across the stages of change, with subjects further along in the stages generally experiencing greater confidence and less temptation. A number of studies have shown the predictive power of self-efficacy for smoking cessation and the maintenance of abstinence (DiClemente, 1981; DiClemente, Prochaska, & Gibertini, 1985; Prochaska, 1985). Self-efficacy for abusive men reflects their level of temptation to use violence in a variety of challenging situations. Three major categories of tempting situations were found for men in domestic violence treatment: (a) partner behavior (e.g., "when my partner is violent toward me"), (b) alcohol and other drug use (e.g., "when I'm high on alcohol or other drugs"), and (c) daily hassles (e.g., "when I'm having problems at work") (Levesque et al., 2001). Identifying tempting situations is critical for relapse prevention among batterers in the later stages, especially batterers in the action or high relapse group.

TTM-BASED EXPERT SYSTEM INTERVENTIONS

Expert systems are broadly defined as computer programs that mimic the reasoning and problem solving of a human "expert." Advanced expert systems use empirically validated theories and accumulated data, which include both *deep knowledge* and *surface knowledge.* Deep knowledge refers to basic principles and the theoretical structure of the decision rules. Surface knowledge involves heuristics and the empirical database, including the specific scoring systems for the input variables and the use of empirically based decision rules (Harmon & King, 1985; Waterman, 1986).

The TTM and the interrelationships between its core constructs (stage of change, decisional balance, self-efficacy, and processes of change) provide the *deep knowledge* or theoretical basis for the expert system. An empirical database and heuristics provide the *surface knowledge* used to establish decision rules (e.g., cutoff scores) that guide the construction of individualized, stage-matched interventions. The empirical data were accumulated across several studies examining the core TTM constructs among domestic violence offenders.

The first expert system based on the TTM was developed for smoking cessation (Prochaska, DiClemente, Velicer, & Rossi, 1993). Multiple clinical trials have documented the ability of standardized, individualized expert system interventions to recruit, retain, and effectively intervene on large populations (Prochaska, Velicer, Fava, Rossi, & Tsoh, 2001; Prochaska, Velicer, Fava, Ruggiero, et al., 2001). First-generation expert systems for a variety of behaviors, including smoking (Prochaska et al., 1993), diet (Greene et al., 1999), mammography screening (Rakowski et al., 1998), and sun exposure (Rossi, Weinstock, Redding, Cottrill, & Maddock, 1997), have produced effective outcomes.

The *Journey to Change* Program

Only the baseline portion of *Journey to Change,* the TTM-based multimedia expert system for domestic violence offenders, was pilot tested in the present project. The session begins with a description of the *Journey to Change* program, instructions on how to use the computer program, and operational definitions of violence and ending the violence. Participants are then assessed and given individualized feedback on the following TTM constructs:

1. *Stage.* A description of the participant's current stage of change for ending the violence
2. *Decisional balance.* The participant's pros and cons of ending the violence and how his scores compare to those of peers who have

changed successfully; strategies for increasing the pros and decreasing the cons

3. *Processes of change.* Feedback on how frequently the participant is using up to six stage-appropriate processes and how he compares with others who were most successful in progressing to the next stage of change

4. *Self-efficacy.* Situations in which the participant is most tempted to use violence and ideas for coping with these situations

5. *Strategies.* Strategies for taking small steps to progress to the next stage of change for ending the violence

At baseline, the program compiles approximately 150 text feedback paragraphs, along with associated audio and graphics files, resulting in more than 2,000 unique sessions that provide immediate, personalized feedback on how the participants' responses compare to the responses of a sample of successful individuals making the same behavior change. Written text for all assessment questions and feedback paragraphs appears on the computer screen, and audio files read all text verbatim, making the program more accessible to participants with low literacy. The graphics are designed to make the program more visually appealing and to illustrate the concepts at hand. To ensure the appropriateness of the program for a culturally diverse group of domestic violence offenders, the paragraphs, voices, and images were reviewed by experts on domestic violence treatment and research, cultural issues, and the TTM and by domestic violence group facilitators and focus groups comprised of domestic violence offenders. To increase interactivity and to begin activating the processes of change, some feedback screens include type-in boxes in which participants are asked to type in their own ideas. For example, feedback screens for decisional balance ask participants to type in their biggest pro of ending the violence. Feedback screens for helping relationships ask participants to type in the names of people they can turn to for support.

The expert system also refers participants to sections of the *Journey to Change* manual that are stage appropriate and most likely to facilitate change. For example, a participant who is in the contemplation stage and underestimating the pros of ending violence against an intimate partner is asked to go to sections of the manual that identify the pros. Participants in the action stage are guided to sections that provide information and exercises on anger management, stress management, and coping with tempting situations.

In two follow-up sessions, not administered in this pilot test, participants receive the same assessments and updated feedback on how their responses compare to the responses of individuals in the normative group and to their own previous responses. The program tracks stage transitions and changes in decisional balance, processes of change, and self-efficacy scores over time. The follow-up sessions are designed to be administered around the middle and end of treatment.

In the pilot test, the interactive session concluded with 14 evaluation questions to assess participants' reactions to the intervention. Twelve closed-ended questions assessed ease of use, clarity, appeal of multimedia components, applicability to the participant, usefulness, whether the participant would return to the program, and whether he would recommend the program to others. Two open-ended questions asked the participant to type in what he liked least about the program and what he liked most. The entire session lasted an average of 30 minutes. At the end of the session, the expert system printed a report that contained all the feedback received during the session. All participants were encouraged to take their manual and individualized report home with them and use them. Guidance on how to use the manual is provided in the feedback report and the introduction to the manual.[1]

To view a demonstration of the expert system intervention that includes the introduction, sample assessment questions, and sample feedback paragraphs, go to http://prochange.com/domesticviolencedemo.

Stage-Matched Manual

Stage-matched manuals developed for smoking and other health behaviors are based on TTM research on how self-changers progress through each stage of change and how to cope with setbacks if they relapse. The *Journey to Change* manual, 67 pages in length, can be used alone or in conjunction with the expert system. The first section of the manual starts by acknowledging that being forced to attend a family violence program—or to make any kind of change—is difficult, especially for people who are not ready. But regardless of one's readiness to make particular changes, there are benefits to reading this guide. The manual then introduces the stages of change and asks readers to identify their own stage. The second section presents the goals of the manual and addresses readers' doubts about whether the guide is really for them (e.g., "I've never been violent or abusive," "I don't have a partner"). The next five sections focus on the five stages of change and

17 strategies representing different TTM principles and processes of change.

Like the expert system intervention, the manual was reviewed by the experts and focus groups to ensure its appropriateness for a culturally diverse group of domestic violence offenders. The manual text and images were revised on the basis of feedback from consultants and focus groups to increase appropriateness, readability, acceptability, and cultural sensitivity.

METHOD

Participants

Pilot-test participants were 58 male domestic violence offenders recruited from two Rhode Island agencies providing batterer treatment. Only clients who were age 18 or older and who were able to read at least some English were eligible to participate. Thirty-four consecutive clients were recruited at treatment intake—33, or 97%, agreed to participate—and 25 clients were recruited from ongoing groups in response to announcements. All participants received a $10 gift certificate good at a nearby grocery store.

Of these participants, 57% were White, non-Hispanic; 26% were Black, non-Hispanic; 12% were Hispanic; and 5% were other. Forty-one percent were unemployed, and 41% had incomes of $10,000 or less. Average years of education was 10.4. Twenty-two percent had a prior history of legal trouble related to partner violence, 38% had a prior history of arrest for assaulting someone who was not a wife or girlfriend, 16% had been arrested on alcohol or drug-related charges, and 59% had been arrested for other types of criminal offenses.

Procedure

Agency staff provided each eligible participant with an overview of the study and reviewed the informed consent document, stressing that the decision to participate—whatever it may be—would have no effect on the participant's treatment or standing with courts. However, the answers given during the computer session might be reviewed by his counselor. (In this regard, we wanted to test the program under conditions similar to those under which the program might be used in the future.) After obtaining informed consent, staff instructed the participant on how to use the computer, provided headphones to increase privacy, and then left him to complete the session on his own. However, staff remained available to help with questions or problems that arose during the session. At the completion of the computer session, staff returned to give the participant his printed feedback report, self-help manual, and gift certificate.

RESULTS

The majority of participants (64%) were in pre-action stages for ending the violence against their partner: 16% were in precontemplation, 16% in contemplation, and 33% in preparation. Only 7% were in action/low relapse group, and 30% were in the action/high relapse group.

Feedback on the interactive session is provided in Table 3.1. Overall, responses were very positive. About 90% reported that they found the program easy or very easy to use, 95% found the personalized feedback to be clear or very clear, and a majority liked the pictures and voices somewhat or very much. Sixty-five percent responded "yes" to the question, "Did it seem like the program was made for people like you?" Unfortunately, this question may not be specific enough to accurately tap the dimension it was meant to tap: cultural sensitivity. Instead, the question may assess the extent to which participants are willing to label themselves as batterers—the obvious target of the intervention (i.e., the group for whom the program was made).

Of all of the pilot-test participants, 98% said that they found the program to be useful or very useful, 88% said it gave them something new to think about, and 98% said it could probably or definitely help them change their attitudes or behaviors. Eighty-one percent reported that they would return to the program in a few months to see how they've changed; 90% said that they would recommend it to a friend.

Participants' verbatim responses to the two open-ended questions— "What did you like least about the program?" and "What did you like most about the program?"—perhaps provide the best gauge of the acceptability of the program.

When asked the first open-ended question, "What did you like least about the program?" 52% of participants described elements that they didn't like; the remainder listed things that they liked (21%) or gave a neutral response or no response at all (28%). A few participants found

Table 3.1

EVALUATION OF MULTIMEDIA EXPERT SYSTEM INTERVENTION

EVALUATION QUESTIONS	PERCENT (*N* = 58)
How easy was this program to use?	
Very easy	75.9
Easy	13.8
Somewhat difficult	8.6
Very difficult	1.7
How clear were the instructions?	
Very clear	72.4
Clear	15.5
Somewhat confusing	6.9
Very confusing	5.2
How clear were the questions you were asked to answer?	
Very clear	62.1
Clear	27.6
Somewhat confusing	8.6
Very confusing	1.7
How clear was the personal feedback the program gave you?	
Very clear	58.6
Clear	36.2
Somewhat confusing	5.2
Very confusing	0.0
How much did you like the pictures?	
Very much	15.5
Somewhat	51.7
A little	20.7
Not at all	12.1
How much did you like the voices?	
Very much	25.9
Somewhat	36.2
A little	20.7
Not at all	17.2
Did it seem like the program was made for people like you?	
Yes	67.2
No	32.8

(Continued)

Table 3.1

EVALUATION OF MULTIMEDIA EXPERT SYSTEM INTERVENTION (*Continued*)

EVALUATION QUESTIONS	PERCENT (*N* = 58)
How useful did you find this program?	
Very useful	50.0
Useful	48.3
Not useful	1.7
Would you return to do the program again in a few months, to see how you've changed?	
Yes	81.0
No	19.0
Would you recommend this program to a friend?	
Yes	89.7
No	10.3
Did this program give you something new to think about?	
Yes	87.9
No	12.1
Do you think this program could help to change your attitudes or behaviors?	
Definitely could help	62.1
Probably could help	36.2
Probably could not help	0.0
Definitely could not help	1.7

the assessment questions repetitive, and a few thought that the questions did not pertain to them. Some respondents objected to one or more of the voices. Others stated that they'd never been violent and that they would have liked an opportunity to tell their side of the story, or that they would have preferred to have talked to a real person.

When asked the open-ended question, "What did you like most about the program?" 90% of participants described elements of the program that they liked, 2% described elements they didn't like, and 9% gave a neutral response or no response at all. About 30% of participants stated that the program gave them something new to think about, opened up their minds, or provided information or advice (e.g., "it told me a lot about myself," "good information and support," "it gave me a few ideas," "it makes you realize how violence affects children!"). About 20% of participants reported that they liked the questions (e.g., "good question asking," "the reality of the questions"), and another 10% reported that they liked the personalized feedback ("it was cool," "the feedback after finishing each section").

DISCUSSION

An intervention's acceptability can influence the degree to which individuals are willing to participate in or use it; this, in turn, can influence its efficacy. This pilot study demonstrated that a computer-administered multimedia stage-matched expert system intervention is acceptable to domestic violence offenders, a population whose resistance to traditional intervention programs has been well documented (e.g., Daniels & Murphy, 1997; Ganley, 1987; Hamberger & Hastings, 1986). We were able to recruit offenders from all stages of change for ending the violence, and a majority found the program to be informative, helpful, and easy to use and said they would be willing to return to the program in the future. Furthermore, all but one of the pilot-test participants believed that the program probably or definitely could help change their attitudes or behaviors. The high participation rate and the quantitative and qualitative feedback suggest a high degree of client–treatment congruence for this population.

But can the program increase motivation to participate in and benefit from traditional batterer treatment programs? A clinical trial involving 585 domestic violence offenders assessed the efficacy of the stage-matched expert system intervention. Participants were randomly assigned to (a) the TTM intervention group that completed an expert system session at intake, 2 months postintake, and around the time of program completion, or (b) a comparison group that completed two brief computer sessions that delivered an assessment and one-size-fits-all feedback highlighting important topics discussed in the group (e.g., how to conduct a "time-out"). The intervention did not improve batterer program attendance, except among participants who were in the action/high relapse stage at program intake. However, data from the final computer session show that offenders assigned to the TTM intervention were significantly more likely to be in the Action stage (55% vs. 24%)

for using healthy strategies to stay violence-free. The intervention also increased use of help-seeking outside of group (e.g., intervention group participants were more likely to talk to a medical professional—39% vs. 24%—and attend other group counseling—34% vs. 17%). Based on victim reports, offenders in the TTM intervention group were less likely to engage in violence (16% vs. 38%) and threats (45% vs. 62%) during the first 6 months follow-up; during the next 6 months (months 7–12 of the study), rates of violence were similarly low for both treatment and control (15% vs. 14%), but the treatment group remained significantly less likely to engage in threats (33% vs. 60%) (Levesque, Driskell, Greene, Castle, & Prochaska, 2008). Thus, the low-cost TTM intervention has the potential to facilitate engagement in the change process and enhance the benefits of traditional treatment.

NOTE

1. Information on the *Journey to Change* client and facilitators' guides is available at www.prochange.com.

ACKNOWLEDGMENT

This project was funded by Research Grant #R43 MH62858 from the National Institute of Mental Health.

REFERENCES

Babcock, J. C., Green, C. E., & Robie, C. (2004). Does batterers' treatment work? A meta-analytic review of domestic violence treatment. *Clinical Psychology Review, 23*, 1023–1053.

Baekeland, F., & Lundwall, L. (1975). Dropping out of treatment: A critical review. *Psychological Bulletin, 82*, 738–783.

Bandura, A. (1977). Self-efficacy: Toward a unifying theory of behavior change. *Psychological Review, 84*, 191–215.

Begun, A. L., Shelley, G., Strodthoff, T., & Short, L. (2002). Adopting a stages of change approach for individuals who are violent with their intimate partners. *Journal of Aggression, Maltreatment and Trauma (Special Issue: Domestic violence offenders: Current interventions, research, and implications for policies and standards), 5*, 105–127.

Beitman, B. D., Beck, N. C., Deuser, W., Carter, C., Davidson, J., & Maddock, R. (1994). Patient stages of change predicts outcome in a panic disorder medication trial. *Anxiety, 1*, 64–69.

Brogan, M. M., Prochaska, J. O., & Prochaska, J. M. (1999). Predicting termination and continuation status in psychotherapy using the transtheoretical model. *Psychotherapy, 36*, 105–113.

Cadsky, O., Hanson, R. K., Crawford, M., & Lalonde, C. (1996). Attrition from a male batterer treatment program: Client-treatment congruence and lifestyle instability. *Violence and Victims, 11,* 51–64.

Daly, J. E., & Pelowski, S. (2000). Predictors of dropout among men who batter: A review of studies with implications for research and practice. *Violence and Victims, 15,* 137–160.

Daly, J. E., Power, T. G., & Gondolf, E. W. (2001). Predictors of batterer program attendance. *Journal of Interpersonal Violence, 16,* 971–991.

Daniels, J. W., & Murphy, C. M. (1997). Stages and processes of change in batterers' treatment. *Cognitive and Behavioral Practice, 4,* 123–145.

DeMaris, A. (1989). Attrition in batterers' counseling: The role of social and demographic factors. *Social Service Review, 63,* 142–154.

DiClemente, C. C. (1981). Self-efficacy and smoking cessation maintenance: A preliminary report. *Cognitive Therapy and Research, 5,* 175–187.

DiClemente, C. C., & Hughes, S. O. (1990). Stages of change profiles in outpatient alcoholism treatment. *Journal of Substance Abuse, 2,* 217–235.

DiClemente, C. C., Prochaska, J. O., & Gibertini, M. (1985). Self-efficacy and the stages of self-change of smoking. *Cognitive Therapy and Research, 9,* 181–200.

Dutton, D. G., Bodnarchuk, M., Kropp, R., Hart, S. D., & Ogloff, J. R. P. (1997). Wife assault treatment and criminal recidivism: An 11-year follow-up. *International Journal of Offender Therapy and Comparative Criminology, 41,* 9–23.

Eckhardt, C. I. (2001, July). *Stage of change clusters in partner assaultive men.* Paper presented at the Seventh International Family Violence Research Conference, Portsmouth, NH.

Ganley, A. (1987). Perpetrators of domestic violence: An overview of counseling the court-mandated client. In D. J. Sonkin (Ed.), *Domestic violence on trial: Psychological and legal dimensions of family violence* (pp. 155–173). New York: Springer.

Greene, G. W., Rossi, S. R., Rossi, J. S., Velicer, W. F., Fava, J. L., & Prochaska, J. O. (1999). Dietary applications of the stages of change model. *Journal of the American Dietetic Association, 99,* 673–678.

Hamberger, L. K., & Hastings, J. E. (1986). Characteristics of spouse abusers: Predictors of treatment acceptance. *Journal of Interpersonal Violence, 1,* 363–373.

Harmon, P., & King, D. (1985). *Expert systems: Artificial intelligence in business.* New York: Wiley.

Janis, I. L., & Mann, L. (1977). *Decision making: A psychological analysis of conflict, choice and commitment.* New York: Free Press.

Levesque, D. A. (1998). *Violence desistance among battering men: Existing interventions and the application of the transtheoretical model of change.* Unpublished doctoral dissertation, University of Rhode Island, Kingston, RI.

Levesque, D. A., & Chell, D. (1999, November). *Stage of change and attrition from batterer treatment.* Paper presented at the 51st annual meeting of the American Society of Criminology, Toronto.

Levesque, D. A., Driskell, M. M., Greene, R. N., Castle, P. H., & Prochaska, J. M. (2008). *Efficacy of a computerized stage-matched intervention for domestic violence offenders.* Manuscript in preparation.

Levesque, D. A., Driskell, M. M., & Prochaska, J. M. (2001, July). *Development of a situational temptation scale for domestic violence offenders.* Paper presented at the Seventh International Family Violence Research Conference, Portsmouth, NH.

Levesque, D. A., & Gelles, R. J. (1998, July). *Does treatment reduce violence recidivism among men who batter? Meta-analytic evaluation of treatment outcome research.* Paper presented at Program Evaluation and Family Violence Research: An International Conference, Durham, NH.

Levesque, D. A., Gelles, R. J., & Velicer, W. F. (2000). Development and validation of a stages of change measure for men in batterer treatment. *Cognitive Therapy and Research, 24,* 175–199.

Marcus, B. H., Bock, B. C., Pinto, B. M., Forsyth, L. H., Roberts, M. B., & Traficante, R. M. (1998). Efficacy of an individualized, motivationally-tailored physical activity intervention. *Annals of Behavioral Medicine, 20,* 174–180.

Murphy, C. M., & Baxter, V. A. (1997). Motivating batterers to change in the treatment context. *Journal of Interpersonal Violence, 12,* 607–619.

Petrik, N. D., Gildersleeve-High, L., McEllistrem, J. E., & Subotnik, L. S. (1994). The reduction of male abusiveness as a result of treatment: Reality or myth? *Journal of Family Violence, 9,* 307–316.

Pirog-Good, M., & Stets, J. (1986). Programs for abusers: Who drops out and what can be done. *Response, 9*(2), 17–19.

Prochaska, J. O. (1984). *Systems of psychotherapy: A transtheoretical approach.* Homewood, IL: Dow Jones-Irwin.

Prochaska, J. O. (1985). Predicting change in smoking status for self-changers. *Addictive Behaviors, 10,* 395–406.

Prochaska, J. O. (1994). Strong and weak principles for progressing from precontemplation to action on the basis of 12 problem behaviors. *Health Psychology, 13,* 47–51.

Prochaska, J. O., & DiClemente, C. C. (1982). Transtheoretical therapy: Toward a more integrative model of change. *Psychotherapy: Theory, Research, and Practice, 19,* 276–288.

Prochaska, J. O., & DiClemente, C. C. (1984). Self change processes, self efficacy and decisional balance across five stages of smoking cessation. *Progress in Clinical and Biological Research, 156,* 131–140.

Prochaska, J. O., & DiClemente, C. C. (1985). Common processes of change in smoking, weight control, and psychological distress. In S. Shiffman & T. Wills (Eds.), *Coping and substance use: A conceptual framework* (pp. 345–363). New York: Academic Press.

Prochaska, J. O., & DiClemente, C. C. (1986). Toward a comprehensive model of behavior change. In W. R. Miller & N. Heather (Eds.), *Treating addictive behaviors: Processes of change* (pp. 3–27). New York: Plenum Press.

Prochaska, J. O., DiClemente, C. C., & Norcross, J. C. (1992). In search of how people change: Applications to addictive behaviors. *American Psychologist, 47,* 1102–1114.

Prochaska, J. O., DiClemente, C. C., Velicer, W. F., & Rossi, J. S. (1993). Standardized, individualized, interactive, and personalized self-help programs for smoking cessation. *Health Psychology, 12,* 399–405.

Prochaska, J. O., Velicer, W. F., DiClemente, C. C., & Fava, J. (1988). Measuring processes of change: Applications to the cessation of smoking. *Journal of Consulting and Clinical Psychology, 56,* 520–528.

Prochaska, J. O., Velicer, W. F., Fava, J. L., Rossi, J. S., & Tsoh, J. Y. (2001). Evaluating a population-based recruitment approach and a stage-based expert system intervention for smoking cessation. *Addictive Behaviors, 26,* 583–602.

Prochaska, J. O., Velicer, W. F., Fava, J. L., Ruggiero, L., Laforge, R. G., Rossi, J. S., et al. (2001). Counselor and stimulus control enhancements of a stage-matched expert system for smokers in a managed care setting. *Preventive Medicine, 32,* 23–32.

Prochaska, J. O., Velicer, W. F., Rossi, J. S., Goldstein, M. G., Marcus, B. H., Rakowski, W., et al. (1994). Stages of change and decisional balance for twelve problem behaviors. *Health Psychology, 13,* 39–46.

Rakowski, W., Ehrich, B., Goldstein, M. G., Rimer, B. K., Pearlman, D. N., Clark, M. A., et al. (1998). Increasing mammography among women aged 40–74 by use of a stage-matched, tailored intervention. *Preventive Medicine, 27,* 748–756.

Rondeau, G., Brodeur, N., Brochu, S., & Lemire, G. (2001). Dropout and completion of treatment among spouse abusers. *Violence and Victims, 16,* 127–143.

Rossi, J. S., Weinstock, M. A., Redding, C. A., Cottrill, S. D., & Maddock, J. E. (1997). Effectiveness of stage-matched interventions for skin cancer prevention: A randomized clinical trial of high-risk beach bathers [Abstract]. *Annals of Behavioral Medicine, 19,* S194.

Saunders, D. G., & Parker, J. C. (1989). Legal sanctions and treatment follow-through among men who batter: A multivariate analysis. *Social Work Research and Abstracts, 25,* 21–29.

U.S. Attorney General's Task Force on Family Violence. (1984, September). *Attorney General's Task Force on Family Violence: Final report.* Washington, DC: Department of Justice.

Velicer, W. F., DiClemente, C. C., Prochaska, J. O., & Brandenburg, N. (1985). Decisional balance measure for assessing and predicting smoking status. *Journal of Personality and Social Psychology, 48,* 1279–1289.

Velicer, W. F., Prochaska, J. O., Fava, J. L., Laforge, R. G., & Rossi, J. S. (1999). Interactive versus non-interactive interventions and dose-response relationships for stage-matched smoking cessation programs in a managed care setting. *Health Psychology, 18,* 21–28.

Waterman, D. A. (1986). *A guide to expert systems.* Reading, MA: Addison-Wesley.

Wierzbicki, M., & Pekarik, G. (1993). A meta-analysis of psychotherapy dropout. *Professional Psychology: Research and Practice, 24,* 190–195.

Motivational Interviewing as a Pregroup Intervention for Partner-Violent Men

4

PETER H. MUSSER, JOSHUA N. SEMIATIN, CASEY T. TAFT, AND CHRISTOPHER M. MURPHY

The efficacy of standard group interventions in reducing partner-violent behavior remains in question. One recent meta-analysis uncovered very small average effects of counseling relative to minimal treatment or probation controls (Babcock, Green, & Robie, 2004). A number of factors may account for the limited program effects, most notably high rates of session nonattendance and treatment dropout (e.g., Brown, O'Leary, & Feldbau, 1997; Cadsky, Hanson, Crawford, & Lalonde, 1996; Chen, Bersani, Myers, & Denton, 1989; Gondolf & Foster, 1991; Hamberger & Hastings, 1989), low motivational readiness to change (Eckhardt, Holtzworth-Munroe, Norlander, Sibley, & Cahill, 2008), problems in the establishment of a therapeutic alliance (Taft, Murphy, Musser, & Remington, 2003b), and limited engagement in treatment activities such as homework assignments (Taft, Murphy, King, Musser, & DeDeyn, 2003a). Thus, treatment innovations are needed to enhance motivational readiness to change, treatment involvement, and session attendance.

Motivation to change has been defined as the probability that a person will enter into, continue, and adhere to a specific change strategy (Miller & Rollnick, 1991). Many counseling programs for partner-violent men emphasize active change techniques that are most appropriate for individuals who are ready and willing to change. Yet, the vast majority of abusive clients appear to be in pre-action stages of change (precontemplation or contemplation; Prochaska & DiClemente, 1984), when they present for services (Alexander & Morris, 2008; Eckhardt et al., 2008; Levesque, Gelles & Velicer, 2000). In addition, some abuser counseling programs promote direct confrontation of denial and excuses in a fashion that may inadvertently enhance defensiveness or impede the establishment of a collaborative working alliance (Murphy & Baxter, 1997). Based on an extensive review of motivation for treatment, Miller (1985) concluded that therapists expressing high levels of empathy have more success than confrontational therapists in helping clients to enter, continue, comply with, and succeed in treatment. Despite this extensive research in other areas of behavior change, supportive, alliance-building strategies are rarely discussed in the clinical literature on partner violence interventions.

Two prior controlled studies have examined supportive pregroup preparation strategies for partner-violent men. One involved an intensive 12-hour workshop conducted over 2 days (Tolman & Bhosley, 1990), and the other involved a 20-minute dramatic video portraying an individual who overcomes his initial resistance to partner violence treatment, followed by a structured group discussion of the video and its effects (Stosny, 1994). Both studies found that supportive pregroup intervention can enhance subsequent program attendance in this population. The measurement of treatment involvement variables other than session attendance, however, was extremely limited in both studies, and neither study presented data on partner violence outcomes. In addition, other methodological weaknesses limit the strength of conclusions, and the format of the interventions may preclude widespread adoption in community agencies.

Research on other clinical populations indicates that motivational interviewing may prove to be a practical and effective alternative pregroup intervention strategy for partner-violent men. In motivational interviewing, therapists use empathy, reflective listening, and resistance-reduction techniques to explore the client's perspectives on change, and to enhance client articulation of the desire and ability to change. Personalized assessment feedback, a menu of change strategies, and structured change planning often accompany motivational interviewing to further promote movement through the stages of intentional behavior change (Miller, 1983; Miller & Rollnick, 1991, 2002). Recent reviews have located 30 controlled clinical trials of interventions based on motivational interviewing. These reviews indicate that brief motivational interventions produce changes in target behaviors of alcohol use, drug use, diet, and exercise that are considerably better than no-treatment or placebo controls, and roughly equal to more lengthy interventions based on traditional therapy strategies. Motivational interviewing has been effective both as a stand-alone intervention, and as a preparation strategy or adjunctive treatment to promote involvement in traditional therapies (Burke, Arkowitz, & Dunn, 2002; Burke, Arkowitz, & Menchola, 2003; Dunn, DeRoo, & Rivara, 2001).

The current investigation examined motivational interviewing as a pregroup preparatory intervention for partner-violent men. The goals of the motivational interview intervention were to increase readiness to change abusive behavior, to facilitate additional help seeking, to promote cooperative and constructive behavior during subsequent group cognitive behavioral treatment sessions, and to enhance involvement in treatment as indicated by cognitive behavioral treatment (CBT) session attendance, the collaborative working alliance between group therapists and the clients, and compliance with CBT homework tasks. Effects on abusive behavior outcomes after group CBT were also explored. The design compared an intake procedure that included two sessions of MI (Miller & Rollnick, 1991) to a standard intake procedure consisting of structured interviewing only.

Efforts were made to address several practical and methodological limitations of prior research on pregroup preparation programs for partner-violent men. First, outcomes included proximal indicators of treatment involvement as well as more distal indicators of abusive behavior after subsequent group treatment and were derived from multiple sources, including client self-reports, therapist reports, observational coding of in-session behavior from videotapes, and collateral partner reports of abusive behavior after group CBT. Second, to control for potential effects of group interaction on the outcomes of interest, including the prospect of treatment diffusion or compensatory rivalry (Cook & Campbell, 1979), each sequential series of cases was exposed to the same intake condition, and then assigned together to a CBT group. Participants had no opportunity to interact with individuals who received the other intake. Third, the motivational interviewing procedures were well specified and manualized (Miller & Rollnick, 1991), and therapist training and adherence to the treatment principles were documented. Finally, the experimental intake procedures were designed in light of practical constraints on therapist time. The motivational intake required only a modest amount of additional intake therapist time, specifically two 45-minute motivational interviews (one of which included personalized feedback on aspects of the client's intake assessment), and a small amount of additional activity designed to promote a collaborative alliance (e.g., sending the client a handwritten note after the first intake).

METHOD

Participants

Participants were 108 men presenting for treatment at the Domestic Violence Center of Howard County, Maryland, between July 1999 and October 2000. All were age 18 or older and provided written informed consent for study participation at the outset of clinic intake. Of 125 consecutive intake cases approached, 12 declined participation, 3 were deemed ineligible for services at the agency because their difficulties did not involve partner abuse, and 2 were referred for individual therapy. Of the 108 remaining participants, 55 (51%) were assigned to the motivational intake (MI) condition, and 53 (49%) were assigned to the standard intake (SI) condition.

With respect to referral status at the time of intake, 79% of the men were court ordered to treatment, 6% had a court case pending, and 16% had no legal involvement for domestic abuse. The sample was predominantly White (50%) and African American (44%), with a smaller number reporting their ethnic identification as Asian (3%), American Indian/Alaskan Native (2%), or Hispanic/Latino (2%). Their mean age was 35.7 years ($SD = 8.6$), and the mean level of formal educational was 13.1 years ($SD = 2.6$). The majority of participants were employed full time (82%) or part time (9%); a smaller number were unemployed (7%) or temporarily laid off from seasonal work (2%). Their average gross yearly income was in the $25,000–$30,000 range.

Measures

Outcome Measures

Readiness to Change Abusive Behavior was assessed with the Safe-at-Home Instrument for Assessing Readiness to Change Intimate Partner Violence (SIRC; Begun et al., 2003). The SIRC contains 35 self-report items administered with a 5-point scale of endorsement. The items were designed to assess stages from the transtheoretical model of change (Prochaska & DiClemente, 1984). Items were developed from a large set of statements generated by abuser group counselors who were given training in the transtheoretical model and asked to come up with statements characteristic of abusive clients at each stage of change. Exploratory and confirmatory factor analyses using data from more than 1,300 men at several different treatment agencies supported a 3-factor solution, with subscales measuring *Precontemplation* (e.g., "It's no big deal if I lose my temper from time to time"; "There's nothing wrong with the way I handle situations, but I get into trouble for it anyway"), *Contemplation* (e.g., "I want to do something about my problem with conflict"; "It's time for me to listen to the people telling me I need help"); and *Preparation/Action* (e.g., "Even though I get angry, I know ways to keep from losing control"; "It's becoming more natural for me to be in control of myself"). The resulting scales had adequate internal consistency in the development sample, with coefficient alpha equal to .91, .79, and .59 for the Contemplation, Preparation/Action, and Precontemplation scales, respectively. Support for construct validity was apparent in predicted subscale correlations with the assumption of personal responsibility for abusive behavior and differences between court-referred and self-referred clients (Begun et al., 2003). As suggested by the scale authors, a readiness-to-change composite score was also derived from a subset of 24 scale items by adding Contemplation and Preparation/Action item totals and subtracting the Precontemplation item total. The SIRC was administered to study participants at the outset of their first intake appointment (before they met with the intake therapist) and again at the outset of the first CBT group session. Although the wait time from intake to the first CBT group session varied across participants as a result of the time needed to constitute treatment groups, the SIRC was administered at the first CBT session to have maximum clinical relevance for determining whether the motivational intake increased readiness to change at the outset of group treatment.

The Working Alliance was assessed with the therapist and client using versions of the Working Alliance Inventory (WAI; Horvath & Greenberg, 1989), a widely used and well-validated measure of the alliance construct. The WAI was developed for use across different schools and forms of therapy. It assesses three components: the bond between therapist and client, agreement on goals of treatment, and agreement on the tasks required to achieve treatment goals. Prior research has established excellent psychometric properties of the WAI (Tracey & Kokotovic, 1989; Tryon & Kane, 1993). The measure appears to have a three-factor structure with a second-order global alliance factor (Tracey & Kokotovic, 1989).

For the current study, clients were asked to complete the long form (36 items) of the WAI, providing separate ratings for alliance with the male and female cotherapists. Each group therapist completed the short form (12 items) of the WAI on each client in their group. The working alliance was assessed twice early in treatment (at sessions 3 and 5), and twice late in treatment (at sessions 11 and 13). For the current study, the global alliance score was used in all analyses, as the subscales tend to be highly intercorrelated (Connors, Carroll, DiClemente, Longabaugh, & Donovan, 1997; Tracey & Kokotovic, 1989). Client ratings of the two cotherapists were highly correlated, and therefore composited for analyses. Likewise, the two cotherapists' ratings of clients were substantially correlated, and were composited for analyses. The average of early ratings (3rd and 5th sessions) and late ratings (11th and 13th sessions) was analyzed.

CBT Homework Compliance was assessed with the Assignment Compliance Rating Scale (ACRS; Bryant, Simons, & Thase, 1999; Primakoff, Epstein, & Covi, 1986). The group therapists collected a written homework summary from each participant during group sessions 2 through 14. One of the therapists rated each individual's homework on a 6-point scale ranging from "The client did not attempt the assigned homework" to "The client did more of the assigned homework than was requested." Composite scores were obtained for homework compliance early in treatment (sessions 2–7) and late in treatment (sessions 8–14) by averaging the ACRS ratings for individuals who attended at least half of the relevant sessions. The resulting composites had adequate internal consistency (alpha = .79 and .82 for early and late treatment composites, respectively).

Session Attendance was recorded by the group therapists after each session. The total number of group treatment sessions attended by each client (range 0–16) was analyzed. Individuals who dropped out during the intake process were assigned a score of 0 on this variable.[1]

Other Help Seeking was assessed via a self-report questionnaire at the end of the CBT group program. For the period from intake to the end of treatment, participants indicated whether they had obtained help from any of six sources, and, if so, about how often using the options "once," "2–3 times," "about once a month," "2–3 times a month," "about once a week," or "twice a week or more." The help sources were Alcoholics Anonymous, Narcotics Anonymous, other drug or alcohol counseling, marital/couples therapy, individual therapy, or other forms of counseling or therapy. Three variables were extracted from these reports: (a) a dichotomous indicator of any other help seeking; (b) the number of different sources of help sought; and (c) the estimated number of contacts, computed by recording the response options to a frequency count and summing across help sources.

Abusive Behavior was assessed with the physical aggression and psychological aggression subscales from the original Conflict Tactics Scale (CTS; Straus, 1979) and the injury subscale from the revised CTS-2 (Straus, Hamby, Boney-McCoy, & Sugarman, 1996). This hybrid version was used to provide motivational intake participants with feedback on their abusive behavior using published population norms, which were available for the original CTS scales, but not for the CTS-2. Only collateral partner reports of abuse were analyzed in the current study, as such ratings are less affected by social desirability than self-reports (Arias & Beach, 1987). Collateral partners completed the CTS with respect to the 6 months before treatment in a phone interview at baseline, and with respect to the 6 months after scheduled completion of group CBT in a follow-up phone interview. The CTS is the most widely used measure of abusive relationship behavior and exhibits sound psychometric properties (Straus, 1979, 1990). Each aggressive act and injury category was rated on a frequency scale ranging from "never" to "more than 20 times" during the prior 6 months. CTS subscale scores were computed by summing the number of positively endorsed items. This computational method, known as the "variety score," has desirable psychometric properties (Moffitt et al., 1997), reducing skewness caused by a small number of high-rate offenders, limiting estimation errors common in recall of high frequency behaviors, and circumventing the need to weight different aggressive acts by their presumed severity.

Observational Coding of In-Session Behavior

Videotapes of CBT group treatment sessions were coded by trained undergraduate research assistants using a system that was developed to assess personal responsibility assumption for abusive behavior (Elliott, 2002) and revised for the current study to include other dimensions of constructive versus counterproductive group behavior. In order to evaluate effects of intake condition that might vary over the course of treatment, for each CBT group, a total of six sessions were coded, two each from the early, middle, and late phases of the 16-week program. Using a 5-point scale, client verbalizations were rated during 5-minute intervals on three variables described later. Each participant received an average rating across session intervals on each of the three variables. Ratings from the two coded sessions were composited to form an early, middle, and late treatment score.

Raters were trained using transcribed statements extracted from treatment sessions. Criterial performance was defined as a correlation above .80 with the standard ratings. Interrater agreement was checked on 30% of treatment session tapes. The pooled reliability correlation (r) across the three coded variables for averaged session ratings was .50, $N = 439$, $p < .001$.

Denial/Acknowledgment of Behavior/Responsibility

This rating scale focused on verbal assertions that refer directly to the participant's view of personal responsibility for his abusive actions, the consequences of these actions, and the need for personal change to avoid future problems with abuse. Raters were instructed to consider the extent to which the individual (a) acknowledged that his abusive behavior(s) occurred; (b) acknowledged that abusive behavior was harmful; (c) asserted that abusive behavior was the result of his own maladaptive cognitive, emotional, or behavioral processes; (d) assumed personal responsibility for the abuse, rather than attributing it to external forces, his partner's behavior, or the legal system; and (e) conveyed a desire to change his behavior for personal reasons, and not simply because of external pressures.

A rating of 1 on this scale was given if the participant denied that his abusive behavior occurred in the first place or claimed that it was a direct result of external, nonpersonal factors, and stated or implied that there is no need to work on altering his self-control, relationship behaviors, or coping skills. A rating of 3 indicated ambivalence, for example, acknowledgment of responsibility for the abuse and its harmful effects along with negative assertions about the need for personal change. This "sitting on the fence" was viewed as part of the change process and therefore was assigned a neutral rating instead of one that inferred denial and avoidance of responsibility. A rating of 5 represented the verbalizations of an "ideal" client who accepted that past abusive behavior had occurred and was harmful, accepted personal responsibility for his abuse, and expressed the desire to work on personal change to eliminate abusive behavior.

Client Role Behavior

This rating scale was created to elucidate change-oriented cognition and behavior expressed on the interpersonal level of group functioning. The scale focused on verbal responses from the participant toward others in the group, most notably advice given to other participants and verbal reactions to others' situations and experiences. Raters were instructed to conceptualize these verbalizations within the context of role modeling. Specifically, the coding system addressed four types of client role behavior defined along two axes: confrontation versus confirmation and positive progress versus negative progress. Positive confrontation involved efforts to change another participant's denial of abuse, externalization of responsibility, minimization of abuse effects, or avoidance of the need for change. In positive confrontation, the individual attempted to convince another group member (or multiple members) that his views or actions were maladaptive, may lead to further abuse and suffering, and need to be changed. Such role behavior constituted a rating of 4 or 5 on this scale, depending on the degree to which the behavior was supportive, generalized, and/or persistent in the face of opposition from peers.

In contrast, negative confrontation involved efforts to change another's acceptance of responsibility and desire to change, including attempts to degrade those views as unnecessary and efforts to reinforce attributions of blame against external forces such as the partner, the legal system, or the counseling process. These assertions were seen as directly opposing positive change and were therefore assigned a rating of 1 or 2 on this measure, depending on the severity and persistence of the negative confrontation. Positive confirmation involved concurrence with the acceptance of responsibility and initiatives toward future change of one or more group peers, including direct affirmation of these positive views or peripheral attempts to reinforce these views in other group members. Finally, negative confirmation involved efforts to support and reinforce the responsibility avoidance of other group participants, such as affirming the view that the partner (or the system) is to blame and should carry the burden of change. A rating of 3 on this scale was used to indicate mixed and ambivalent expressions of client role behavior.

Group Value

This rating scale was designed to capture general sentiments about the counseling experience. It focused on client verbalizations regarding the perceived value of the group, the treatment program, and counseling in general. Raters were instructed to consider client statements regarding the necessity, relevance, and perceived personal value of treatment, and the extent to which each participant viewed the group as a positive force in men's efforts to end abuse. A rating of 1 or 2 was assigned to statements indicating resistance to the group, negative statements about the value of the program, and/or reluctance to participate in the group. A rating of 3 was assigned to ambivalent statements. A rating of 4 or 5 was assigned to statements reflecting a positive attitude toward the group and its ability to facilitate positive change.

Instruments Used to Provide Feedback in Motivational Interviewing

In an attempt to foster motivation to change and articulation of change goals, information gathered from the participant as part of the routine clinical assessment at the agency research site was used to provide feedback during the second motivational interviewing session following general guidelines outlined by Miller and Rollnick (1991). This feedback was not provided to individuals in the standard intake condition. All motivational intake participants were provided with normative feedback on the following self-report measures: the State Trait Anger Expression Inventory (Spielberger, 1988), the Dyadic Adjustment Scale (Spanier, 1976), and the Conflict Tactics Scale (Straus, 1979). Feedback used normative data from the instrument manuals for the STAXI (Spielberger, 1988) and the DAS (Spanier, 1989), and from the 1985 National Family Violence Survey for the CTS (Straus & Gelles, 1990). Feedback also listed out specific item endorsements for perceived pros and cons of abusive behavior from a measure currently under development. Individuals who reported alcohol or drug use at the time of violence or who exceeded a screening threshold indicating possible substance abuse problems were provided with additional feedback on the Alcohol Use Disorders Identification Test (AUDIT; Babor, de la Fuente, Saunders, & Grant, 1992) and the Drug Abuse Screening Test (DAST; Skinner, 1982). To protect victim confidentiality, no feedback was provided from collateral partner report data. In addition, no feedback was provided on the SIRC, as this measure was used to assess outcome.

Procedure

Assignment to Condition

Assignment to condition was unsystematic, but not technically random. Participants were assigned to Motivational Intake (MI) versus Standard Intake (SI) in alternating cohorts, with each sequential block of 12 cases assigned to the same study condition. Each cohort of 12 intake cases then constituted a treatment group and was referred to a standard 16-week CBT program (Murphy & Scott, 1996). Each treatment group consisted entirely of men who had been exposed to one of the two experimental conditions and were participating in the study. Individuals in the two intake conditions had no opportunity to intermingle or share information at the research site during the study.

Therapists and Therapist Training

Nine doctoral students in clinical psychology (1 male, 8 female) served as intake counselors. All received training in the administration of both MI and SI from the study authors and administered both intakes. Training in the SI condition involved didactic presentation, review of structured intake assessment instruments, and instruction on the administration of the interview for Antisocial Personality Disorder in the Structured Clinical Interview for *DSM–IV* Axis II Personality Disorders (SCID-II; First, Gibbon, Spitzer, & Williams, 1997). Therapists were instructed in the SI condition to respond cordially to clients, answer all client questions, and provide factual information about the program in a supportive fashion.

Multiple methods were used to teach MI skills to project therapists. First, they were given background readings that describe the basic philosophy and procedures of MI and the rationale for its use with partner-violent individuals (e.g., Miller & Rollnick, 1991; Murphy & Baxter, 1997).[2] Next, they attended a 15-hour workshop involving discussion of the philosophy of MI, role plays of specific MI techniques, and ideas on how to adapt MI for partner-abusive clients. This training was supplemented by the Professional Videotape Training Series on Motivational Interviewing (Miller, Rollnick, & Moyers, 1998). After completing the workshop, therapists participated in two 45-minute role plays with study authors, who depicted treatment-resistant clients. A videotape of each role play was reviewed with the trainees. The tapes were rated for MI adherence by investigators at the University of Maryland, Baltimore County, and the University of Oregon, and additional feedback was provided on adherence ratings to promote MI skill acquisition.

Procedures for Evaluating Therapist Proficiency and MI Adherence

To evaluate whether therapists were trained to a competent level of MI performance, the role-play sessions were coded by three independent raters using the First Pass Ratings Scale for Motivational Interviewing (Miller, 2000). Therapist certification required average First Pass Global Ratings of 5 or greater, with at least 70% of therapist behaviors during the first and last 10 minutes of each role-play session being coded as consistent with MI techniques, and all raters providing an affirmative answer to the global question: "Did the therapist adhere to Motivational Interviewing?" Throughout the course of data collection, the first author reviewed and rated audiotapes of the first three motivational interviews conducted by each project therapist, and every eighth session thereafter. Therapists were informed that tapes were being periodically reviewed, but they did not know which ones. In all sessions rated, the therapists exceeded the established criterion of 70% MI-consistent behaviors.

Description of Conditions

Both intake conditions were conducted over two sessions, approximately 2 weeks apart. Although efforts were made to equate the time for the two conditions, MI took about 4 hours to complete, whereas SI took about 3.5 hours. In both conditions, after three missed intake appointments, clients were terminated from the treatment program and a notice of non-attendance was provided to referral sources in court-mandated cases.

Standard Intake Condition (SI)

The SI condition was designed to be similar to intake procedures used by domestic violence agencies in the general locale of the research site. The goals were to gather clinically important information and to inform clients about agency rules and the philosophy and structure of the group counseling program. The first SI session was conducted in an individual format. In sequence, the intake worker reviewed agency policies and forms (for confidentiality, grievance procedures, release of information, etc.), set fees for counseling, completed a set of structured interviews, and administered a set of self-report measures. The second SI session consisted of a treatment orientation conducted in small-group format. The therapist reviewed written material about the program rules and philosophy, answered questions about the 16-session group CBT program, and administered a second set of self-report measures.

    In an effort to equate therapist contact time across conditions, individuals in SI were administered two structured interviews that were not administered to individuals in MI, and were used to investigate correlates of personality dysfunction in this population (Remington,

2002). Specifically, these were the Antisocial Personality Disorder Section of the SCID-II (First et al., 1997) and structured interview questions about casual sexual relationships, violence in prior intimate relationships, anticipatory (planning) behaviors before engaging in partner violence, conciliatory behaviors after partner violence, and emotional reactions to violence.

In the SI condition, therapists were instructed to answer questions openly and without defensiveness in a matter-of-fact style. They were instructed to listen empathically to client communications, but to refrain from using other techniques of motivational interviewing that are designed to counter resistance or elicit statements of a desire to change. If the client did not attend one of the two standard intake sessions and did not call to reschedule, the therapist was instructed to wait 1 week (to allow the client to take the initiative) before attempting to reschedule.

Motivational Intake (MI) Condition

Therapists in the MI condition were trained to use the five basic principles of motivational interviewing: express empathy, develop discrepancy, avoid argumentation, roll with resistance, and support self-efficacy. As in the SI condition, during the first MI session clients completed a brief demographic questionnaire and the stages of change measure before meeting with the therapist to review clinic policies and relevant forms. Next, the therapist conducted a 45-minute motivational interview with the client. After that, the client was asked to complete the same self-report questionnaire packet as administered in SI. Consistent with the philosophy of MI, the therapists attempted to elicit the client's cooperation and interest in completing the assessment as a means of self-exploration and personal evaluation. After completion of the questionnaire, the intake counselor spent 5 minutes wrapping-up, providing a short summary of material covered during the motivational interview, and addressing any client concerns or questions.

After the first MI session, the counselor sent a personalized, handwritten note to encourage the client to attend the subsequent meeting and to facilitate collaboration. The individualized letter included a joining statement (e.g., "It was nice to meet you," or "I am very glad that you made contact with our program") and a statement of optimism and hope (e.g., "I look forward to working together" or "I felt very good about the work we did in our first session").

The second MI session was conducted approximately 2 weeks after the first session. The therapist provided personalized feedback (using the techniques described by Miller and Rollnick, 1991) regarding the client's responses to measures of partner abuse, anger, and relationship adjustment. If the client exceeded screening cutoffs, feedback was also provided on risky drinking and signs of drug abuse. Feedback was presented with a data form that included information on the client's responses relative to population norms. The feedback portion of the session lasted 10 to 15 minutes, after which the therapist engaged the client in a second motivational interview for approximately 30 minutes. A set of self-report questionnaires was administered to the client at the end of the second intake session.

In MI, when a client missed a scheduled appointment, the therapist was instructed to phone the client as soon as possible to clarify reasons for the missed appointment and to express supportive concern, interest in meeting with the client, and, when appropriate, optimism about the prospect of change. In addition, a personalized, handwritten note was sent to the client after the missed appointment. In research with substance-abusing clients, it has been shown that a prompt note and telephone call of this type significantly increased the likelihood that the client would return (Intagliata, 1976; Koumans & Muller, 1965; Koumans, Muller, & Miller, 1967; Nirenberg, Sobell, & Sobell, 1980), and prior research from our team indicated that such procedures reduced dropout in group treatment for partner-violent men as well (Taft, Murphy, Elliott, & Morrel, 2001).

RESULTS

Comparability of Study Conditions

Tests were run to determine the effectiveness of assignment to conditions in establishing comparable study groups. Those assigned to MI versus SI did not differ significantly in average age, education, income, ethnicity, court-mandated status, readiness to change at baseline, or baseline collateral partner reports of abusive behavior on the CTS. Background demographics of participants in the two study conditions are presented in Table 4.1.

Motivation to Change

To test the effects of intake condition on motivational readiness to change, mixed-design analysis of variance tests (ANOVAs) were conducted with

Table 4.1

INITIAL COMPARABILITY OF PARTICIPANTS IN THE MOTIVATIONAL INTAKE (MI) AND STANDARD INTAKE (SI) CONDITIONS

| | INTAKE CONDITION | | | | | | |
| | MI (N = 55) | | SI (N = 53) | | | | |
VARIABLE	MEAN	SD	MEAN	SD	t	df	p
Age	35.8	7.9	35.6	9.4	0.1	106	.898
Education (Years)	13.3	2.9	12.8	2.1	1.2	106	.234
Income[a]	31.7	24.0	29.7	24.3	0.4	106	.668
Readiness-to-change	4.6	1.3	4.4	1.2	0.8	104	.416
CTS (Collateral report)[b]							
Physical	3.7	2.6	3.9	2.4	0.3	77	.752
Psychological	4.7	1.5	4.9	1.4	0.5	76	.601
Injuries	2.2	1.8	2.2	1.5	0.1	76	.941
Dichotomous Variables:	MI		SI		χ^2	df	p
% Ethnic minority	45		55		0.9	1	.336
% Court-mandated	80		77		0.1	1	.737

[a]Income in thousands (U.S. dollars). [b]Baseline collateral partner interviews were completed for 42 cases in the MI condition and 37 cases in the SI condition.

intake condition (MI vs. SI) as the grouping variable and time (before first intake session vs. first CBT group session) as the within-subjects factor. The three SIRC subscales (Precontemplation, Contemplation, and Preparation/Action) and the composite readiness to change score served as dependent variables in separate analyses. Contrary to the hypothesis, no significant condition by time interaction effect was found for the SIRC subscales or readiness to change composite. Table 4.2 presents descriptive statistics and ANOVA results for these analyses. The only significant result, a main effect of time for the Contemplation subscale, was unexpected, as scores decreased significantly across conditions from before to after intake.

DESCRIPTIVE STATISTICS AND MIXED-DESIGN ANALYSES OF VARIANCE FOR READINESS TO CHANGE VARIABLES

Table 4.2

| | TIME 1 | | | | TIME 2 | | | | SOURCE (df = 1, 76) | | | |
| | MI (N = 34) | | SI (N = 31) | | MI (N = 34) | | SI (N = 31) | | TIME | | X TIME | |
VARIABLE	MEAN	(SD)	MEAN	(SD)	MEAN	(SD)	MEAN	(SD)	F	p	F	p
Precontemplation	2.56	(.57)	2.49	(.53)	2.48	(.58)	2.51	(.63)	0.1	.755	0.7	.402
Contemplation	3.24	.83	3.28	1.07	3.09	.84	3.14	1.03	4.3	.041	0.1	.896
Preparation/Action	3.85	.54	3.61	.57	3.87	.49	3.62	.64	0.4	.519	0.0	.960
Readiness-to-Change composite	4.52	1.33	4.39	1.31	4.48	1.17	4.24	1.46	0.7	.407	0.2	.655

Treatment Involvement

The hypothesis of enhanced involvement in group CBT was tested using a one-way MANOVA with intake condition as the grouping variable and CBT session attendance, working alliance (client and therapist ratings early and late in treatment), and homework compliance (early and late in treatment) as the dependent variables. As hypothesized, the analysis revealed a significant effect of intake condition, $F(7, 66) = 5.30$, $p < .001$. A set of follow-up univariate one-way ANOVAs was then conducted to examine differences in each of the treatment involvement variables as a function of intake condition. The means and standard deviations of these variables across conditions and tests of significance are provided in Table 4.3. Significant differences (in the medium to large range of magnitude; Cohen, 1987) favored the MI condition on CBT homework compliance both early (effect size $d = .54$) and late

Table 4.3

TREATMENT INVOLVEMENT VARIABLES

| | INTAKE CONDITION | | | | |
| | MI | SI | | | |
VARIABLE	MEAN (*SD*)	MEAN (*SD*)	*t*	*df*	*p*
CBT sessions attended	10.0 (6.7)	10.5 (6.0)	0.39	106	.700
CBT homework compliance					
Early in treatment	3.8 (1.2)	3.1 (1.3)	2.49	80	.015
Late in treatment	3.7 (1.4)	2.3 (1.1)	4.77	72	.001
Client working alliance					
Early in treatment	195.1 (35.1)	197.1 (28.3)	0.29	79	.773
Late in treatment	203.4 (37.2)	204.5 (30.5)	0.13	74	.894
Therapist working alliance					
Early in treatment	53.8 (11.3)	54.0 (12.9)	0.12	80	.905
Late in treatment	59.7 (11.9)	52.6 (13.8)	2.40	74	.019

(d = 1.23) in treatment, as well as therapist ratings of the working alliance late in treatment (d = .51). The intake conditions did not differ significantly on number of sessions attended, client reports of the working alliance, or therapist reports of the working alliance early in treatment. The motivational intake participants were not more likely to begin CBT groups in the first place: 73% of those assigned to MI, and 81% of those assigned to SI attended at least one CBT group session, χ^2 = 1.1, df = 1, N = 108, p = .301.

Observational Ratings of CBT Session Behavior

Observational ratings of in-session behavior were analyzed using separate MANOVAs for early, middle, and late treatment sessions, with intake condition as the grouping variable and the three observational coding categories (responsibility assumption, role behavior, and group value) as the dependent variables. A significant multivariate effect of intake condition was observed during the early sessions of group CBT (Table 4.4). Univariate follow-up tests revealed that individuals in the MI condition, as compared to individuals in the SI condition, displayed significantly greater responsibility assumption (d = .59) and endorsement of group value (d = .76) during these early treatment sessions, with effect sizes in the medium range of magnitude (Cohen, 1987). The intake conditions did not differ significantly in role behavior.[3]

Interestingly, these intake effects dissipated by the middle phase of group CBT, as revealed by nonsignificant multivariate tests for the middle and late treatment sessions (see Table 4.4). Examination of the means indicates that MI participants displayed more constructive group behavior during the early sessions of CBT, but SI participants caught up to the MI condition in their display of constructive group behavior by the middle sessions of treatment.[4]

Other Help-Seeking Behavior

The data supported the hypothesized effect of MI on other help-seeking behavior. By client self-report at the end of the group CBT program, 66% of individuals in the MI condition had received help from outside sources since intake, compared to 41% in the SI condition (χ^2 = 4.2, df = 1, N = 69, p < .05). MI clients sought help from a greater number of different sources (M = 1.3, SD = 1.3) than did SI clients (M = .8, SD = 1.3), Mann–Whitney U = 435, z = 2.04, p < .05, and attended a greater number

Table 4.4

CONSTRUCTIVE BEHAVIOR IN GROUP CBT FROM OBSERVATIONAL CODING OF TREATMENT SESSIONS

| | INTAKE CONDITION | | | | |
| | MI | SI | | | |
VARIABLE	MEAN (*SD*)	MEAN (*SD*)	*t*	*df*	*p*
Early treatment sessions	Multivariate $F(3, 67) = 4.64$, $p = .005$				
Responsibility for abuse	3.11 (.95)	2.67 (.74)	2.27	73	.026
Role behavior	3.42 (.91)	3.17 (.64)	1.31	69	.194
Group value	3.66 (.82)	3.03 (.83)	3.25	72	.002
Middle treatment sessions	Multivariate $F(3, 60) = 0.78$, $p = .508$				
Responsibility for abuse	3.02 (.61)	2.86 (.69)	0.98	63	.331
Role behavior	3.20 (.82)	3.11 (.81)	0.42	63	.672
Group value	3.44 (.68)	3.20 (.75)			
Late treatment sessions	Multivariate $F(3, 64) = 1.94$, $p = .131$				
Responsibility for abuse	3.13 (.77)	3.20 (.84)	0.34	69	.733
Role behavior	3.44 (.74)	3.23 (.72)	1.23	63	.223
Group value	3.53 (.83)	3.36 (.90)	0.79	68	.434

Note. The *N*s vary as a result of missed sessions and insufficient verbalization for coding. The *N*s for early, middle, and late treatment analyses in the two study conditions are as follows: For Responsibility Assumption: 39, 30, and 38 in MI; 36, 35, and 33 in SI; for Role Behavior: 39, 30, and 36 in MI; 32, 35, and 33 in SI; and for Group Value: 41, 31, and 37 in MI; 33, 35, and 33 in SI. Analyses were repeated after imputing missing observations from available observational data at other time points, and yielded the same substantive findings.

of other help sessions ($M = 26.1$, $SD = 39.0$) than did SI clients ($M = 16.3$, $SD = 45.9$), Mann–Whitney $U = 445$, $z = 2.22$, $p < .05$.[5]

Abusive Behavior Outcomes

Given that the target goals of MI were to enhance treatment engagement and motivational readiness to change, effects on abusive behavior outcomes were not specifically hypothesized, but were explored with available data. Collateral partner reports of psychological aggression, physical assault, and injury for the 6-month period after scheduled completion of the CBT group were the dependent variables in these analyses. The presence versus absence of any physical aggression and injury during the follow-up period were also analyzed, as these variables provide a straightforward indication of clinically significant outcome. Individuals who completed two sessions of intake were eligible for inclusion in these analyses whether or not they attended subsequent group sessions. Collateral data on abuse at the 6-month follow-up assessment were available for 68% of these cases in the MI condition ($N = 34$), and 66% of these cases in the SI condition ($N = 31$).

The rates of abuse during follow-up evaluation were somewhat lower for those in the MI versus SI condition, but these effects were not statistically significant (Table 4.5). The result for physical assault approached standard significance levels at the cutoff sometimes used in exploratory data analyses ($p < .10$). Regarding dichotomous outcomes for physical assault and injury, 12% of the female partners of MI clients (4 of 34) versus 26% of female partners of SI clients (8 of 31) reported experiencing one or more acts of physical assault during the follow-up period. Injuries during the follow-up period were reported by 6% of the partners

Table 4.5

ABUSIVE BEHAVIOR DURING THE 6 MONTHS AFTER GROUP CBT FROM COLLATERAL PARTNER REPORTS (CTS VARIETY SCORES)

| | INTAKE CONDITION | | | | | | |
| | MI ($N = 34$) | | SI ($N = 31$) | | | | |
VARIABLE	MEAN	SD	MEAN	SD	F[a]	df	p
Physical assault	0.18	0.52	0.61	1.28	3.38	(1, 61)	.071
Injury	0.01	0.38	0.35	0.88	1.46	(1, 61)	.232
Psychological aggression	2.09	1.91	2.81	2.14	1.65	(1, 61)	.204

[a]ANCOVA controlling for baseline scores on the same variable.

in the MI condition (2 of 34) versus 16% of partners in the SI condition (5 of 31). These differences were not statistically significant (for physical assault, $\chi^2 = 2.1$, $df = 1$, $p = .145$; for injuries, $\chi^2 = 1.8$, $df = 1$, $p = .183$). Thus, although the prevalence rates for assault and injury were more than twice as high in the control group than in the MI group, these differences were not statistically reliable given the current sample size and the relatively low base rates of these outcomes in both conditions.

DISCUSSION

The results provide qualified support for the utility of motivational interviewing as a pretreatment preparation strategy for partner-violent men. When compared to a highly structured control intake, two sessions of motivational interviewing significantly enhanced treatment engagement and help-seeking behavior, but did not significantly alter treatment session attendance or subjective self-reports of readiness to change. These participants displayed more constructive behavior in session when they began attending subsequent group cognitive behavioral therapy (CBT), articulating greater perceived value of treatment and assuming more personal responsibility for their abusive behavior. Throughout treatment, these motivational intake (MI) participants completed substantially more of the assigned CBT homework than did standard intake (SI) participants. By the later stages of treatment, their therapists came to see the MI participants as having a stronger working alliance than SI participants. In addition, more of the MI participants reported that they had obtained help from sources outside of the domestic violence program during treatment. According to collateral partner report for the 6 months after group CBT, participants who received the SI intake were over twice as likely as MI participants to physically assault or injure their partners, but these findings were not statistically significant given the low overall rates of posttreatment violence and the modest sample size.

The clinical importance of the findings is bolstered by the observation that some of the factors affected by MI have predicted abusive behavior outcomes in prior research with this population. In our prior study with an expanded sample that included participants in the current investigation, those with higher levels of CBT homework compliance had significantly lower levels of psychological abuse during the 6 months after group treatment. In addition, higher therapist ratings of the working alliance predicted lower levels of both physical and psychological abuse during follow-up evaluation, and therapist ratings of the working alliance were the strongest predictors of physical and psychological abuse outcomes from among a set of treatment process variables (Taft et al., 2003a). Likewise, in a self-referred sample of couples affected by husband-to-wife violence, Brown and O'Leary (2000) found that the working alliance, assessed through objective ratings from the first group treatment session, was associated with significant reductions in physical and psychological abuse. Thus, the treatment involvement variables measured in the current study have predictive validity as proximal indicators of successful intervention. Together with the findings of lower physical assault during the follow-up period in the MI condition (which approached significance), the current results provide cautious optimism for continued experimentation with motivational therapies for partner-violent individuals.

The nature and strength of the findings were consistent with previous research on motivational interventions for substance abuse problems, health-behavior promotion, and relationship concerns (Cordova, Warren, & Gee, 2001). Although there is considerable evidence that motivational interventions are effective in altering problem behavior, there is little evidence to date that MI exerts its effects through enhancing motivation to change (Burke et al., 2002). In substance use applications, brief motivational interventions, on average, produce abstinence rates that are twice as high as control conditions (Burke et al., 2003). This result is consistent with the partner violence rate observed in the current study, which was cut roughly in half with MI. In Project MATCH, a large-scale clinical trial designed to identify factors associated with successful outcome in different types of alcoholism treatment, one of the few significant findings was that clients with high levels of anger responded more favorably to motivational enhancement therapy than to coping skills therapy (Project MATCH Research Group, 1997). Clinical impressions from the current study likewise indicate that motivational interviewing is particularly helpful in diffusing initial client hostility and resistance to therapist direction.

Despite these consistencies with prior research, the lack of significant findings on treatment session attendance is puzzling, particularly given that this was one of the primary reasons for experimenting with MI. Our previous research had demonstrated that supportive, personalized communication (handwritten notes and telephone calls) after missed group sessions, in the context of greater communication about the importance of session attendance, significantly decreased dropout (Taft et al., 2001). These interventions were incorporated into the MI condition in the current study, but with no apparent impact on treatment attendance. It is important to note, however, that participants in both intake conditions received personalized communication if they missed sessions once they reached the group CBT phase of treatment, so differences in the intake conditions may have been insufficient to affect subsequent group attendance. It is also possible that other motivations to attend treatment, such as fear of negative repercussions from the court or changes in relationship status, may override intake effects on session attendance. In addition, motivation to attend treatment sessions may be distinct from motivation to change abusive behavior, which was the ostensible focus of the MI intervention.

It is also interesting to note that the observed effects of MI on session behavior were most noticeable early in treatment. This finding may reflect the fact that the standard CBT intervention provided to all participants used some motivational strategies during the early group sessions, including group discussion of the pros and cons of acting abusively and commitment to change, which may have allowed participants in the SI condition to catch up to those in the MI condition in their expression of positive group behavior by the middle of treatment. Nevertheless, those in the SI condition completed less CBT homework (which typically reflected a drop-off in initial homework compliance over the course of treatment) and were less likely to seek help outside of the abuser treatment program. This pattern of behavioral results suggests that reduction in treatment-resistant attitudes and enhancement of treatment-receptive attitudes early on in treatment produces noticeable benefits in subsequent treatment activities.

The study had several important limitations, both in terms of research design and clinical implementation, which should be considered. First, the assignment to conditions was unsystematic, but not technically random. Although preliminary analyses indicated that the two study conditions did not differ on baseline measures of demographic and clinical variables, it is possible that other undetected differences between conditions may have influenced the results. Second, the findings may have been influenced by attrition from treatment, as only participants who attended group CBT sessions were available to provide data on the readiness-to-change instrument and treatment involvement measures. Third, the follow-up rate for collateral partner reports of abusive behavior was modest, as is common in this area of research (Gondolf,

1997), and therefore missing data may have influenced the abusive behavior outcomes. Fourth, generalization is limited by the fact that the study was conducted in a suburban context, with a population that was almost exclusively White and African American, 80% court mandated to counseling, and consisting solely of male clients who abused female partners. Fifth, the format of the second intake differed between study conditions, conducted individually for MI participants and in a small group format for SI participants. Therefore it is possible that negative group interactions reduced subsequent treatment engagement for SI participants. However, the second SI session was devoted primarily to structured provision of information regarding agency procedures and group rules, information that was likewise reviewed (albeit individually) with MI participants. Therefore, differences due to session format would most likely reflect the opportunity for supportive discussion to reduce client resistance to program information in the MI condition, an effect that is consistent with the conceptual foundation of this approach as implemented in the current project.

Several aspects of the clinical implementation also deserve careful scrutiny. First, the project therapists were novices with respect to MI. Although all met the minimum competency requirements, greater experience and training may be necessary to facilitate advanced level practice. Second, the target goals of MI were somewhat vague, and therefore the typical MI emphasis on self-directed change may have been watered down by focusing on engagement into subsequent treatment. Finally, other features of the treatment context may have clashed with core philosophical elements of MI. Most important, MI emphasizes personal autonomy and choice in the decision to change and the menu of change strategies. The court mandate to treatment, as well as the fact that the target behavior produces harm to others, creates complexities in maintaining this emphasis on personal autonomy.

In conclusion, two sessions of motivational interviewing during the intake process at a community domestic violence agency produced significant benefits during subsequent group counseling on several indicators of treatment involvement. The current findings should be evaluated in light of prior clinical outcome studies that have yielded quite small average effects of treatment for partner-violent men, with no specific intervention consistently superior to any other (Babcock et al., 2004). As suggested by prior clinical writings (e.g., Daniels & Murphy, 1997; Dutton, 1995; Murphy & Baxter, 1997), the current findings indicate that treatment of partner-violent men can be enhanced by intervention strategies that are sensitive to the client's readiness for change and designed to promote a collaborative working alliance.

NOTES

1. The data on session attendance were reanalyzed after dropping subjects who did not complete the intake process, and none of the substantive results reported here were altered.

2. The treatment manual for motivational interviewing was revised after this project was under way (Miller & Rollnick, 2002). Only the first edition of the manual was available for therapist training in the current investigation.

3. The Ns vary somewhat for these analyses as a function of missing data arising from session nonattendance and inadequate verbalization during treatment sessions to allow coding for some individuals.

4. A multivariate analysis with all three observational codes as dependent variables revealed a significant condition by time interaction, statistically verifying the observation that SI participants caught up to MI participants in constructive group behavior over the course of treatment.

5. Nonparametric tests were used for these latter two variables because their distributions did not approximate normal theory assumptions.

ACKNOWLEDGMENTS

This project was supported by grants from the Directed Research Initiative Fund of the University of Maryland, Baltimore County, and the National Institute of Mental Health (1RO3MH56373) to the fourth author and an Individual National Research Service Award to the third author from the National Institute of Mental Health (1F31MH12234). The authors gratefully acknowledge the therapists who conducted motivational interviewing and CBT groups during the period of this investigation and the generous support of the agency staff at the Domestic Violence Center of Howard County, Maryland.

REFERENCES

Alexander, P. C., & Morris, E. (2008). Stages of change in batterers and their response to treatment. *Violence and Victims, 23*(4), 476–492.

Arias, I., & Beach, S. R. H. (1987). Validity of self-reports of marital violence. *Journal of Family Violence, 2,* 139–149.

Babcock, J. C., Green, C. E., & Robie, C. (2004). Does batterers' treatment work? A meta-analytic review of domestic violence treatment. *Clinical Psychology Review, 23,* 1023–1053.

Babor, T. F., de la Fuente, J. R., Saunders, J., & Grant, M. (1992). *AUDIT: Alcohol use disorders identification test: Guidelines for use in primary health care.* Geneva, Switzerland: World Health Organization.

Begun, A. L., Murphy, C. M., Bolt, D., Weinstein, B., Strodthoff, T., Short, L., et al. (2003). Characteristics of the safe at home instrument for assessing readiness to change intimate partner violence. *Research on Social Work Practice, 13,* 80–107.

Brown, P. D., & O'Leary, K. D. (2000). Therapeutic alliance: Predicting continuance and success in group treatment for spouse abuse. *Journal of Consulting and Clinical Psychology, 68,* 340–345.

Brown, P. D., O'Leary, K. D., & Feldbau, S. R. (1997). Dropout in a treatment program for self-referring wife abusing men. *Journal of Family Violence, 12,* 365–387.

Bryant, M. J., Simons, A. D., & Thase, M. E. (1999). Therapist skill and patient variables in home-work compliance: Controlling an uncontrolled variable in cognitive therapy outcome research. *Cognitive Therapy and Research, 23,* 381–399.

Burke, B. L., Arkowitz, H., & Dunn, C. (2002). The efficacy of motivational interviewing. In W. R. Miller & S. Rollnick (Eds.), *Motivational interviewing: Preparing people for change* (2nd ed., pp. 217–250). New York: Guilford Press.

Burke, B. L., Arkowitz, H., & Menchola, M. (2003). The efficacy of motivational interviewing: A meta-analysis. *Journal of Consulting and Clinical Psychology, 71,* 843–861.

Cadsky, O., Hanson, R. K., Crawford, M., & Lalonde, C. (1996). Attrition from a male batterer treatment program: Client-treatment congruence and lifestyle instability. *Violence and Victims, 11,* 51–64.

Chen, H., Bersani, C., Myers, S. C., & Denton, R. (1989). Evaluating the effectiveness of a court-sponsored abuser treatment program. *Journal of Family Violence, 4,* 309–322.

Cohen, J. (1987). *Statistical power analysis for the behavioral sciences* (Rev. ed.). Hillsdale, NJ: Lawrence Erlbaum.

Connors, G. J., Carroll, K. M., DiClemente, C. C., Longabaugh, R., & Donovan, D. M. (1997). The therapeutic alliance and its relation to alcoholism treatment participation and outcome. *Journal of Consulting and Clinical Psychology, 65,* 588–598.

Cook, T. D., & Campbell, D. T. (1979). *Quasi-experimental design and analysis: Issues for field settings.* Chicago: Rand McNally.

Cordova, J. V., Warren, L. Z., & Gee, C. B. (2001). Motivational interviewing as an intervention for at-risk couples. *Journal of Marital and Family Therapy, 27,* 315–326.

Daniels, J. W., & Murphy, C. M. (1997). Stages and processes of change in batterers' treatment. *Cognitive and Behavioral Practice, 4,* 123–145.

Dunn, C., DeRoo, L., & Rivara, F. P. (2001). The use of brief interventions adapted from motivational interviewing across behavioral domains: A systematic review. *Addiction, 96,* 1725–1742.

Dutton, D. G. (1995). *The domestic assault of women: Psychological and criminal justice perspectives* (Rev. ed.). Vancouver, British Columbia: UBC Press.

Eckhardt, C., Holtzworth-Munroe, A., Norlander, B., Sibley, A., & Cahill, M. (2008). Readiness to change, partner violence subtypes, and treatment outcomes among men in treatment for partner assault. *Violence and Victims, 23*(4), 446–475.

Elliott, J. D. (2002). *Responsibility acceptance and aggression changes in group therapy for relationship abuse perpetrators.* Unpublished doctoral dissertation, University of Maryland, Baltimore County.

First, M. A., Gibbon, M., Spitzer, R. L., & Williams, J. B. W. (1997). *Structured clinical interview for DSM-IV Axis-II personality disorders (SCID-II user's guide).* Washington, DC: American Psychiatric Press.

Gondolf, E. W. (1997). Patterns of reassault in batterer programs. *Violence and Victims, 12*, 373–387.

Gondolf, E. W., & Foster, R. A. (1991). Preprogram attrition in batterer programs. *Journal of Family Violence, 6*, 337–350.

Hamberger, L. K., & Hastings, J. E. (1989). Counseling of male spouse abusers: Characteristics of treatment completers and dropouts. *Violence and Victims, 4*, 275–286.

Horvath, A. O., & Greenberg, L. S. (1989). The development and validation of the working alliance inventory. *Journal of Counseling Psychology, 36*, 223–233.

Intagliata, J. (1976). A telephone follow-up procedure for increasing the effectiveness of a treatment program for alcoholics. *Journal of Studies on Alcohol, 37*, 1330–1335.

Koumans, A. J. R., & Muller, J. J. (1965). Use of letters to increase motivation for treatment in alcoholics. *Psychological Reports, 16*, 11–52.

Koumans, A. J. R., Muller, J. J., & Miller, C. F. (1967). Use of telephone calls to increase motivation for treatment in alcoholics. *Psychological Reports, 21*, 327–328.

Levesque, D. A., Gelles, R. J., & Velicer, W. F. (2000). Development and validation of a stages of change measure for men in batterer treatment. *Cognitive Therapy and Research, 24*, 175–199.

Miller, W. R. (1983). Motivational interviewing with problem drinkers. *Behavioural Psychotherapy, 11*(2), 147–172.

Miller, W. R. (1985). Motivation for treatment: A review with special emphasis on alcoholism. *Psychological Bulletin, 98*, 84–107.

Miller, W. R. (2000). *Motivational interviewing skill coding (MISC)*. Unpublished coding manual, University of New Mexico, Albuquerque.

Miller, W. R., & Rollnick, S. (1991). *Motivational interviewing: Preparing people to change addictive behavior*. New York: Guilford Press.

Miller, W. R., & Rollnick, S. (2002). *Motivational interviewing: Preparing people for change* (2nd ed.). New York: Guilford Press.

Miller, W. R., Rollnick, S., & Moyers, T. (1998). *Motivational interviewing: Professional training videotape series*. Albuquerque: University of New Mexico.

Moffitt, T. E., Caspi, A., Krueger, R. F., Magdol, L., Margolin, G., Silva, P. A., et al. (1997). Do partners agree about abuse in their relationship? A psychometric evaluation of interpartner agreement. *Psychological Assessment, 9*, 47–56.

Murphy, C. M., & Baxter, V. A. (1997). Motivating batterers to change in the treatment context. *Journal of Interpersonal Violence, 12*, 607–619.

Murphy, C. M., & Scott, E. (1996). *Cognitive-behavioral therapy for domestically assaultive individuals: A treatment manual*. Unpublished manuscript, University of Maryland, Baltimore County.

Nirenberg, T. D., Sobell, L. C., & Sobell, M. B. (1980). Effective and inexpensive procedures for decreasing client attrition in an outpatient alcohol treatment program. *American Journal of Drug and Alcohol Abuse, 7*, 73–82.

Primakoff, L., Epstein, N., & Covi, L. (1986). Homework compliance: An uncontrolled variable in cognitive therapy outcome research. *Behavior Therapy, 17*, 433–446.

Prochaska, J. O., & DiClemente, C. C. (1984). *The transtheoretical approach: Crossing traditional boundaries of therapy*. Melbourne, FL: Krieger.

Project MATCH Research Group. (1997). Project MATCH secondary a priori hypotheses. *Addiction, 92*, 1671–1698.

Remington, N. A. (2002). *Correlates of antisocial personality characteristics with the relationship dynamics and treatment outcomes of domestically violent men.* Unpublished doctoral dissertation, University of Maryland, Baltimore County.

Skinner, H. A. (1982). The drug abuse screening test. *Addictive Behaviors, 7,* 363–371.

Spanier, G. (1976). Measuring dyadic adjustment: New scales for assessing the quality of marriage and similar dyads. *Journal of Marriage and the Family, 3,* 15–28.

Spanier, G. B. (1989). *Manual for the dyadic adjustment scale.* North Tonawanda, NY: Multi-Health Systems, Inc.

Spielberger, C. D. (1988). *Manual for the state-trait anger expression inventory (STAXI).* Odessa, FL: Psychological Assessment Resources.

Stosny, S. (1994). "Shadows of the heart": A dramatic video for the treatment resistance of spouse abusers. *Social Work, 39,* 686–694.

Straus, M. A. (1979). Measuring intrafamily conflict and violence: The conflict tactics scales. *Journal of Marriage and the Family, 41,* 75–88.

Straus, M. A. (1990). The conflict tactics scales and its critics: An evaluation and new data on validity and reliability. In M. A. Straus & R. J. Gelles (Eds.), *Physical violence in American families* (pp. 49–73). New Brunswick, NJ: Transaction Publishers.

Straus, M. A., & Gelles, R. J. (1990). *Physical violence in American families: Risk factors and adaptations to violence in 8,145 families.* New Brunswick, NJ: Transaction Publishers.

Straus, M. A., Hamby, S. L., Boney-McCoy, S., & Sugarman, D. B. (1996). The revised conflict tactics scales (CTS-2). *Journal of Family Issues, 7,* 283–316.

Taft, C. T., Murphy, C. M., Elliott, J. D., & Morrel, T. M. (2001). Attendance enhancing procedures in group counseling for domestic abusers. *Journal of Counseling Psychology, 48,* 51–60.

Taft, C. T., Murphy, C. M., King, D. W., Musser, P. H., & DeDeyn, J. M. (2003a). Process and treatment adherence factors in group cognitive-behavioral therapy for partner-violent men. *Journal of Consulting and Clinical Psychology, 71,* 812–820.

Taft, C. T., Murphy, C. M., Musser, P. H., & Remington, N. A. (2003b). Personality, interpersonal, and motivational predictors of the working alliance in group cognitive-behavioral therapy for partner-violent men. *Journal of Consulting and Clinical Psychology, 71,* 812–820.

Tolman, R. M., & Bhosley, G. (1990). A comparison of two types of pregroup preparation for men who batter. *Journal of Social Service Research, 13,* 33–43.

Tracey, T. J., & Kokotovic, A. M. (1989). Factor structure of the working alliance inventory. *Psychological Assessment, 1,* 207–210.

Tryon, G. S., & Kane, A. S. (1993). Relationship of working alliance to mutual and unilateral termination. *Journal of Counseling Psychology, 40,* 33–36.

Readiness to Change, Partner Violence Subtypes, and Treatment Outcomes Among Men in Treatment for Partner Assault

5

CHRISTOPHER ECKHARDT, AMY HOLTZWORTH-MUNROE,
BRADLEY NORLANDER, ASHLEY SIBLEY, AND MELISSA CAHILL

Despite the criminalization of male abuse against female intimate partners and the addition of rehabilitative postadjudication sentences designed to reduce assault continuance, a relatively high rate of men mandated to attend batterer's intervention programs (BIPs) continue to reassault their female partners. While some researchers point to an overall positive effect of BIPs on domestic violence recidivism (e.g., Gondolf, 1999), others note that existing treatment approaches for men who batter do little beyond other potential postadjudication sanctions (e.g., intensive probation monitoring) (Babcock, Green, & Robie, 2004; Babcock & La Taillade, 2000; Dunford, 2000). In addition, researchers have consistently noted that between 40% and 90% of men initially mandated by the court to attend batterer intervention programs do not attend or complete such programs (Daly & Pelowski, 2000). These findings suggest that the effectiveness of court-mandated BIPs is a complicated issue that is determined by a variety of interdependent factors, including program practices specific to a given BIP, the overall community response to domestic violence, sanctions existing within the criminal justice system for BIP nonattendance, and the individual characteristics of the perpetrator (Healey, Smith, & O'Sullivan, 1998). In the present study, we focused on the latter domain as a predictor of BIP outcomes. Specifically, we investigated relationships among pretreatment motivation to change violent behavior (i.e., "readiness to change"; Prochaska, DiClemente, & Norcross, 1992), differing "subtypes" of intimate partner violence perpetrators (e.g., Holtzworth-Munroe & Stuart, 1994), and BIP-related outcomes (attrition and recidivism) among a postadjudication sample of men convicted of misdemeanor partner assault offenses.

While the data regarding the general effectiveness of BIPs are not uniformly encouraging, it is also apparent that there is substantial individual variation in how men respond to BIP (Daniels & Murphy, 1997; Edelson, 1996). The question remains how criminal justice professionals can identify those abusers whose history and characteristics indicate that treatment as usual is not likely to be effective and who are at risk for program dropout and/or recidivism. It is clear from decades of psychotherapy research that treatment outcome is due in large part to the extent that clients are *ready* to receive the intervention being offered regardless of the specific intervention modality (Prochaska, 1979). Thus, one of the important variables that may predict attrition (i.e., whether men are getting an adequate "dose" of treatment) and subsequent recidivism is men's readiness to change their abusive behavior at the commencement of BIP. According to the transtheoretical model of behavior change (TTM; Prochaska, 1979), individuals confronted with the task of changing a problematic behavior are not uniformly ready to change that behavior at the commencement of treatment. Some are committed to action, some barely recognize the existence of a problem, and others wish to change but are not sure how. After over two decades of research, Prochaska and colleagues (e.g., Prochaska et al., 1992) have indicated that intentional behavior change consists of five stages (precontemplation, contemplation, preparation, action, and maintenance) through which individuals pass as they attempt to change a problematic behavior. Movement through the stages of change, as assessed by the University of Rhode Island Change Assessment Scale (URICA) (McConnaughy, Prochaska, & Velicer, 1983), has predicted client persistence in treatment, willingness to change outside the therapy session, treatment effectiveness, and overall therapy outcome in samples of individuals with a wide range of negative health behaviors (for a review, see Prochaska et al., 1992).

Clinicians and researchers (Murphy & Baxter, 1997; Pence & Paymar, 1993) have suggested that partner abuse perpetrators mandated to attend group counseling may minimize or deny the extent of abusiveness in their relationships (Dutton, 1986) and often blame external factors for their violence (Eckhardt & Dye, 2000) and their presence in the BIP (e.g., a "raw deal" from the criminal justice system). Thus, it is unlikely that partner assaultive men as a group will automatically recognize the need to change their behavior solely because of their involvement in the legal process. Accordingly, researchers have hypothesized that the majority of men mandated to treatment for intimate partner violence are in the precontemplative stage of the change process (Daniels & Murphy, 1997; Murphy & Baxter, 1997) and are not using processes that might otherwise result in behavior change. Researchers investigating partner abusive men mandated to attend BIP have reported that 25% to 41% of these men present with characteristics suggestive of the precontemplative stage of change (Eckhardt, Babcock, & Homack, 2004; Levesque, Gelles, & Velicer, 2000; Scott & Wolfe, 2003). Precontemplative men reported using fewer behavior change processes than men in other stages (Eckhardt, Babcock, et al., 2004), reported fewer benefits relative to costs of making a commitment to nonviolence (Levesque et al., 2000), and demonstrated minimal therapeutic change over the course of BIP (Scott & Wolfe, 2003). Research investigating general therapeutic change processes supports the link between therapy outcomes and stage of change, as clients who terminate therapy prematurely are more likely to be in the precontemplative stage of change (Brogan, Prochaska, & Prochaska, 1999) and to utilize fewer processes of change at the outset of counseling relative to nonterminating clients (O'Hare, 1996; Smith, Subich, & Kalodner, 1995).

In addition, partner assaultive men are likely to possess other psychological and behavioral traits that predict a poor response to treatment (for a review, see Schumacher, Feldbau-Kohn, Slep, & Heyman, 2001). Indeed, ample data indicate that partner assaultive men are a heterogeneous group of males that may cluster into *particular violence subtypes* (for reviews, see Holtzworth-Munroe, 2000; Holtzworth-Munroe & Stuart, 1994). While the precise number of subtypes varies according to the researcher, three dimensions typically underlie these subtypes: presence and degree of psychopathology, severity of intimate partner violence, and the extent of general violence (Holtzworth-Munroe & Stuart, 1994). Using a community sample, Holtzworth-Munroe and colleagues (Holtzworth-Munroe, Meehan, Herron, Rehman, & Stuart, 2000) cluster analyzed these dimensions and suggested the presence of four batterer subtypes: (a) family-only (FO) batterers, who evidence minimal family violence, engage in the least violence outside the home, and show little or no psychopathology; (b) borderline/dysphoric (BD) batterers, who present with moderate to severe partner assault and moderate general violence, and who present with the most affective distress and personality disturbances related to borderline and dependent personality disorders; (c) generally violent/antisocial (GVA) batterers, who engage in moderate to severe partner violence and the highest levels of violence outside the home and evidence antisocial and/or psychopathic personality traits; and (d) low-level antisocial (LLA) batterers, who score moderately on measures of partner violence, violence generality, and antisociality. These subtypes, as well as conceptually similar typologies reported by other researchers (e.g., Waltz, Babcock, Jacobson, & Gottman, 2000), differ across a variety of cognitive, affective, and behavioral domains in both cross-sectional (Holtzworth-Munroe et al., 2000) and longitudinal (Holtzworth-Munroe, Meehan, Herron, Rehman, & Stuart, 2003) studies involving community samples.

Currently, there are few published data that link these partner violence subtypes to men adjudicated for partner assault offenses (see Hamberger, Lohr, Bonge, & Tolin, 1996; Langinrichsen-Rohling, Huss, & Ramsey, 2000), and additional evidence would add important information on the generalizability of the subtype construct. In addition, there are no published data that examine whether partner violence subtypes relate to readiness-to-change variables and only limited data on subtypes as predictors of BIP outcomes. For instance, research examining the TTM and general psychotherapy outcome suggests that individuals who enter treatment at the precontemplative stage show more psychopathology than individuals entering treatment at later stages (McConnaughy, DiClemente, Prochaska, & Velicer, 1989). In the context of partner-abusing males, one might therefore predict that abusers who exhibit greater levels of psychopathology (men in BD and GVA subtypes) will report lackluster motivation to change their violent behavior and thus an increased probability of postadjudication recidivism or BIP noncompletion. The GVA men might not see their violent behavior as particularly problematic and thus see little need for change, while BD men may have such serious mood-related problems that they are unaware of the need or unable to cease their violence. Conversely, one could also hypothesize that FO men, who present with the least amount of intimate partner violence and psychopathology, may simply not define themselves as batterers and may resist the idea that they are in need of a batterers program. Consequently, they may report low motivation to change since they do not perceive the presence of problematic behaviors in need of modification and thus be more likely to prematurely terminate BIP (which for some individuals may potentiate risk for partner violence continuance).

In the present research, we addressed these issues by investigating pre-BIP stages-of-change profiles and partner violence subtypes as predictors of BIP dropout and criminal recidivism 6 months post-BIP among males mandated to attend BIP for a misdemeanor domestic violence assault conviction involving a female intimate partner. First, using cluster analysis, we predicted that men commencing BIP would group into distinct readiness-to-change clusters based on a self-report measure of domestic violence–related stages of change. Second, we expected a second set of cluster analyses to reveal four batterer subtypes (FO, BD, GVA, and LLA) similar to those reported by Holtzworth-Munroe and colleagues (2000). Third, we predicted that men falling into more change-resistant stages-of-change clusters would group into the more disturbed batterer subtypes (GVA, BD). Fourth, we expected that men who eventually dropped out of BIP would be in stages-of-change clusters reflective of the precontemplative stage and fall into more antisocial batterer subtypes (GVA, LLA). Finally, we expected that postadjudication criminal recidivism would be predicted by a combination of factors, including BIP dropout, low readiness to change, and membership in more psychopathological and violent subtypes (BD, GVA).

METHOD

Participants

Male participants consisted of 199 men convicted of a misdemeanor assault offense involving an intimate female partner in Dallas County, Texas. Inclusion criteria were a guilty or no-contest plea of misdemeanor assault (class A) with a positive finding of family violence (as determined by the arresting police officer in the arrest report), the ability to read and speak English fluently, and being 18 years of age or older. Participants were paid a total of $120 for their involvement in this study. Demographic data (Table 5.1) generally indicate that participants were in their early 30s, predominantly African American, equally likely to have either some college or a high school education or less, in blue-collar professions earning less than $30,000 per year, and equally likely to be married, divorced, or separated and had at least one child.

To improve the reliability index of postadjudication partner violence recurrence, female intimate partners (*n* = 65) of male study participants were also contracted. Study interviewers (all female) proceeded with the

DEMOGRAPHIC CHARACTERISTICS OF THE SAMPLE

VARIABLE	SAMPLE ($N = 199$)
M Age (*SD*)	33.0 (8.8)
Ethnicity	
% African American	45.7
% White	32.3
% Hispanic	19.9
% Other	1.1
Marital Status	
% Single	29.0
% Living together	14.5
% Married	29.0
% Separated	14.0
% Divorced	12.9
M Relationship length (years)	4.2
Children	
% One or more	81.2
Education (highest completed)	
% Some high school	46.8
% GED or high school diploma only	8.1
% Some college/trade school	40.8
% College degree	4.3
Employed	
% Yes	84.7
Occupational Status	
% Managerial/Profession Specialty	9.3
% Technical, Sales, & Administration Support	23.6
% Service	8.8
% Precision Production, Craft, & Repair	22.0
% Operators, Fabricators, & Laborers	20.9
% Unemployed/Student	15.4
M Income (thousands)	29.0
M Prior Arrests (*SD*)	1.8 (2.5)
M Prior Assault Arrests (*SD*)	0.3 (0.7)

Note. GED = general equivalency diploma.

recruitment phone call to female partners, *only* if the individual answering the phone was female. Telephone contact was then maintained if female partners (a) expressed interest in learning more about the study, and (b) felt sufficiently safe to answer questions concerning their experience as victims of domestic violence, with safety determined by administration of the Danger Assessment Inventory (Campbell, 1995). Only after receipt of a signed consent form and clear documentation of their desired method of contact did administration of questionnaires occur. Female participants were also paid $120.

Procedure

Recruitment and Screening

Men were individually recruited during the batterer intervention intake orientation at the Family Violence Court in Dallas, Texas.[1] If the male expressed interest in the study, project representatives scheduled the pre-BIP interview date/time/location and gave the man a flyer describing the study in detail. Out of the approximately 550 men who were eligible to enroll in this study, 450 expressed interest in participating. Of these, 199 men actually kept their scheduled appointment and/or were able to be rescheduled for a different day or time and are the focus of the present report. Recruitment lasted for 18 months.

Interviews

All measures were completed using a computer-assisted structured interview (CASI) program designed specifically for this study. Pilot testing revealed that a majority of men from this population had difficulty with self-administration of our measures (via paper and pencil or computer), largely because of reading difficulties and poor computer navigation skills. The Microsoft Access–based CASI program presented each question from each scale of the project questionnaire battery (see the following discussion) to the interviewer to read aloud, who then recorded participants' responses by pointing and clicking on the appropriate response option. All data were organized in the CASI database on each laptop computer for eventual download into a desktop computer. Interviewers were primarily female undergraduate or graduate students in psychology.

This chapter utilized data from the pre-BIP interview and the review of criminal justice outcomes 6 months post-BIP. The initial interview (pre-BIP) took place approximately 2 weeks before the start of the participant's treatment program at various locations in the Dallas metroplex of convenience to the participant (e.g., public libraries, university lab, probation department offices). This initial interview (pre-BIP) took approximately 60 minutes to complete.

Female participants were interviewed via telephone at similar time intervals as males. When possible, we interviewed female participants at the same time their male partners were being interviewed at other locations.

Measures

Except where noted, all measures were administered via the CASI at the pre-BIP interview and consisted exclusively of male self-reports.

University of Rhode Island Change Assessment Scale–Domestic Violence

The University of Rhode Island Change Assessment Scale–Domestic Violence (URICA-DV; Levesque et al., 2000) is a 20-item questionnaire designed to assess the stages of change according to the dimensions of the TTM. The scale provides subscale scores for the Precontemplation (e.g., "The violence in my relationship isn't a big deal"), Contemplation (e.g., "I'm beginning to see that the violence in my relationship is a problem"), Action (e.g., "I'm finally doing something to end my violent behavior"), and Maintenance (e.g., "Although I haven't been violent in a while, I know it's possible for me to be violent again") stages as well as a global Readiness to Change Index (Contemplation + Action + Maintenance—Precontemplation).There are five items per stage. Responses are scored along a 5-point Likert scale with 1 = strongly disagree and 5 = strongly agree. Eckhardt, Babcock, and colleagues (2004) reported the following internal consistency estimates (coefficient alpha) for each URICA-DV subscale—Precontemplation (.63), Contemplation (.77), Action (.85), and Maintenance (.75) scales—which were similar to those obtained by Levesque and colleagues (2000) during scale validation. In the present sample of partner assaultive males, the following alpha coefficients were obtained: Precontemplation (.58), Contemplation (.83), Action (.91), and Maintenance (.77).

Partner Abuse Measures

Conflict Tactics Scale–Revised

The 78-item Conflict Tactics Scale–Revised (CTS-2; Straus, Hamby, Boney-McCoy, & Sugarman, 1996) was administered to determine the frequency and severity of intimate partner violence. Of the five CTS-2 scales, we will report only data from the Physical Assault scale (12 items; $\alpha = .77$). Items were scored according to a frequency-weighted scoring system (Straus, 2001) that utilizes a 0 (never), 1 (once in previous year), 2 (twice in previous year), 4 (3–5 times), 8 (6–10 times), 15 (11–20 times), and 25 (more than 20 times) scaling format. A scoring algorithm for this scale was used to provide subscale scores and prevalence data for *minor* (pushing, shoving, twisting arm/hair, grabbing, slapping) versus *severe* (punching, hitting, choking, burning, kicking, weapon threat/usage) assault. At the pre-BIP interview, respondents answered CTS-2 items in reference to assaultive behavior that occurred during the previous year. For administrations of the CTS-2 occurring after BIP commencement, item wording was modified to refer to behaviors occurring since the respondent's last interview (6–8 weeks during BIP, 6 months at the follow-up interview).

Multidimensional Measure of Emotional Abuse

The 28-item Multidimensional Measure of Emotional Abuse (MMEA; Murphy & Hoover, 1999) was used to determine the presence and severity of partner emotional abuse across four dimensions over the past 6 months. The four dimensions are dominance/intimidation (behaviors that produce fear or submission through the display of symbolic aggression), restrictive engulfment (behaviors that try to limit perceived threats by increasing partner dependence and availability), hostile withdrawal (behaviors that increase partner anxiety and insecurity about the relationship), and denigration (behaviors that reduce the partner's self-esteem and self-worth). The response choices are 0 = never, 1 = once, 2 = twice, 3 = 3 to 5 times, 4 = 6 to 10 times, 5 = 11 to 20 times, 6 = more than 20 times, and 7 = not in the past 6 months, but it did happen before. In the present sample of males, we utilized the total score, with higher scores reflecting greater enactment of emotionally abusive behaviors, which had a strong internal consistency estimate ($\alpha = .90$).

Other Variables

Millon Clinical Multiaxial Inventory–III

We utilized three scales from the Millon Clinical Multiaxial Inventory–III (MCMI-III; Millon, 1994), hypothesized to be relevant to the partner violence typology construct: Antisocial, Borderline, and Dependent (Holtzworth-Munroe & Stuart, 1994). The Antisocial subscale consists of 17 items, with high scorers endorsing a variety of illegal, aggressive, irresponsible, and/or psychopathic behaviors. The 16-item Borderline subscale assesses the degree to which respondents endorse a tendency toward intense and variable moods, an unstable identity, and impulsively destructive attempts to secure close relationships. The Borderline and Antisocial scales share four items. The 16-item Dependent subscale assesses respondents' fear of negative evaluation by a loved one, concerns about being abandoned by a romantic partner, and reliance on others to make important decisions. The Dependent and Borderline scales share one overlapping item. All items were presented in a true–false format and were scored using the weighting algorithms provided by Millon (1994).

General Violence Measure

For the General Violence Measure (Waltz et al., 2000), participants were asked to report the presence of prior aggressive altercations with family members, friends, coworkers/bosses, acquaintances, strangers, or police officers or in military/combat situations. Respondents' reports concerning the categories of people toward whom he was aggressive during the previous year were converted into a binary presence/absence score for each item summed into a total violence generality score ($\alpha = .93$).

Alcohol Use Disorders Identification Test

The Alcohol Use Disorders Identification Test (AUDIT; Saunders, Aasland, Babor, de la Fuente, & Grant, 1993) is a brief 10-item screening measure that assesses amount and frequency of alcohol use (three items), alcohol dependence (three items), and alcohol-related problems (four items) over a 1-year period of time. Despite its limited number of items, the AUDIT has been shown to possess strong psychometric properties (Bradley et al., 1998; Clements, 1998) with internal consistency estimates (coefficient α) of .87 and higher (McCann, Simpson, Ries, & Roy-Byrne, 2000). Scores of 8 and above have traditionally been used to identify those with probable alcohol problems. In the present sample, we obtained a similar internal consistency estimate (α = .89).

Drug Abuse Screening Test

The 28-item Drug Abuse Screening Test (DAST; Skinner, 1982) assessed the presence and degree of consequences relating to signs of drug-associated problems. Questions were presented in true–false format and addressed, for example, the presence of blackouts, flashbacks, legal problems, social or occupational impairments, and drug cessation attempts. The DAST has high internal consistency estimates (α = .92; Skinner, 1982), and principal components analyses suggest that the DAST assesses a unitary construct (McCann et al., 2000). In the present sample, we also obtained a high internal consistency estimate (α = .97).

Hostile Automatic Thoughts Inventory

The 30-item Hostile Automatic Thoughts Inventory (HAT; Snyder, Crowson, Houston, Kurylo, & Poirier, 1997) assesses the presence and degree of automatic thoughts associated with hostility and anger arousal. Items on the HAT are clustered into three factors: Physical Aggression (11 items; e.g., "I want to kill this person!"), Derogation of Others (10 items; e.g., "What an idiot!"), and Revenge (9 items; e.g., "This person needs to be taught a lesson"). Respondents are asked to think about situations that occurred the previous week, including those involving a female intimate partner, and on a 5-point scale rate the frequency that each thought occurred. Snyder and colleagues (1997) reported that the HAT had excellent internal consistency (overall α = .94) and was more strongly correlated with measures of hostility (r = .55–.62) than measures of negative emotion (r = .29–.33). In the present report, we used the total score, which had adequate internal consistency (α = .74).

Acceptance of Interpersonal Violence

The Acceptance of Interpersonal Violence (AIV; Burt, 1980) assessed the degree to which men endorse the use of violence in close relationships ("A man is never justified in hitting his wife"). The six items are scored along a 7-point scale, with 1 = strongly agree, 4 = unsure, and 7 = strongly disagree. The items (some reverse scored) are summed such that higher scores indicate greater acceptance of interpersonal violence. The AIV has been used in previous studies of violence-related attitudes in a partner violent sample (Holtzworth-Munroe et al., 2000), with marginal internal consistency estimates (α = .58). In the present sample, internal consistency was very poor (α = .27). Consequently, readers should judge any results involving the AIV with caution.

Hostility Toward Women Inventory

The 30-item Hostility Toward Women Inventory (HTWI; Check, Malamuth, Elias, & Barton, 1985) was administered in order to obtain an index of men's attitudes toward women. Item content concerns resentment of women in general ("Women irritate me a great deal more than they are aware of") and a general suspicion of women's motivations ("It is safer not to trust women"). Responses are given in a true–false format (scored 1 and 0, respectively), with higher scores suggestive of hostility toward women. In the present sample, internal consistency was adequate (α = .82).

Social Desirability

Male participants completed a short form of the Marlowe-Crowne Social Desirability Scale (MCSD; Reynolds, 1982) to control for the tendency to "fake good." This version of the Marlowe-Crowne (Form C) contains the 13 items having the highest item-total correlations with the complete 33-item version (Crowne & Marlowe, 1960). According to Reynolds (1982), scores obtained from the short form of the MCSD were strongly correlated with scores on the 33-item version (r = .93). In the present sample, internal consistency was adequate (α = .74).

Trait Anger Scale

The 10-item Trait Anger Scale (TAS; Spielberger, 1988) was administered to assess the frequency that an individual experiences state anger over time and in response to a variety of situations. The TAS consists of two subscales—Angry Temperament and Angry Reaction—with alpha coefficients of .85 and .73, respectively (Fuqua, Leonard, Masters, & Smith, 1991). Ample evidence has been published concerning the psychometric adequacy and construct validity of the TAS (e.g., Deffenbacher et al., 1996; Eckhardt, Norlander, & Deffenbacher, 2004; Spielberger, 1988). The TAS yielded good internal consistency in the present sample (α = .85).

Criminal Justice–Related Data

In order to assess BIP attendance and criminal recidivism, study personnel were given full access to the Dallas County Probation Department's computer records, which provided updated information concerning BIP attendance (as reported by each agency to probation officers on a monthly basis) and arrest history (as compiled by probation staff on a monthly basis). Study personnel reviewed each participant's case during the follow-up period (6 months post-BIP completion, which corresponded to approximately 13 months postadjudication) and recorded relevant information concerning BIP attendance and recidivism on a coding spreadsheet.

BIP Completion

We utilized the dichotomous definition of program completion used by BIP agencies in the Dallas area, wherein successful BIP completion was defined as attendance at all 24 weekly sessions, with up to three excused absences, and attendance at an exit interview. Men who were absent on more than three occasions, regardless of the reason, were considered unsuccessful and in violation of their probation terms. In addition, men who never attended BIP beyond the orientation session, who voluntarily dropped out of the program, or who were dismissed from the program for disciplinary or mental health reasons were also coded as unsuccessful. While some researchers (e.g., Chang & Saunders, 2002; Daly, Power, & Gondolf, 2001) have expressed concerns about dichotomizing BIP attendance given the arbitrary nature of the session cutoffs used to define completion, we nevertheless opted to use a dichotomous definition. The reasoning behind this was that both participants and criminal justice system personnel (BIP staff, probation officers, judges) were acutely aware of and conceivably made decisions about attendance and attendance-based contingencies using this admittedly arbitrary cutoff of three or more missed sessions. Thus, failure to satisfy the cutoff invoked the threat of probation revocation, an arrest warrant, or jail, all of which represent important categorical consequences that might be lost if one opted to use a continuous measure of BIP completion (e.g., number of sessions attended). BIP completion data were available on 186 cases.

Rearrests

Recidivism data were based on Dallas County arrest records obtained from probation department records and were coded according to the nature of the offense. As part of their probationary terms, men were required to reside in Dallas County. As the state of Texas does not have a separate intimate partner assault code in its arrest records, we were able to classify cases only as nonassault rearrest versus assault-related rearrest. Complete arrest data were available on 181 cases.

Self- or Partner-Reported Partner Violence Recidivism

In addition to official recidivism records, we created a new binary variable regarding the occurrence of self- or partner-reported physical assault during the 13-month study period. As described earlier, male participants and available female partners were administered the CTS-2 at five points over a 13-month period of time: the pre-BIP interview three times during the 24-week BIP (corresponding to early-BIP, mid-BIP, and post-BIP) as well as 6 months post-BIP. If male participants indicated the enactment of a new act of CTS-2 physical assault across the 13-month study period during any interview *following* the initial pre-BIP interview or if a female partner reported being the target of male physical assault during any phone interview following the pre-BIP interview (regardless of corroborating evidence for any single IPV event), the male was considered a reoffender. Of the 199 men in the study, we had at least partial recidivism data on 141 men, with the remaining cases coded as missing due to inability to contact either dyad member following the pre-BIP interview (38 cases) or the male reporting no postadjudication contact with a female partner (20 cases).

RESULTS

Criminal Justice–Related Outcomes

Before examining predictors of BIP dropout and criminal recidivism, we first present descriptive data regarding these outcome variables. As a group, the men in this study had difficulty completing the terms of their probation during the course of this evaluation, as 57.6% of the men violated various terms of their probation, 20.8% had their probation revoked, and 17.7% had their revocations pending before the judge. Among those whose probation was revoked or whose revocation was pending during the study period, 39% had active warrants issued for their arrest, 16.9% were considered absconders, and 1.6% were in jail (all others were awaiting the judge's action by the end of the study period).

Regarding BIP attrition and completion, 59.1% of our sample completed their mandated 24-week BIP. Reasons for unsuccessful BIP completion were (a) nonattendance (i.e., never reporting for a BIP session other than orientation) (65.5%), (b) agency dismissal (16.4%), (c) dropout (14.5%), (d) missing the exit interview (1.8%), and (e) nonattendance during appeal of conviction (1.8%).

Approximately 27% of the sample were rearrested during the 13-month study period for any criminal activity. Only 5.4% (n = 10) were rearrested for an assault-related charge, which represents our only available *official* index for domestic violence reoccurrence.

In terms of unofficial self- or partner-reported physical assaults during the index period, 60% of our male respondents (84 of the 141 respondents with a current partner and complete CTS-2 Physical Assault scale data) physically assaulted an intimate partner. Of these, 62 men (74%) were identified as recidivists by their own reports, 11 (13.1%) were identified by female partner reports only, and 11 (13.1%) were identified by both male and female reports on the CTS-2.

BIP attrition was related to the race or ethnicity of the perpetrator, $\chi^2(2)$ = 12.06, p < .002. Relative to those who completed BIP, African Americans/Blacks were overrepresented among BIP dropouts (62.2%), and Latinos/Hispanic Americans (13.5%) and Whites (24.3%) were somewhat underrepresented. Overall, 54.1% of African American/Black individuals dropped out of BIP, relative to 27% of Latinos/Hispanic Americans and 30% of Whites. Racial/ethnic background factors were not significantly related to other outcome variables.

BIP attrition was significantly related to postoffense arrests, $\chi^2(1)$ = 10.50, p < .001. More than twice as many BIP dropouts (39.7%) than completers (17.9%) were rearrested during the 13-month study period. The relationship between BIP completion and the presence of an assault rearrest approached significance, $\chi^2(1)$ = 2.70, p = .10, with almost three times as many BIP dropouts (8.1%) being arrested for an assault-related charge during the index period versus BIP completers (2.8%).

Unfortunately, because of the manner in which these data were obtained by probation staff, we were unable to determine how many men were dismissed from BIP *because* of a new arrest during the study period. However, it should be noted that of the 12 men who were listed as non-completers because of agency dismissal, only three were also arrested for a new criminal offense at some point during the study period. BIP completion was unrelated to frequency of prior arrests, $\chi^2(2) = 0.01$, and self- or partner-reported assault recidivism, $\chi^2(1) = 0.25$.

In order to determine the representativeness of the current sample, we compared our participants on a number of criminal record variables to a pseudo–control group consisting of the first 200 men who were eligible to participate but did not formally enroll in the study. Relative to participants enrolled in the study, nonenrollees tended to be younger (M age = 31.4), were slightly more likely to be classified as BIP non-completers (43.9%), and were somewhat more likely to be arrested for any criminal offense (30%) as well as an assault-related offense (14%). Nonenrollees did not differ from study participants in their racial or ethnic background or on the number of prior arrests. Thus, men enrolled in this study may represent a somewhat less severe subgroup of men than men generally adjudicated for misdemeanor charges of assaulting a partner.

STAGES OF CHANGE

URICA-DV Cluster Analyses

While it is not possible to determine an individual's precise stage of change by looking at a single scale from the URICA-DV, inspection of individuals' pattern of URICA-DV subscale scores may provide information about how their scores cluster together to form stagelike profiles. Toward this end, cluster analysis was used to classify the 199 males who completed the pre-BIP interview into a smaller number of homogeneous clusters based on URICA-DV subscale profiles. Squared Euclidean distance was selected as the similarity/dissimilarity measure, and Ward's (1963) hierarchical agglomeration method was used as the clustering method. Participants' scores on the separate URICA-DV dimensions were first summed and converted to z scores, and Ward's method was used to cluster individual cases and then groups of cases in a manner that minimized within-group error sums of squares. Since there are no

completely satisfactory methods available for determining the number
of clusters to retain, the decision in this case was based on hierarchical dendogram inspection and profile interpretability. K-means analysis
cluster was used to confirm the results of the cluster analysis. K-means
analysis was conducted using cluster means derived from the hierarchical cluster analysis as seeds for K-means groups.

We had complete URICA-DV data for 166 of the 199 men. Missing data were imputed using a multiple imputation method based on
the Expectation-Maximization algorithm (Rubin, 1987).[2] The cluster
analysis using the fully imputed data set yielded a four-cluster solution.
The URICA-DV Precontemplation, Contemplation, Action, and Maintenance subscale raw scores for each cluster are reported in Table 5.2,
and standardized (T scores: $M = 50$, $SD = 10$) mean subscale scores for
each cluster are presented in Figure 5.1. The four clusters are described
next in an order that appears to represent a progression from the least
to the most advanced in the change sequence, using the cluster labels
provided by Levesque and colleagues (2000):

1. *Reluctant cluster.* Thirty-five individuals (17.6%) were in this
   cluster. These men scored higher than average on Precontemplation and lower than average (1.5 SD) on Contemplation and Action, suggesting that relative to men in other clusters, they were

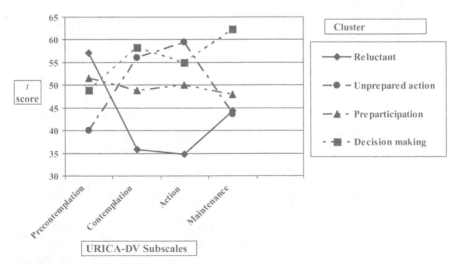

Figure 5.1 URICA-DV Stages-of-change clusters.

Table 5.2

CHARACTERISTICS OF PRE-BIP URICA-DV STAGES-OF-CHANGE CLUSTERS

	URICA-DV CLUSTERS			
	RELUCTANT ($n = 35$)	UNPREPARED ACTION ($n = 32$)	PREPARTICI-PATION ($n = 85$)	DECISION MAKING ($n = 47$)
URICA-DV raw $M/(SD)$				
Precontemplation	12.0	7.1	10.4	9.6
	(3.0)	(2.1)	(1.2)	(3.8)
Contemplation	12.8	21.0	18.1	22.0
	(3.9)	(3.1)	(1.9)	(2.2)
Action	14.8	23.8	20.3	22.1
	(4.1)	(1.4)	(1.1)	(2.4)
Maintenance	12.9	12.6	14.4	20.2
	(3.7)	(3.4)	(2.8)	(2.0)
Readiness Index	28.6	50.3	42.4	54.7
	(9.0)	(5.5)	(4.0)	(6.9)
Race/Ethnicity				
% African American	40.6	53.1	44.0	45.7
% White	50.0	21.9	36.9	28.3
% Hispanic/Latino	9.4	25.0	19.0	26.1
Age (M)	31.4	31.9	33.2	33.4
CTS-2 Assault Freq.				
12-months (weighted M/SD)	8.8	11.5	7.9	11.0
	(23.2)	(16.5)	(12.2)	(11.1)
CTS-2 Assault Severity				
12-months				
% No assault	37.1	15.6	14.1	2.2
% Minor assault only	37.1	40.6	47.4	21.7
% Severe assault	25.7	43.8	38.5	76.1

(Continued)

Table 5.2

CHARACTERISTICS OF PRE-BIP URICA-DV STAGES-OF-CHANGE CLUSTERS (*Continued*)

	URICA-DV CLUSTERS			
	RELUCTANT (*n* = 35)	**UNPREPARED ACTION** (*n* = 32)	**PREPARTICI-PATION** (*n* = 85)	**DECISION MAKING** (*n* = 47)
MEA Total (*M/SD*)	38.4	42.0	37.7	47.7
	(29.8)	(25.8)	(26.6)	(29.4)
Social Desirability (*M/SD*)	8.5	8.3	8.1	6.8
	(3.0)	(2.9)	(3.2)	(2.6)
AUDIT (*M/SD*)	7.3	12.6	7.3	12.4
	(7.6)	(12.1)	(7.6)	(8.8)
DAST (*M/SD*)	7.9	8.3	6.9	7.2
	(6.8)	(7.5)	(6.5)	(6.0)
HTWI (*M/SD*)	10.9	9.1	9.7	12.2
	(6.1)	(5.6)	(4.9)	(4.6)
AIV (*M/SD*)	19.5	18.1	18.3	20.6
	(4.9)	(5.0)	(4.1)	(4.6)
HAT (*M/SD*)	49.4	45.8	45.9	56.2
	(20.4)	(22.6)	(20.4)	(19.1)
TAS (*M/SD*)	16.6	16.2	16.9	20.6
	(4.6)	(4.5)	(5.0)	(5.4)

Note. N = 199. URICA-DV = University of Rhode Island Change Assessment Inventory for Domestic Violence; CTS-2 = Conflict Tactics Scale, 2nd ed.; MEA = Measure of Emotional Abuse; AUDIT = Alcohol Use Disorders Inventory; DAST = Drug Abuse Screening Test; HTWI = Hostility Toward Women Inventory; AIV = Attitudes Toward Interpersonal Violence Scale; HAT = Hostile Automatic Thoughts Inventory; TAS = Trait Anger Scale.

more likely to deny the existence of an abusiveness problem and to be minimally engaged in the change process.

2. *Unprepared Action cluster.* This cluster is composed of 32 individuals (16.1%). In this profile, Contemplation is low (.5 *SD*) relative

to Action, suggesting that while these men may demonstrate an adequate level of change, they may be not be able to sustain the changes they make given the relatively low Contemplation level. Maintenance is low relative to other subscales (.5 SD below the mean and the lowest score across the four clusters), also suggesting a limited degree of awareness concerning the potential for relapse.

3. *Preparticipation cluster.* The 85 individuals (42.7%) in this cluster displayed a leveling out on Precontemplation, Contemplation, Action, and Maintenance. These men were about average on all URICA-DV subscales, suggesting that they may have acknowledged the existence of a problem and have become somewhat engaged in making or sustaining changes in their abusive behavior.

4. *Decision-Making cluster.* This cluster is comprised of 47 men (23.6%). Men in this cluster were characterized by higher-than-average scores on Contemplation and Action and average scores on Precontemplation. Men in this cluster had much higher than average Maintenance scores (1.25 SD) and had the highest overall score on this dimension across the four clusters. The profile presents with an average level and a moderate degree of scatter. As suggested by Levesque and colleagues (2000), this cluster may represent a "transitional stage" whereby men contemplating the benefits of behavior change are starting to take action but acutely aware of both the difficulty of the task and the probability for relapse.

In stages-of-change terms, the Reluctant cluster may be akin to the Precontemplative stage, the Preparticipation cluster is suggestive of the Contemplation stage with some Precontemplation elements, and the Decision-Making cluster is parallel to a Preparation-Action hybrid stage. The Unprepared Action cluster is more difficult to characterize in that individuals within this group exhibit elements from later stages of change (average Action stage scores) but also aspects of earlier stages (moderate Contemplation, low Maintenance).

Characteristics of the URICA-DV Clusters

Using one-way analyses of variance (ANOVAs) and post hoc least significant differences (LSD) group comparison analyses, we examined how the URICA-DV clusters differed on demographic factors, drug and alcohol use, and several measures of cognitive and affective processes. Table 5.2

shows descriptive statistics. With regard to demographics, there were no significant differences in racial or ethnic distribution across the clusters, $\chi^2(6) = 8.06$, $p = .23$. The clusters did not differ in age, $F(3, 181) = .75$, $p = .52$; years of education, $\chi^2(9) = 14.78$, $p = .10$; or occupational status, $\chi^2(6) = 5.09$, $p = .53$. There were significant differences on self-reported CTS-2 physical assault toward an intimate partner in the 12 months prior to the study, $\chi^2(6) = 33.95$, $p < .001$. More men in the Decision-Making cluster (76.1%) reported engaging in severe violence than other clusters (the next highest was Unprepared Action, with 43.8% of men engaging in severe violence). Relative to men in other clusters, Reluctant cluster males were less likely to report any physical assault (37.1%) or usage of minor violence only (37.1%). The clusters differed on social desirability, with men in the Decision-Making cluster scoring significantly lower than men in the three remaining clusters, who in turn did not differ from each other. Significant differences among the clusters emerged on the HTWI, $F(3, 195) = 3.10$, $p < .03$, with the Decision-Making cluster scoring significantly higher than Unprepared Action ($p < .01$) and Preparticipation ($p < .01$); the AIV, $F(3, 195) = 3.11$, $p < .03$, with the Decision-Making cluster scoring significantly higher than Unprepared Action ($p < .01$) and Preparticipation ($p < .03$); the HAT, $F(3, 195) = 3.84$, $p < .01$, with the Decision-Making cluster scoring significantly higher than Unprepared Action ($p < .02$) and Preparticipation ($p < .01$); the TAS, $F(3, 195) = 7.17$, $p < .001$, with the Decision-Making cluster scoring significantly higher than all other clusters (all p values $< .002$); and the AUDIT, $F(3, 162) = 4.53$, $p < .01$, with the Decision-Making and Unprepared Action clusters scoring higher than the Preparticipation and Reluctant clusters (p values $< .02$).

PARTNER VIOLENCE SUBTYPES

Using the same imputation and cluster analytic strategies as were described previously, we standardized and entered the three MCMI scales (Antisocial, Borderline, and Dependency), the measure of violence generality, and previous year CTS-2 frequency-weighted Physical Assault scale scores (male report) into a hierarchical cluster analysis, followed by a K-means analysis. These procedures resulted in a four-cluster solution, with each cluster discussed next in terms of between-group differences on the clustering variables using one-way ANOVAs and post hoc LSD multiple comparison analyses. Table 5.3 provides means for each subtype across the clustering variables.

Table 5.3

CHARACTERISTICS OF PARTNER VIOLENCE SUBTYPES

	PARTNER VIOLENCE SUBTYPES			
	FAMILY ONLY ($n = 61$)	**LOW-LEVEL ANTISOCIAL** ($n = 86$)	**BORDER-LINE/ DYSPHORIC** ($n = 40$)	**GENERALLY VIOLENT/ ANTISOCIAL** ($n = 12$)
MCMI-III (*M T*-scores)				
Antisocial	39.6	51.5	58.6	63.4
Borderline	40.1	49.9	62.2	60.3
Dependent	42.2	48.2	64.4	54.4
General violence				
(*M T*-scores)	44.7	48.9	56.7	62.1
CTS-2 assault frequency				
12-months (weighted *M/SD*)	2.8	7.3	11.0	52.7
	(3.8)	(6.8)	(9.0)	(28.8)
CTS-2 assault severity, 12-months				
% No assault	34.4	7.7	7.5	0.0
% Minor assault only	47.5	43.6	22.5	8.3
% Severe assault	18.0	48.7	70.0	91.7
Race/Ethnicity				
% African American	47.5	35.7	59.0	58.3
% White	35.6	40.5	23.1	25.0
% Hispanic/Latino	16.9	23.8	17.9	16.7
Age (*M*)	34.7	30.7	31.6	35.8
MEA total (*M/SD*)	30.2	39.1	51.0	72.8
	(27.4)	(23.8)	(28.5)	(20.3)
Social desirability (*M/SD*)	9.8	7.6	6.4	5.0
	(2.3)	(2.7)	(3.0)	(2.7)
AUDIT (*M/SD*)	5.2	9.7	11.9	17.8
	(5.8)	(8.4)	(10.6)	(10.9)

(*Continued*)

Table 5.3

CHARACTERISTICS OF PARTNER VIOLENCE SUBTYPES (*Continued*)

	PARTNER VIOLENCE SUBTYPES			
	FAMILY ONLY **(*n* = 61)**	**LOW-LEVEL ANTISOCIAL** **(*n* = 86)**	**BORDER-LINE/ DYSPHORIC** **(*n* = 40)**	**GENERALLY VIOLENT/ ANTISOCIAL** **(*n* = 12)**
DAST (*M/SD*)	3.6	6.5	9.6	15.6
	(3.3)	(5.9)	(6.9)	(6.7)
HTWI (*M/SD*)	7.8	10.0	13.2	16.3
	(4.8)	(4.6)	(4.4)	(6.2)
AIV (*M/SD*)	18.4	17.8	21.8	21.2
	(4.8)	(4.0)	(6.0)	(4.2)
HAT (*M/SD*)	41.5	49.1	54.8	65.4
	(11.4)	(16.0)	(19.0)	(33.5)
TAS (*M/SD*)	14.2	17.7	21.0	22.4
	(3.0)	(4.1)	(5.8)	(7.0)

Note. N = 199. URICA-DV = University of Rhode Island Change Assessment Inventory for Domestic Violence; CTS-2 = Conflict Tactics Scale, 2nd ed.; MEA = Measure of Emotional Abuse; AUDIT = Alcohol Use Disorders Inventory; DAST = Drug Abuse Screening Test; HTWI = Hostility Toward Women Inventory; AIV = Attitudes Toward Interpersonal Violence Scale; HAT = Hostile Automatic Thoughts Inventory; TAS = Trait Anger Scale.

The first cluster consisted of 61 (30.7%) men. These men reported significantly lower levels of intimate partner violence, violence generality, and MCMI Antisocial, Borderline, and Dependent scales relative to the other clusters (all p values < .01), and are thus similar to Holtzworth-Munroe and colleagues' (2000) FO subtype.

The 86 (43.2%) men in cluster two reported average levels of psychopathology, intimate partner violence, and violence generality. Men in this cluster score significantly higher than FO men on the MCMI Antisocial (p < .001), MCMI Borderline (p < .001), and MCMI Dependent (p < .001) scales but significantly lower than the remaining two clusters (BD, GVA; see the following discussion) on these dimensions. Men in this cluster also scored significantly higher than FO men on CTS-2 Physical Assault (p < .004) and violence generality (p < .004) but significantly lower than men in the remaining two clusters (BD, GVA). Thus, men in this cluster do not appear to possess distinctive psychopathological traits, although they report engaging in more aggressive acts both within and outside the home relative to men in the FO cluster but significantly less than the remaining two clusters. As such, we label this group LLA.

The 40 (20.1%) men in the third cluster resemble the BD subtype reported by Holtzworth-Munroe and colleagues (2000). While these men scored highest on the MCMI Borderline scale, their mean did not differ significantly from those of the fourth cluster of GVA men (see the following discussion; p = .34). However, as predicted, men in this cluster had significantly higher scores on the MCMI Dependency scale relative to all other groups (p < .001). They also had significantly (p < .001) higher scores on violence generality than all other clusters except the GVA cluster and significantly higher CTS-2 Physical Assault scores than FO and LLA men (p values < .001) but significantly lower levels of intimate partner violence than GVA men (p < .001). This group also scored significantly lower on the MCMI Antisocial scale than the remaining GVA cluster (p < .02) but higher than FO and LLA men (p values < .001). Given the higher Dependency scores in conjunction with the high scores on the Borderline measure, men in this cluster can be labeled BD.

The 12 (6.0%) men in the fourth cluster closely resemble Holtzworth-Munroe and colleagues' (2000) GVA subtype. These men scored significantly higher than those in other clusters on MCMI Antisociality (1.3 SD above the mean; p values < .001), CTS-2 Physical Assault (3 SD above the mean; p values < .001), and violence generality (+1 SD above the mean; p values < .001). However, there was no significant difference between this cluster's MCMI Borderline scale and that of the BD subtype (p = .34). Nevertheless, these men report the highest levels of antisocial traits, intimate partner violence, and violence generality and are thus labeled the GVA subtype.

Characteristics of the Subtypes

Using chi-square tests for independence, one-way ANOVAs, and post hoc LSD group comparison analyses, we examined how the partner violence subtypes differed on the same variables reported previously for the stages-of-change clusters. Table 5.3 shows descriptive statistics.

With regard to demographics, there were no significant differences in racial or ethnic distribution across the four subtypes, $\chi^2(6) = 7.52$, $p = .28$. The subtypes differed significantly in age, $F(3, 179) = 4.40$, $p < .01$, with BD and LLA men significantly younger than GVA and FO men ($p < .01$). The relationship between partner violence subtype and educational attainment approached significance, $\chi^2(9) = 16.29$, $p = .06$, with more FO (53.3%) and LLA (40.5%) men reporting at least some college involvement than the other subtypes. Men in the BD and GVA subtypes tended to report completing less than a high school education (BD: 65.8%; GVA: 66.7%). There was no significant relationship between partner violence subtype and occupational status, $\chi^2(3) = 3.74$, $p = .29$. As predicted, there were significant differences on self-reported CTS-2 physical assault toward an intimate partner in the 12 months prior to the study, $\chi^2(6) = 48.68$, $p < .001$. More men in the GVA subtype (91.7%) reported engaging in severe violence than other forms of violence (the next highest was BD, with 70.0% of men engaging in severe violence). Relative to men in other clusters, FO males were more likely to report that they did not engage in any physical assault during the previous year (34.4%).

Across the various psychological measures administered, the subtypes differed in predictable directions based on previous research in this area (Holtzworth-Munroe et al., 2000). One-way ANOVAs and post hoc LSD tests for group differences revealed that relative to all other subtypes, GVA men reported more hostility toward women, $F(3, 195) = 16.84$, $p < .001$; hostile automatic thoughts, $F(3, 195) = 9.31$, $p < .001$; alcohol problems, $F(3, 195) = 9.29$, $p < .001$; drug usage, $F(3, 195) = 14.37$, $p < .001$; and emotional abuse, $F(3, 195) = 12.65$, $p < .001$. GVA and BD men scored significantly higher than FO and LLA men on attitudes approving interpersonal violence, $F(3, 195) = 7.68$, $p < .001$, and trait anger, $F(3, 195) = 25.28$, $p < .001$. GVA and BD men scored significantly lower than FO and LLA men on the measure of social desirability, $F(3, 195) = 18.25$, $p < .001$. On every measure reported in Table 5.3 except the AIV and AUDIT, LLA men scored significantly higher than FO men and significantly lower than BD men. Regarding those exceptions, LLA men scored significantly lower than BD men on the AIV ($p < .01$) but were not significantly different from FO men ($p = .42$). There was not a significant difference between BD and LLA participants' scores on the AUDIT ($p = .26$), although LLA men reported significantly more alcohol problems than FO men ($p < .03$).

PARTNER VIOLENCE SUBTYPES AND STAGES-OF-CHANGE CLUSTERS

We examined the relationships among the four batterer subtypes and four URICA-DV–assessed stages-of-change clusters by first examining stages-of-change subscale scores across the four subtypes and then examining the degree of dependence between URICA-DV clusters and batterer subtypes.

As can be seen in Table 5.4, the four partner violence subtypes did not differ on the URICA-DV subscales of Precontemplation, $F(3, 195) = .36, p = .78$, and Action, $F(3, 195) = 1.68, p = .17$. One-way ANOVAs revealed significant differences among the subtypes for URICA-DV Con-

Table 5.4

PARTNER VIOLENCE SUBTYPES AND THE STAGES OF CHANGE

	PARTNER VIOLENCE SUBTYPES			
	FO	LLA	BD	GVA
URICA-DV				
Subscales (raw *M/SD*)				
Precontemplation	9.9	9.8	10.4	9.9
Contemplation	16.8	18.7	19.8	21.9
Action	19.8	20.5	20.2	22.3
Maintenance	13.2	15.8	16.7	16.4
Index	39.9	45.2	46.4	50.7
URICA-DV				
Clusters				
% Reluctant	27.9	12.8	15.0	8.3
% Unprepared action	14.8	15.1	15.0	33.3
% Preparticipation	47.5	47.7	27.5	33.3
% Decision making	9.8	24.4	42.5	25.0

Note. N = 199. URICA-DV = University of Rhode Island Change Assessment Inventory for Domestic Violence; FO = Family Only subtype; LLA = Low-Level Antisocial subtype; BD = Borderline/Dysphoric subtype; GVA = Generally Violent/Antisocial subtype.

templation, $F(3, 195) = 8.68$, $p < .001$; Maintenance, $F(3, 195) = 8.66$, $p < .001$; and the Readiness to Change Index, $F(3, 195) = 6.03$, $p < .001$. Fisher's LSD multiple comparisons indicated that FO men scored lower than all other subtypes on URICA-DV Contemplation, Maintenance, and the Readiness to Change Index (all p values $< .003$). LLA males scored significantly lower than GVA men on URICA-DV Contemplation ($p < .009$). There were no other significant between-cluster differences. Because we were concerned about the potential effects of social desirability on these analyses, we reran the ANOVAs using the social desirability measure as a covariate. No substantive changes to the results reported previously were found.

Chi-square analyses were used to examine the degree of interdependence between membership in stages-of-change clusters and batterer subtype categories. Stage-of-change clusters were related to batterer subtype, $\chi^2(9) = 22.12$, $p < .009$. As can be seen in Table 5.4, relative to men within the other three partner violence subtypes, twice as many men within the FO subtype (27.9%) were also in the Reluctant cluster. GVA men tended to have more frequent membership in the Unprepared Action cluster (33.3%). Men in the BD subtype had the highest rate of membership in the Decision Making cluster (42.5%). Men in the LLA and FO subtypes tended to have membership in the Preparticipation cluster (47.5% and 47.7%, respectively).

CRIMINAL JUSTICE OUTCOMES

For each criminal justice variable, we used two strategies to evaluate each dichotomous outcome. First, we utilized a *categorical* approach and examined whether stages-of-change clusters and partner violence subtypes were related to BIP completion, postadjudication arrest for any offense over a 13-month period including assault-related arrests, and self-reported recidivism over the same 13-month period. Second, given the controversies surrounding the utility of categorical models in psychopathology (e.g., Livesley, Schroeder, Jackson, & Jang, 1994), we examined the TTM and partner violence subtype models *dimensionally*, entering URICA-DV and violence subtyping measures as continuous predictors of the binary criminal justice outcomes in separate logistic regression analyses in order to examine whether and to what degree the individual dimensions underlying each cluster or subtype contributed to the prediction of each outcome. Table 5.5 shows descriptive statistics.

Table 5.5

URICA-DV CLUSTERS, PARTNER VIOLENCE SUBTYPES, AND CRIMINAL JUSTICE OUTCOMES 13 MONTHS POSTADJUDICATION

	BIP COMPLETION		REARREST		REARREST-ASSAULT		SELF/PARTNER-REPORTED VIOLENCE	
	% YES	% NO	% YES	% NO	% YES	% NO	% YES	% NO
Overall	59.1	40.9	27.1	72.9	5.4	94.6	61.7	38.3
URICA-DV Clusters								
Decision								
making	55.3	44.7	29.8	70.2	8.5	91.5	90.6	9.4
Preparticipation	58.7	41.3	28.2	71.8	6.7	93.3	50.0	50.0
Unprepared								
action	60.0	40.0	16.7	83.3	0.0	100	59.3	40.7
Reluctant	64.7	35.3	30.3	69.7	2.9	97.1	53.8	46.2
Violence Subtypes								
FO	77.0	23.0	17.5	82.5	3.3	96.7	55.1	44.9
LLA	62.7	37.3	24.7	75.3	6.7	93.3	63.3	36.7
BD	38.5	61.5	37.5	62.5	7.5	92.5	62.5	37.5
GVA	9.1	90.9	45.5	54.5	0.0	100	87.5	12.5

Note. $N = 199$. BIP = Batterers Intervention Program; URICA-DV = University of Rhode Island Change Assessment Inventory for Domestic Violence; FO = Family Only subtype; LLA = Low-Level Antisocial subtype; BD = Borderline/Dysphoric subtype; GVA = Generally Violent/Antisocial subtype. BIP completion and rearrest data based on information gathered from Dallas County Community Supervision and Corrections (probation) department files. Self- or partner-reported partner violence recidivism based on presence of physical violence involving male participant during 13 months postadjudication according to either male participant or female partners ($N = 72$).

BIP Completion

Stages-of-change clusters were independent of BIP completion, $\chi^2(3) = .74, p = .87$. Similarly, the four continuous URICA-DV subscales also did not significantly predict BIP completion, $R^2 = .02, \chi^2(4) = 3.37, p = .50$ (60.4% of cases accurately classified).

Partner violence subtypes were related to BIP completion, $\chi^2(3) = 26.79, p < .001$. GVA (90.9%) and BD (61.5%) men were more likely to have dropped out of BIP relative to other subtypes, whereas only 23% of FO men were classified as BIP noncompleters. Dimensionally, while the overall model regressing BIP completion onto partner violence subtype measures was significant, $R^2 = .17, \chi^2(5) = 23.12, p < .001$, no individual predictor emerged as significant (p values ranged from .09 for CTS-2 assault to .87 for the MCMI Antisocial scale). The model correctly classified 69.2% of cases.

Postadjudication Arrest

Stages-of-change clusters were independent of postadjudication arrests, $\chi^2(3) = 2.04, p = .56$. Similarly, when we examined the small number of postadjudication assaults resulting in arrest, stages-of-change clusters were once again not significantly related, $\chi^2(3) = 3.25, p = .35$. However, logistic regression analyses suggested that URICA-DV subscales significantly predicted postadjudication arrest, $R^2 = .10, \chi^2(4) = 12.49, p < .02$, with the model correctly classifying 71.8% of the cases. In terms of individual predictors, higher scores on URICA-DV Precontemplation predicted rearrest, $\beta = .21, z = 8.31, p < .01$, odds ratio (OR) = 1.23. URICA-DV subscales did not predict postadjudication assault-related arrest, $R^2 = .01, \chi^2(4) = .92, p = .92$.

Partner violence subtypes were nonindependent of postadjudication arrests, $\chi^2(3) = 9.24, p < .03$, with GVA (45.5%) and BD (37.5%) men more likely to have been arrested for any charge relative to other subtypes. The FO men (17.5%) were less likely than other subtypes to have been arrested postadjudication. There was no relationship among partner violence subtypes and postoffense assault-related arrests, $\chi^2(3) = 1.72, p = .63$. Logistic regression analyses indicated that partner violence subtype dimensions were significant predictors of postoffense arrest, $R^2 = .14, \chi^2(5) = 18.23, p < .003$, with the model correctly classifying 72.8% of the cases. Only the MCMI Borderline scale emerged as a significant predictor of arrest, $\beta = .13, z = 4.97, p < .03$, OR = 1.14. A separate logistic regression analysis revealed no predictive relationship between partner violence subtype dimensions and postadjudication assault-related arrests, $R^2 = .11$, $\chi^2(5) = 6.54$, $p = .26$.

Self- or Partner-Reported Recidivism

Stages-of-change clusters were significantly related to self-reported partner assault recidivism, $\chi^2(3) = 15.32$, $p < .001$. Within the Decision-Making cluster, 90.6% of men (or female partners of men) reported a new partner violence incident in the 13 months postadjudication. Men in the Preparticipation cluster were less likely to have assaulted their partners during that time (50% no assaults vs. cross-cluster mean of 38% no assaults). Using the continuous measures, URICA-DV subscales significantly predicted the presence of self- or partner-reported violence, $R^2 = .17$, $\chi^2(4) = 18.83$, $p = .001$, with 67.4% of cases accurately classified. Only URICA-DV Maintenance emerged as a significant individual predictor of recidivism, $\beta = .16$, $z = 8.43$, $p < .01$, OR = 1.18, with higher Maintenance scores predicting new incidents of partner violence.

Partner violence subtypes were independent of self- or partner-reported recidivism during the 13-month postadjudication period, $\chi^2(3) = 3.23$, $p = .36$. However, it should be noted that of the 12 GVA men, 11 committed an act of partner assault during the study period. A separate logistic regression analysis revealed no predictive relationship between partner violence subtype dimensions and the presence of postadjudication self-reported partner violence, $R^2 = .06$, $\chi^2(5) = 5.86$, $p = .32$.

DISCUSSION

The purpose of the present investigation was to empirically evaluate the ability of the TTM of behavior change (Prochaska et al., 1992) and the partner violence typology construct (Holtzworth-Munroe et al., 2000) to predict BIP completion, criminal recidivism, and new incidents of intimate partner violence. The men in this postadjudication or probation sample had fairly typical BIP dropout rates as reported in previous reviews of this literature (e.g., Daly & Pelowski, 2000), with 40% of men failing to successfully complete their court-mandated BIP, primarily for reasons relating to nonattendance (rather than being forced to leave or leaving after a few sessions). African Americans had a significantly higher rate of BIP attrition versus men of Latino/Hispanic or White racial or ethnic background. As has been found in previous research (Chen, Bersani, Myers, & Denton, 1989; Daly & Pelowski, 2000), BIP dropout reliably predicted criminal recidivism in terms of both general rearrest for any offense and assault-related rearrest. The next step was to examine whether the TTM and/or the partner violence subtype construct was predictive of or related to these important criminal justice outcomes.

We first predicted that using cluster analysis, men in treatment for partner assault would cluster into distinct readiness-to-change groupings based on the URICA-DV. In support of this hypothesis, the cluster analysis suggested the presence of four readiness-to-change clusters: Reluctant men, who are in a Precontemplative phase; Unprepared Action men, who may be "going through the motions" of behavior change; Preparticipation men, who are moderately aware of the problem and making at some minimal change attempts; and Decision-Making individuals, who appear to be in the Preparation stage of change and taking steps necessary to actively change their behavior. Between 18% and 35% of men commencing BIP appear to be either steadfastly opposed to the very idea that change is desirable or will not likely be sufficiently prepared to initiate change attempts (i.e., the Reluctant and Unprepared Action clusters). Another 30% to 40% of men will perhaps be thinking about change but will most likely neither initiate nor sustain behavior change (Preparticipation stage). Finally, a paltry 20% to 25% of men starting BIP appear ready to change (those in the Decision-Making cluster) and are at the point where they may realize the need for change, are treating the BIP as an opportunity to make those changes, and are likely perceiving the program as at least having the potential to be useful. Noticeably absent from the present set of clusters was a grouping of men clearly in the Action stage, which is in keeping with previous research in this area (Eckhardt, Babcock, et al., 2004; Levesque et al., 2000; Scott & Wolfe, 2003). Thus, in accordance with clinical predictions made by Murphy and colleagues some years ago (Daniels & Murphy, 1997; Murphy & Baxter, 1997), our cluster analysis revealed that the present sample was comprised of men primarily in the Precontemplative and Contemplative stages.

Our second hypothesis predicted that the four partner violence subtypes previously identified by Holtzworth-Munroe and colleagues (2000) using a community sample would also emerge in the present criminal justice sample. This hypothesis was confirmed, as the cluster analysis based on indices of psychopathology (antisocial, borderline, and dependent personality traits), previous-year intimate partner violence, and frequency of previous-year cross-situational violence revealed four distinct group-ings closely aligned with the Holtzworth-Munroe subtypes (Holtzworth-Munroe et al., 2000; Holtzworth-Munroe & Stuart, 1994): FO men, who reported the least amount of partner violence, general violence, and psychopathology; LLA men, who reported moderate levels of vio-lence toward an intimate partner as well as to others in general but had relatively mild levels of psychopathology; BD men, who evidenced traits consistent with borderline and dependent personality disturbances and relatively high levels of intimate partner violence and general violence; and GVA men, who exhibited the highest levels of antisocial personal-ity characteristics, intimate partner violence, and general violence rela-tive to the other subtypes. The distribution of men from this sample into subtype categories differs somewhat from previous researchers' re-ports using similar clustering variables and community volunteers (i.e., Holtzworth-Munroe et al., 2000; Waltz et al., 2000). The percentage of FO men in the present sample (31%) is consistent with the 36% reported by Holtzworth-Munroe and colleagues (2000) but slightly lower than the 53% reported by Waltz and colleagues (2000) using different clustering methods. More LLA (43%) and BD men (20%) were present in this sam-ple relative to the 33% and 15%, respectively, reported by Holtzworth-Munroe and colleagues (2000), with the percentage of BD men similar to that of Waltz and colleagues' (2000) Pathological subtype (23%). Most striking was the relatively small number of GVA men in the present sample ($n = 12$; 6%) relative to comparable groups in previous research (16 of 102 reported by Holtzworth-Munroe et al., 2000; 18 of 75 reported by Waltz et al., 2000). The reasons for this latter differential may be that men with more antisocial tendencies, who are likely to have lengthy criminal histo-ries and prior arrests, may have their partner violence cases adjudicated in felony courts and are thus poorly represented within this sample of misde-meanor offenders. Likewise, GVA men may be less likely to have a treat-ment condition (i.e., BIP) tagged to their postadjudication requirements in favor of other options (e.g., jail).

Our third prediction was that readiness-to-change clusters would be meaningfully related to partner violence subtypes. Specifically, it was expected that men falling into more change-resistant stages-of-change clusters would also group into the more disturbed batterer subtypes (e.g., GVA and/or BD). While there was indeed a relationship between readiness-to-change clusters and partner violence subtypes, it was not in the predicted direction. FO men scored lower than all other subtypes on the Contemplation, Action, and Maintenance scales of the URICA-DV and were more likely than other subtypes to group into the Reluctant readiness-to-change cluster. Thus, FO men report relatively infrequent partner violence episodes but also express little interest in thinking about or doing anything active to modify problems relating to partner assault. While some men may perhaps be in denial of a partner abuse problem, it is also plausible that men who report infrequent, nonsevere forms of violence and who do not report using violence outside the home do not view themselves as having a problem in need of psychoeducational modification. Thus, there is little if anything they desire to change at BIP commencement and appear precontemplative and change resistant on the URICA-DV.

LLA men, who tended to score at the mean level on violence subtype measures, also tended to group into an average or "leveled-out" readiness-to-change cluster (the Preparticipation cluster). Thus, these men are likely to exhibit some degree of contemplation about the consequences of their intimate partner violence and make moderate attempts to change their behavior. GVA men were more likely than other subtypes to be categorized in the Unprepared Action cluster, which is perhaps in keeping with the idea of men in this cluster going through the motions and impulsively attempting active behavior change in the absence of sufficient contemplative effort (Levesque et al., 2000). The BD men were more likely to be categorized in the Decision-Making cluster, which is surprising in the sense that men in this cluster appear to be the most ready to change but unsurprising in the sense that they also appear to be emotionally and behaviorally volatile and more likely to report a host of other clinical problems, including alcohol-related disturbances, drug use, anger, negative attitudes toward women, positive attitudes toward violence, and increased usage of psychological and physical aggression tactics. One explanation might be a social desirability-related effect, given that Decision-Making men scored significantly lower than the other three clusters on the tendency to present oneself in a favorable light. Thus, men in this cluster may be less prone to censor or edit their personal shortcomings regardless of their self-presentational consequences and may also be more prone to indicate a positive attitude toward change. Similarly, these men might also make up a subgroup with a history of seeking treatment for a wide range of personal problems. Previous research indeed suggests that BD men are more likely than men in other subtypes to have a lengthy history of seeking mental health services (Clements, Holtzworth-Munroe, Gondolf, & Meehan, 2002; Saunders, 1992). Thus, while there was no evidence of a direct overlap between readiness to change and partner violence subtypes, the data suggest linkages between FO men grouping into the Precontemplative stage, LLA men in the Contemplative/Preparation stages, GVA men in a stage that suggests action without contemplation, and BD men in a Preparation-like stage with a high probability of assault continuance.

Our fourth hypothesis concerned the ability of readiness-to-change variables and partner violence subtypes to predict criminal justice–related outcomes, including BIP completion, rearrest, and partner violence recidivism. Regarding BIP, the results suggested that membership in a particular stages-of-change cluster pre-BIP was not significantly associated with our BIP-completion and recidivism-dependent variables. Similarly, we were unable to satisfactorily predict BIP completion from URICA-DV subscales assessed pre-BIP. However, partner violence subtypes were related to BIP completion, with GVA (91%) and BD (62%) men showing higher rates of BIP noncompletion relative to other subtypes. Using logistic regression, we investigated subtype dimensions that uniquely predicted BIP completion. These analyses indicated that while the set of measures used to form the subtypes significantly predicted BIP completion, no single dimension was uniquely related to this outcome. Thus, rather than any one individual attribute, it is the combination of factors (i.e., the subtype) that is important in predicting completion of BIP.

We also examined rearrest for any criminal offense as well as new arrests for an assault offense (the only available charge relevant to intimate partner violence in Texas) during the probationary period. While the small number of new assault-related arrests ($n = 10$) did not allow for sufficient power in our statistical analyses, general rearrest was significantly predicted by higher levels of URICA-DV Precontemplation but was not related to any particular readiness-to-change cluster. Thus, the tendency to deny or minimize the need to change abusive behavior patterns predicted additional contact with law enforcement for new criminal offenses while men were on probation for partner assault. One could hypothesize that men who score high on Precontemplation may not view their involvement in the criminal justice system on a domestic violence charge as particularly serious and may therefore not approach their probationary terms as conscientiously as those who see it more soberly, resulting in a greater tendency toward rearrest (although we have no direct data to support or refute this idea). Likewise, some men may harbor lingering anger and resentment about what they perceive as an unjust arrest and may perhaps be more prone toward impulsive and reckless behavior resulting in arrest. In terms of partner violence subtypes, GVA (45%) and BD (38%) subtypes were once again overrepresented among rearrestees, which is in keeping with their tendency toward impulsive and illegal behaviors. Interestingly, however, only high scores on the MCMI Borderline scale emerged as a unique predictor of rearrest, again highlighting contentions by previous researchers concerning the relationship among borderline personality organization and acts of impulse and aggression among intimately violent males (e.g., Dutton, Bodnarchuk, Kropp, Hart, & Ogloff, 1997; Dutton & Starzomski, 1993).

Self- or partner-reported IPV was frequent during respondents' probationary period, with almost 62% of men assaulting a female intimate partner during the probationary period. The Decision-Making readiness-to-change cluster was related to partner violence recidivism, with almost 91% of men in this cluster committing new acts of intimate partner violence. As discussed earlier, this may have to do with the unstable psychological and behavioral nature of men in this cluster, or it may relate to a tendency toward revealing negative personal information. In addition, partner violence was predicted by higher Maintenance scores (which were highest among men in the Decision-Making cluster). The Maintenance scale findings are difficult to interpret given that they are based on a pretreatment assessment, although recent research on predictors of alcoholism treatment suggested that scoring high on Maintenance at the commencement of treatment is associated with treatment *success* (Carbonari & DiClemente, 2000). As URICA-DV Maintenance-scale items represent the individual's awareness of the difficulty regarding maintenance of treatment gains over time, it is once again the realistic appraisal of that difficulty that may in turn spark a more realistic appraisal of other aspects of the self. Thus, it is not clear whether scoring high on Maintenance is meaningfully associated with other clinically relevant factors (such as partner violence) or whether it merely reflects greater awareness that these behaviors are indeed occurring and are problematic.

New incidents of partner violence were not significantly predicted by partner violence subtype or the individual dimensions underlying those subtypes. However, 11 of the 12 men in the GVA subtype assaulted a female intimate partner during their probationary period, which is in keeping with the notion of these men being more prone to violent behavior both within and outside the home. Obviously, the small sample size of GVA men undermined the power of this analysis.

LIMITATIONS

The data reported herein should be interpreted in light of several methodological shortcomings. First, most of the variables reported herein are based on self-reports among men involved in the criminal justice system, which may set the stage for distortion, denial, and inaccurate reporting of sensitive topics. While one could make the decision to simply covary out these social desirability effects for all statistical analyses, we would argue that this self-presentational style is part of their clinical picture. In addition, this is the clinical picture that criminal justice professionals and BIP counselors must confront daily, and it is important to examine whether and how impression management tactics might relate to clinical decision making rather than statistically eliminating such tendencies. Second, it should be noted that men in this sample were not randomly selected from the population of men adjudicated on partner assault charges in this jurisdiction. Participation was voluntary and no doubt some men may have been attracted to or turned off by the research project for reasons potentially related to the outcome variables of interest. Third, these data were collected pre-BIP and as such reflect a particular moment in time that may have changed once men began their court-mandated BIP program. The next step is to examine how readiness to change and psychological functioning changed over time and in turn how these changes predict criminal justice outcomes. Fourth, we were able to provide only general rearrest data for respondents rather than official indices of new incidents of intimate partner violence. This is in part due to the fact that the state of Texas does not have a separate domestic assault charge available to police officers, who must provide narrative in the police report as to whether the assault offense involved a domestic violence incident. Even if domestic violence cases are flagged, it is often difficult to know whether the domestic violence incident involved a child, another family member, or an intimate partner. Nevertheless, only 5% of the present sample were rearrested for an assault-related offense during their probationary period.

Because we were concerned that official indices of domestic violence would differ substantially from the frequency of unreported acts of intimate partner violence, we also obtained reports of intimate partner violence recurrence during the males' probationary period from 65 female partners. However, it should be noted as a limitation that we were able to recruit only a relatively small number of female partners into the study. One of the advantages of doing research in a BIP agency is that female partners have typically been contacted by the agency, which provides researchers with a more centralized recruitment and tracking system. But recruiting a courthouse-based sample of men such as those assessed in the present study, who are more representative of partner assaultive men in general than those recruited from BIPs, does not afford one of those luxuries; we became aware of female partner names and phone numbers at the discretion of the male perpetrators, who could not decide whether to keep that information private or share it with the researchers. Once we had that contact information (from about 50% of the men), we still faced difficulties convincing female partners to participate and obtaining signed consent forms after verbal agreement and had the usual troubles tracking their whereabouts when phone numbers were suddenly out of service and mail was returned as undeliverable.

CLINICAL IMPLICATIONS

Our data indicate that most men who are assigned to BIP present with little to no motivation to change their abusive behavior. Interestingly, about 20% to 30% of men will readily reveal their unwillingness to change (being on probation would seem a prime situation for a moderately high baseline level of social desirability), and another 30% to 40% will merely go through the motions—doing some of what was asked of them by their BIP providers but in the absence of change outside of BIP. While pretreatment motivation to change surprisingly did not predict attrition from BIP, some limited implications for how the abuser approaches and accepts the treatment being offered and that in turn may impact attendance and treatment outcome can be offered. Murphy and colleagues (Daniels & Murphy, 1997; Murphy & Baxter, 1997) have suggested that there is an interaction between an abuser's stage of change at treatment onset and the change-related assumption of the BIP such that the majority of men are likely to present in the Precontemplative stage, but the majority of programs have programmatic content that presumes rapid ascent into the Action stage. Thus, Duluth model–based programs (Pence & Paymar, 1993) often include early confrontations with men about issues relating to responsibility for violent actions and admittance of a patriarchal power and control ideology. Similarly, programs based on cognitive-behavioral therapy often presume that men will be ready to immediately implement action-oriented behavior change tactics (cognitive restructuring and mood management). The question, however, is whether these more general client–treatment matching ideals are important in the context of BIPs, given the coercive reason for referral and criminal justice elements involved in such programs. Future research is needed that more directly evaluates how abuser stage of change interacts with particular treatment modalities to predict treatment completion and recidivism.

The present findings suggest that the partner violence subtype construct may be important from a treatment planning perspective. As has been extensively documented, partner assaultive men are a heterogeneous group that present with a variety of family-of-origin experiences, economic and societal circumstances, cognitive capabilities, and emotional or behavioral dysfunction. The notion that one intervention can be successfully applied to such a diverse group may therefore be tenuous, and numerous authors have suggested that interventions can indeed be tailored to fit specific subtypes of intimate partner violence (Holtzworth-Munroe et al., 2000; Saunders, 1996). Thus, BD males, who tend to fit the Decision-Making readiness-to-change profile, may require interventions that more carefully address their various emotional and interpersonal vulnerabilities, whereas GVA males (the Unprepared Action readiness-to-change profile) may require more structured interventions that are more behaviorally focused and that rely less on cognitive or affective precursors to behavior change attempts (see Saunders, 1996). The FO or Reluctant males, who are resistant to change and often oppose the idea that the criminal justice system is telling them how to handle their private lives, present a significant clinical dilemma since they tend to make up the bulk of BIP clients. It is important for future researchers to further delineate between those men whose low motivation to change merely reflects their low level of violence and those men who, despite clinically significant levels of IPV, refuse to believe they have done anything wrong or perceive the need for change. Whether any of the strategies discussed here can be effectively applied in group counseling formats typically used in BIPs remains to be evaluated.

The present results suggest that men in treatment for partner assault are not uniform in their readiness to change their abusive behavior and that a variety of cognitive, affective, and behavioral factors may impart critical information to criminal justice personnel concerning appropriate postadjudication interventions for men who assault women. It is therefore critical to work together with the prosecutors and judges who routinely mandate group counseling for partner-assaultive men and the agencies providing such services to foster research-informed treatment recommendations.

NOTES

1. This biweekly orientation was held in the central jury room of the Dallas County courthouse and was implemented by the domestic violence court judge in order to increase attendance rates at area BIP programs. The idea behind having a courthouse-based orientation procedure as opposed to an agency-based orientation was to bring the agencies to the men rather than requiring the men to go to the agencies. Following a presentation by the judge and officer of the court concerning probation terms and expectations, a representative from a local BIP agency gave a presentation about their particular approach to treatment. Following this presentation, men adjudicated in the domestic violence court during the previous 2 weeks registered at one of five different area agencies and pledged to attend an intake session. The interval between agency sign-up and the required intake appointment at BIP varied by agency, although 2 to 4 weeks was typical.

2. As discussed by numerous authors (e.g., Collins, Schafer, & Kam, 2001; Schafer & Olson, 1998), unnecessary loss of statistical power and increased type I and type II error rates can result given the presence of missing questionnaire data. Rather than removing whole cases because they are missing one or two answers on a given questionnaire, the Expectation-Maximization algorithm (Dempster, Laird, & Rubin, 1977) allows for estimation of unobserved values by using properties of observed values. In multiple imputation (Rubin, 1987), each missing value is replaced by a range of possible predicted values based on existing relationships among observed variables. Each individual data set is then combined, resulting in an overall estimate for each missing value that takes into account observed relationships among nonmissing values of the variables of interest as well as the inherent uncertainty surrounding missing values. The primary assumption that must be met prior to usage of multiple imputation is that data must be missing at random or that missing values of the variable under consideration must not be missing because of the variable itself. While it is not possible to completely establish whether truly random reasons underlie missing data (since it would require further information about the unobserved data that are unobtainable), we nevertheless found no significant differences between cases that provided complete data on the URICA-DV and partner violence subtype measures and those that did not on the study's major outcome variables.

ACKNOWLEDGMENTS

This research was supported in part by grant 99-WT-VX-0012 from the National Institute of Justice awarded to the first author. The authors wish to thank Judge David Finn, Ron R. Goethals, Mike Hurlburt, Bernie Auchter, Katherine Darke, Ifeoluwa Togun, Elizabeth Franks, Liv Sharp, Kevin Impelman, Lauren Innes, Anna Brandon, and the Stages of Change Project interviewers.

REFERENCES

Babcock, J. C., Green, C. E., & Robie, C. (2004). Does batterers' treatment work? A meta-analytic review of domestic violence treatment. *Clinical Psychology Review, 23,* 1023–1053.

Babcock, J. C., & La Taillade, J. (2000). Evaluating interventions for men who batter. In J. Vincent & E. Jouriles (Eds.), *Domestic violence: Guidelines for research-informed practice* (pp. 37–77). Philadelphia: Jessica Kingsley.

Bradley, K. A., McDonell, M. B., Bush, K., Kivlahan, D. R., Diehr, P., & Fihn, S. D. (1998). The AUDIT alcohol consumption questions: Reliability, validity, and responsiveness to change. *Alcoholism: Clinical and Experimental Research, 22,* 1842–1848.

Brogan, M. M., Prochaska, J. O., & Prochaska, J. M. (1999). Predicting termination and continuation status in psychotherapy using the transtheoretical model. *Psychotherapy: Theory, Research, Practice, Training, 36,* 105–113.

Burt, M. (1980). Cultural myths and supports for rape. *Journal of Personality and Social Psychology, 38,* 217–230.

Campbell, J. C. (1995). Predicting homicide of and by battered women. In J. C. Campbell (Ed.), *Assessing dangerousness: Violence by sexual offenders, batterers, and child abusers* (pp. 47–68). Thousand Oaks, CA: Sage.

Carbonari, J. P., & DiClemente, C. C. (2000). Using transtheoretical model profiles to differentiate levels of alcohol abstinence success. *Journal of Consulting and Clinical Psychology, 68,* 810–817.

Chang, H., & Saunders, D. G. (2002). Predictors of attrition in two types of group programs for men who batter. *Journal of Family Violence, 17,* 273–292.

Check, J., Malamuth, N., Elias, B., & Barton, S. (1985, April). On hostile ground. *Psychology Today,* 56–61.

Chen, H., Bersani, C., Myers, S. C., & Denton, R. (1989). Evaluating the effectiveness of a court-sponsored abuse treatment program. *Journal of Family Violence, 4,* 309–322.

Clements, K., Holtzworth-Munroe, A., Gondolf, E., & Meehan, J. C. (2002, November). *Testing the Holtzworth-Munroe & Stuart (2000) batterer typology among court-referred maritally violent men.* Paper presented at the annual convention of the Association for Advancement of Behavior Therapy, Reno, NV.

Clements, R. (1998). A critical evaluation of several alcohol screening instruments using the CIDISAM as a criterion measure. *Alcoholism: Clinical and Experimental Research, 22,* 450–465.

Collins, L. M., Schafer, J. L., & Kam, C. M. (2001). A comparison of inclusive and restrictive strategies in modern missing data procedures. *Psychological Methods, 6,* 330–351.

Crowne, D. P., & Marlowe, D. (1960). A new scale of social desirability independent of psychopathology. *Journal of Consulting Psychology, 24,* 349–354.

Daly, J. E., & Pelowski, S. (2000). Predictors of dropout among men who batter: A review of studies with implications for research and practice. *Violence and Victims, 17,* 137–160.

Daly, J. E., Power, T. G., & Gondolf, E. W. (2001). Predictors of batterer program attendance. *Journal of Interpersonal Violence, 16,* 971–991.

Daniels, J. W., & Murphy, C. M. (1997). Stages and processes of change in batterers' treatment. *Cognitive and Behavioral Practice, 4,* 123–145.

Deffenbacher, J. L., Oetting, E. R., Thwaites, G. A., Lynch, R. S., Baker, D. A., Stark, R. S., et al. (1996). State-trait anger theory and the utility of the trait anger scale. *Journal of Counseling Psychology, 43,* 131–148.

Dempster, A. P., Laird, N. M., & Rubin, D. B. (1977). Maximum likelihood from incomplete data via the EM algorithm. *Journal of the Royal Statistical Society, 39,* 1–38.

Dunford, F. W. (2000). The San Diego navy experiment: An assessment of interventions for men who assault their wives. *Journal of Consulting and Clinical Psychology, 68,* 468–476.

Dutton, D. G. (1986). The outcome of court-mandated treatment for wife assault: A quasi-experimental evaluation. *Violence and Victims, 1,* 163–175.

Dutton, D. G., Bodnarchuk, M., Kropp, R., Hart, S. D., & Ogloff, J. P. (1997). Client personality disorders affecting post-treatment recidivism. *Violence and Victims, 12,* 37–50.

Dutton, D. G., & Starzomski, A. J. (1993). Borderline personality in perpetrators of psychological and physical abuse. *Violence and Victims, 8,* 327–337.

Eckhardt, C. I., Babcock, J., & Homack, S. (2004). Partner assaultive men and the stages and processes of change. *Journal of Family Violence, 19,* 81–93.

Eckhardt, C. I., & Dye, M. L. (2000). The cognitive characteristics of maritally violent men: Theory and evidence. *Cognitive Therapy and Research, 24,* 139–158.

Eckhardt, C. I., Norlander, B., & Deffenbacher, J. (2004). The assessment of anger and hostility: A critical review. *Aggression and Violent Behavior: A Review Journal, 9,* 17–43.

Edelson, J. (1996). Controversy and change in batterers' programs. In J. L. Edelson & Z. C. Eisikovits (Eds.), *Future interventions with battered women and their families* (pp. 154–169). Thousand Oaks, CA: Sage.

Fuqua, D. R., Leonard, E., Masters, M. A., & Smith, R. J. (1991). A structural analysis of the state-trait anger expression inventory. *Educational and Psychological Measurement, 51,* 439–446.

Gondolf, E. W. (1999). A comparison of four batterer intervention systems: Do court-referral, program length, and services matter? *Journal of Interpersonal Violence, 14,* 41–61.

Hamberger, L. K., Lohr, J. M., Bonge, D., & Tolin, D. F. (1996). A large sample empirical typology of male spouse abusers and its relationship to dimensions of abuse. *Violence and Victims, 11,* 277–292.

Healey, K., Smith, C., & O'Sullivan, C. (1998). *Batterer intervention: Program approaches and criminal justice strategies.* Washington, DC: National Institute of Justice.

Holtzworth-Munroe, A. (2000). A typology of men who are violent toward their female partners: Making sense of the heterogeneity in husband violence. *Current Directions in Psychological Science, 9,* 140–143.

Holtzworth-Munroe, A., Meehan, J. C., Herron, K., Rehman, U., & Stuart, G. L. (2000). Testing the Holtzworth-Munroe & Stuart (1994) batterer typology. *Journal of Consulting and Clinical Psychology, 68,* 1000–1019.

Holtzworth-Munroe, A., Meehan, J. C., Herron, K., Rehman, U., & Stuart, G. L. (2003). Do subtypes of maritally violent men continue to differ over time? *Journal of Consulting and Clinical Psychology, 71,* 728–740.

Holtzworth-Munroe, A., & Stuart, G. L. (1994). Typologies of male batterers: Three subtypes and the differences among them. *Psychological Bulletin, 116,* 476–497.

Langinrichsen-Rohling, J., Huss, M., & Ramsey, S. (2000). The clinical utility of batterer typologies. *Journal of Family Violence, 15,* 37–53.

Levesque, D. A., Gelles, R. J., & Velicer, W. F. (2000). Development and validation of a stages of change measure for men in batterer treatment. *Cognitive Therapy and Research, 24,* 175–200.

Livesley, W. J., Schroeder, M. L., Jackson, D. N., & Jang, K. (1994). Categorical distinctions in the study of personality disorder: Implications for classification. *Journal of Abnormal Psychology, 103,* 6–17.

McCann, B. S., Simpson, T. L., Ries, R., & Roy-Byrne, P. (2000). Reliability and validity of screening instruments for drug and alcohol abuse in adults seeking evaluation for attention-deficit/hyperactivity disorder. *American Journal on Addictions, 9,* 1–9.

McConnaughy, E. A., DiClemente, C. C., Prochaska, J. O., & Velicer, W. F. (1989). Stages of change in psychotherapy: A follow-up report. *Psychotherapy, 26,* 494–503.

McConnaughy, E. A., Prochaska, J. O., & Velicer, W. F. (1983). Stages of change in psychotherapy: Measurement and sample profiles. *Psychotherapy, 20,* 368–375.

Millon, T. (1994). *Manual for the Millon Clinical Multiaxial Inventory* (3rd ed.). Minneapolis, MN: National Computer Systems.

Murphy, C. M., & Baxter, V. A. (1997). Motivating batterers to change in the treatment context. *Journal of Interpersonal Violence, 12,* 607–619.

Murphy, C. M., & Hoover, S. A. (1999). Measuring emotional abuse in dating relationships as a multifactorial construct. *Violence and Victims, 39,* 39–53.

O'Hare, T. (1996). Court-ordered versus voluntary clients: Problem differences and readiness for change. *Social Work, 41,* 417–422.

Pence, E., & Paymar, M. (1993). *Education groups for men who batter: The Duluth model.* New York: Springer.

Prochaska, J. O. (1979). *Systems of psychotherapy: A transtheoretical analysis.* Homewood, IL: Dorsey Press.

Prochaska, J. O., DiClemente, C. C., & Norcross, J. C. (1992). In search of how people change: Applications to addictive behaviors. *American Psychologist, 47,* 1102–1114.

Reynolds, W. M. (1982). Development of reliable and valid short forms of the Marlowe-Crowne social desirability scale. *Journal of Clinical Psychology, 38,* 119–125.

Rubin, D. B. (1987). *Multiple imputation for nonresponse in surveys.* New York: Wiley.

Saunders, D. G. (1992). A typology of men who batter: Three types derived from cluster analysis. *American Journal of Orthopsychiatry, 62,* 264–275.

Saunders, D. G. (1996). Feminist-cognitive-behavioral and process-psychodynamic treatments for men who batter. *Violence and Victims, 11,* 393–414.

Saunders, J. B., Aasland, O. G., Babor, T. F., de la Fuente, J. R., & Grant, M. (1993). Development of the alcohol use disorders identification test (AUDIT): WHO collaborative project on early detection of persons with harmful alcohol consumption–II. *Addiction, 88,* 791–804.

Schafer, J. L., & Olson, M. K. (1998). Multiple imputation for multivariate missing data problems: A data analyst's perspective. *Multivariate Behavioral Research, 33,* 545–571.

Schumacher, J. A., Feldbau-Kohn, S., Slep, A., & Heyman, R. E. (2001). Risk factors for male-to-female partner physical abuse. *Aggression and Violent Behavior, 6,* 281–352.

Scott, K. S., & Wolfe, D. (2003). Readiness to change as a predictor of outcome in batterer treatment. *Journal of Consulting and Clinical Psychology, 71,* 879–889.

Skinner, H. A. (1982). The drug abuse screening test. *Addictive Behaviors, 7,* 363–371.

Smith, K. J., Subich, L. M., & Kalodner, C. (1995). The transtheoretical model's stages and processes of change and their relation to premature termination. *Journal of Counseling Psychology, 42,* 34–39.

Snyder, C. R., Crowson, J. J., Houston, B. K., Kurylo, M., & Poirier, J. (1997). Assessing hostile automatic thoughts: Development and validation of the HAT scale. *Cognitive Therapy and Research, 21,* 477–492.

Spielberger, C. D. (1988). *Manual for the state-trait anger expression inventory.* Odessa, FL: Psychological Assessment Resources.

Straus, M. A. (2001). *Scoring and norms for the CTS2 and CTSPC.* Technical report available from the Family Research Laboratory, University of New Hampshire, Durham, NH.

Straus, M. A., Hamby, S. L., Boney-McCoy, S., & Sugarman, D. B. (1996). The revised conflict tactics scales (CTS-2). *Journal of Family Issues, 17,* 283–316.

Waltz, J., Babcock, J. C., Jacobson, N. S., & Gottman, J. M. (2000). Testing a typology of batterers. *Journal of Consulting and Clinical Psychology, 68,* 658–669.

Ward, J. H. (1963). Hierarchical grouping to optimize an objective function. *Journal of the American Statistical Association, 58,* 236–244.

Stages of Change in Batterers and Their Response to Treatment

6

PAMELA C. ALEXANDER AND EUGENE MORRIS

Given the significance of intimate partner violence (IPV) in this country, criminal courts have increasingly begun to rely on court-mandated treatment for intimate partner violence offenders in hopes of turning the tide against this problem. However, the few randomized studies that have compared batterer treatment to a no-treatment control condition find little basis for optimism (Babcock & LaTaillaide, 2000; Davis & Taylor, 1998; Dunford, 2000; Feder & Ford, 1999). Studies comparing different types of treatment have similarly found few differences (Edleson & Syers, 1990; Gondolf, 1997b; Harris, Savage, Jones, & Brooke, 1988). On the other hand, recent promising research on typologies suggests that batterers differ on a number of important dimensions (cf. Hamberger, Lohr, Bonge, & Tolin, 1996; Holtzworth-Munroe, Meehan, Herron, Rehman, & Stuart, 2000; Holtzworth-Munroe & Stuart, 1994; Waltz, Babcock, Jacobson, & Gottman, 2000), and these differences may predict response to treatment (Langhinrichsen-Rohling, Huss, & Ramsey, 2000). Therefore, it is possible that many potentially significant differences between treatment conditions have gone undetected by failing to consider individual differences among group members.

One such potentially important individual difference is the individual's readiness and motivation for change. It is clear that the effectiveness of batterers' treatment programs is frequently limited by the denial and minimization characterizing many batterers regarding their violent behavior (Cadsky, Hanson, Crawford, & Lalonde, 1996; Malloy, McCloskey, & Monford, 1999; Scalia, 1994). Many batterers do not see themselves as having a problem with violence, and, to the degree that they acknowledge that they are abusive, they may frame it in terms of a normal reaction to their partner's provocative behavior. One way of understanding this denial and lack of motivation is through the transtheoretical model of change (TTM), which has frequently been applied to another population characterized by denial and minimization, namely, substance abusers. As articulated by Prochaska and DiClemente (1984), this model assumes that all individuals go through a series of stages before a change in behavior is ever accomplished. Initially, individuals in a stage of *precontemplation* either deny the existence of the behavior, minimize it, or attribute its cause to someone else. In the stage of *contemplation,* they begin to acknowledge the problem's existence as well as its negative effect, but they are still not actively doing anything to change the behavior. In the stage of *preparation,* they are thinking more clearly about what they can do to alter the behavior. In the *action* stage, they are actually focused on making behavior change and are taking active steps to alter the behavior. Finally, in the *maintenance* stage, they are still actively monitoring themselves to ensure that the problematic behavior does not resume.

This model assumes that change is not usually linear. Instead, individuals relapse and achieve the desired behavior change only gradually, although even relapse may be followed by eventual progress. Furthermore, it is expected that different types of symptoms and reactions would characterize different stages. Thus, individuals in the precontemplation stage do not usually experience much distress pertaining to the behavior. On the other hand, individuals in the contemplation stage may experience excessive distress and worry, even more perhaps than those in the preparation or action stage. Finally, it is expected that different change processes characterize individuals in different stages (Eckhardt, Babcock, & Homack, 2004; Prochaska, DiClemente, & Norcross, 1992). Consequently, different types of interventions would be appropriate for individuals in different stages. For example, several smoking cessation programs found that the use of behavioral strategies was highly successful for individuals in an action stage of change but virtually useless for individuals in the precontemplation or contemplation stages (Prochaska et al., 1992). Therefore, considering the readiness to change of an individual is essential for treatment planning.

Several researchers have attempted to assess the applicability of the stages-of-change model to batterers in treatment (cf. Begun, Shelley,

Strodthoff, & Short, 2002; Daniels & Murphy, 1997; Eckhardt et al., 2004; Levesque, Gelles, & Velicer, 2000; Scott & Wolfe, 2003). For example, Begun and colleagues (2003) have demonstrated that the 35-item Safe at Home assessment is comprised of three scales consistent with the pre-contemplation, contemplation, and preparation/action stages outlined in the transtheoretical model. Low readiness to change in the Safe-at-Home measure was correlated with little assumption of personal responsibility for violence and with minimization of psychological aggression, and prep-aration/action scores were significantly correlated with self-efficacy for abstaining from verbal aggression. Surprisingly, precontemplation scores were not associated with minimization of violence (relative to partners' reports), although contemplation scores were. Levesque and colleagues (2000) developed a measure of intimate partner violent offender readi-ness to change and provided evidence of validity based on self-reported strategies used to control the abusive behavior and on partner blame. However, Levesque and colleagues did not compare responses to part-ner report. Scott and Wolfe (2003) collected reports from 13% of the partners at intake but acknowledged being hampered even in this by the short time frame (i.e., 2 months) used to assess recent abusive behavior. Partner report is essential in assessing the relationship between stage-of-change and batterers' reports of their own behavior and symptoms because it is possible that individuals who are assumed to be denying the significance of their behavior may actually have perpetrated less violence and are therefore deservedly experiencing less distress. Finally, in order to assess the relevance of this model to types of treatment, it is important to assess whether an individual's stage of change indeed predicts his re-sponse to treatment (cf. Scott & Wolfe, 2003).

It was the purpose of this study to assess the validity of the stages-of-change model with respect to IPV offenders. To this end, the University of Rhode Island Change Assessment (URICA) scale was administered to 210 participants in a 26-week, court-ordered batterer treatment pro-gram. As is customary with the use of this scale, respondents' scores on the four scales of this measure (precontemplation, contemplation, action, and maintenance) were subjected to a cluster analysis in order to derive clusters of individuals who differed with respect to their re-sponses. It should be noted that cluster analysis of the URICA does not tend to result in clusters of individuals characterized by an elevation on only one scale (suggesting a primary stage of change) but instead leads to different overall profiles on these scales. The validity of this cluster solution was then assessed by testing the differences between clusters on relevant criterion variables (cf. Aldenderfer & Blashfield, 1984).

It was hypothesized that individuals with a profile suggesting an earlier stage of change would report having perpetrated less violence against their partners (thus denying the significance of their behavior), although their partners would report no difference in their behavior as compared to the partners of batterers in a later stage of change. This hypothesis was assessed in several ways. First, the self-reports of batterers with respect to their perpetration of violence (both over the past 6 months and in the lifetime of their relationship with their current partner) were compared as a function of cluster, with the expectation that men in an earlier stage of change would be significantly less likely to acknowledge their abusive behavior. Second, the reports of partners were compared as a function of cluster, with the expectation that partner reports would not vary as a function of their partners' stage of change. Finally, the degree of discrepancy between men and their partners was compared as a function of cluster with the expectation that the reports of men in an earlier stage of change would be more discrepant from that of their partners. Both paired t tests and a multivariate analysis of variance of difference scores (between the men's and the women's reports) were used to make these latter comparisons.

Second, it was hypothesized that those individuals characterized by an earlier stage of change would report experiencing less distress (anxiety, depression, and alcohol abuse) as well as fewer problems with anger. That is, it was hypothesized that an earlier stage of change would be associated with fewer internal motivators (such as distress or guilt) for changing one's behavior.

Finally, it was hypothesized that individuals in an earlier stage of change would exhibit less change over the course of treatment. In other words, standard treatment protocols neither address the emotional distress presumably associated with the causes or consequences of the violent behavior nor result in an actual decrease in the violent behavior. The latter, of course, is the gold standard of treatment effectiveness and was examined with only preliminary follow-up partner reports in this study.

METHOD

Sample

The sample consisted of 210 men who were court-ordered to participate in a 26-week outpatient group for batterers at the Montgomery County, Maryland, Abused Persons Program (APP). The APP's Abuser Intervention Program receives court-referred offenders primarily (a) as a condition of a criminal sentence for a partner abuse charge, or (b) as a part of a civil order for protection against intimate partner violence. Some referrals may also come as a diversion of the prosecution of a partner abuse charge by the court and/or the office of the state's attorney or as part of a juvenile court order where partner abuse contributed to abuse or neglect of a child. Clients are excluded from group treatment if they are actively psychotic, have personality disorders severe enough that they would disrupt a group, or have very poor ability to communicate in English. (Groups for Spanish-speaking individuals are conducted separately and were not included in this study.) Men who are actively abusing alcohol or other drugs are enrolled in substance abuse programs and are required to have 1 month of sobriety before they are eligible to begin group treatment.

Only those men for whom complete data on the URICA (the basis for the cluster analysis) were available were included in this study. Demographics of the sample can be found in Table 6.1.

Measures

Conflict Tactics Scales–Revised

The Conflict Tactics Scale–Revised (CTS-2; Straus, Hamby, Boney-McCoy, & Sugarman, 1996) consists of a 14-item Psychological Aggression scale, a 12-item Physical Assault scale, a 7-item Sexual Coercion scale, and a 6-item Injury scale. Each item is responded to with a frequency rating of 0 to 6 (ranging from "never happened" to "more than 20 times") with respect to either the partner's behavior toward the self or the self's behavior toward the partner. Participants were asked to respond with a time frame of the most recent 6 months as well as lifetime prevalence. In this study, lifetime prevalence was based not on the total frequency of behaviors but on the respondent's acknowledgment of whether a given behavior had ever occurred. Moffitt and colleagues (1997) used these same "variety" scores in which respondents indicated how many of the CTS-2 items had been endorsed at least once. They noted the superiority of these variety scores to frequency scores in that the former are less skewed and more reliable. Good internal consistency and construct and discriminant validity exist for all scales (Straus et al., 1996).

URICA

The URICA (McConnaughy, DiClemente, Prochaska, & Velicer, 1989) is a 28-item questionnaire designed to assess an individual's stage of change as measured by scores on four scales—precontemplation,

Table 6.1

DEMOGRAPHIC CHARACTERISTICS AND ATTRITION AS A FUNCTION OF CLUSTER

SCALE	CLUSTER 1 (N = 108) MEAN (SD)	CLUSTER 2 (N = 102) MEAN (SD)	t	χ^2
Age	35.0 (9.2)	36.5 (9.3)	1.25 ns	
Net monthly income	$1,485 ($1,411)	$1,363 ($1,145)	.31 ns	
Educational level				9.28 ns
<High school	9	12		
High school or GED	34	44		
College <4 years	36	21		
College degree	17	9		
>College degree	4	6		
Vocational/ technical		1		
Ethnicity				4.73 ns
White	28	36		
African American	50	45		
Hispanic	21	13		
American Indian		1		
Asian American	7	4		
Other	1	1		
Marital status				2.39 ns
Single	27	30		
Married	50	38		
Separated	25	23		
Divorced	4	7		
Attrition				.47 ns
Never attended	17	20		
Dropped out	18	17		
Completed	67	61		

Note. GED = general equivalency diploma.

contemplation, action, and maintenance. Results of a principal components analysis determined a clear four-component solution, and internal consistency is good for each scale (McConnaughy et al., 1989). In the current sample, internal consistency estimates were .79 for precontemplation, .87 for contemplation, .64 for action, and .87 for maintenance. For use in this study, individuals were instructed to complete the questions with respect to their abusive behavior.

Beck Depression Inventory–Revised

The Beck Depression Inventory–Revised (BDI-II; Beck, Steer, & Brown, 1996) consists of 21 items and is designed to assess the affective, cognitive, and physiological dimensions of depression. It has excellent internal consistency and concurrent validity.

State-Trait Anxiety Inventory–Trait Anxiety

The State-Trait Anxiety Inventory–Trait Anxiety (STAI-Trait; Spielberger, Gorsuch, & Lushene, 1970) is comprised of 20 items assessing trait anxiety. Test–retest reliability for trait anxiety is .81. Internal consistency ranges from .83 to .92. Good concurrent validity exists for this scale.

State-Trait Anger Expression Inventory

The State-Trait Anger Expression Inventory (STAXI; Spielberger, 1988) is a self-administered instrument developed to assess state anger, trait anger, and expression of angry feelings. The specific scales include Trait Anger (respondents' reports of how they generally reacted with regard to anger during the previous 2 weeks), Anger-Out (the tendency to express anger outwardly and negatively), Anger-In (the tendency to suppress or hold in anger), and Anger-Control (the frequency with which energy is used in monitoring and preventing the expression of anger). Internal consistency estimates, factor structure estimates across criterion groups, concurrent validity, and discriminant validity have been found to be excellent (Fuqua et al., 1991; Spielberger & Sydeman, 1994).

Short Michigan Alcohol Screening Test

The Short Michigan Alcohol Screening Test (SMAST; Selzer, Vinokur, & van Rooijen, 1975) is a short version of the Michigan Alcohol Screening

Test (MAST) and consists of 13 self-administered items regarding behavioral, interpersonal, and psychological indicators of problematic alcohol use. It correlates from .95 to .99 with the MAST (Pokorny, Miller, &
Kaplan, 1972), and its internal consistency ranges from .76 to .93 (Selzer
et al., 1975). In this study, the SMAST was used to assess lifetime alcohol
abuse problems.

Procedure

Prior to assignment to a group, men were interviewed at the APP and
were required to complete the following questionnaires: a demographic
questionnaire, BDI-II, STAI, STAXI, CTS-2, SMAST, and the URICA.
The BDI-II, STAI, STAXI, CTS-2, and URICA were then readminis-
tered at the end of treatment.

The partner was contacted by telephone when the batterer was enrolled in the program and was asked to complete the CTS-2 with respect
to her partner's lifetime prevalence of violent behavior toward her as
well as his violent behavior toward her within the preceding 6 months.
At the time of this data collection, the APP had just instituted a policy of
partner follow-up (at 6 months following the completion of treatment).
Therefore, only a very small number of partners ($N = 15$) were recontacted at follow-up.

The men then participated in a standard cognitive-behavioral gender-
reeducation group format for 26 weeks (39 hours). This program consists
of closed groups of 8 to 12 men with curriculum focusing on education and discussion about intimate partner violence, power, and control,
and the roles of men and women as well as skills-building work in anger
management, communication, and conflict resolution. This program
represents elements of the Duluth model and the cognitive-behavioral
approach, the two most common models in North American programs
offering counseling interventions with partner abuse offenders.

RESULTS

Cluster Composition

Scores on the URICA scales were initially transformed into Z-scores.
Then, as is customary with the use of the URICA, a cluster analysis was
conducted of the men's responses on the four scales of the URICA—
precontemplation, contemplation, action, and maintenance. A two-stage

cluster analysis was conducted. In the first stage, Ward's (1963) method, relying on the squared Euclidean distance as the distance measure, was used to identify the optimal number of clusters in the data. Ward's method indicates the point in the sort at which two relatively dissimilar clusters have been merged, suggesting that the stage preceding this merger is the optimal number of clusters (Aldenderfer & Blashfield, 1984). The result of Ward's method suggested that a two-cluster solution was most appropriate for these data. In the second stage, a K-means cluster analysis with a two-cluster solution specified was used to assign individuals to the specific clusters. The K-means cluster analysis has the advantage over Ward's method of conducting more than one partition of the data and thus compensating for a poor initial specification of the clusters (Aldenderfer & Blashfield, 1984). As can be seen in Figure 6.1, the two clusters derived are similar to Levesque and colleagues' (2000) Participation cluster (cluster 1) and Immotive cluster (cluster 2).

As would be expected, the two clusters differed significantly on their scores on these four scales—namely, precontemplation ($F[1, 208] = 74.95, p < .001$), contemplation ($F[1, 208] = 203.68, p < .001$), action ($F[1, 208] = 126.13, p < .001$), and maintenance ($F[1, 208] = 181.13, p < .001$). As can be seen in Figure 6.1, cluster 1 ($N = 108$) was characterized by lower scores than cluster 2 ($N = 102$) on precontemplation and higher

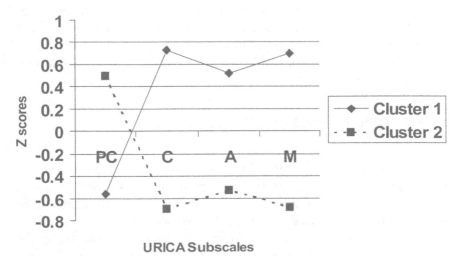

Figure 6.1 Z Scores of two-cluster solution on URICA scales.
Note. PC = Precontemplation; C = Contemplation; A = Action; M = Maintenance. Cluster 1 $N = 108$; cluster 2 $N = 102$.

scores on contemplation, action, and maintenance; therefore, cluster 1 individuals would appear to be at a later stage of change with respect to their acknowledgment of their violent behavior.

The more meaningful indication of the validity of this cluster solution is based on the presence of statistically significant differences between the two clusters on variables external to the cluster analysis (Aldenderfer & Blashfield, 1984). Therefore, clusters 1 and 2 were compared with respect to demographic characteristics, self-reported experiences of current distress and anger problems, self-reported history of violence, partner-reported history of violence, and self-reported change in symptoms and stages of change over the course of treatment.

Demographic Characteristics and Attrition Rates of Clusters 1 and 2

As can be seen in Table 6.1, clusters 1 and 2 were not found to differ significantly with respect to age, net monthly income, educational level, ethnicity, or marital status. Moreover, when attrition was defined as those who never attended the group (but had completed assessment instruments prior to the group), and those who terminated from the group prematurely, as compared to those who completed the group, results of a chi-square analysis suggested that clusters 1 and 2 did not differ with respect to attrition. Finally, a composite Readiness to Change score was calculated consisting of the Z-score of the precontemplation scale subtracted from the total of the Z-scores of the contemplation, action, and maintenance scales. This composite score was not found to vary significantly with either the number of sessions attended ($r = .07$, ns) or with the variable of attrition ($F[2, 197] = .29$, ns).

Self-Reported Violence Perpetrated Against One's Partner

Given the variability of length of time between a complaint of assault, adjudication, and initial attendance at a group, couples varied greatly as to how much actual contact they had had in the 6 months prior to the group; many had seen each other very little in those months. Therefore, while comparisons were made between the clusters on the 6 months preceding the onset of the group, the more meaningful comparisons were based on their self-reported lifetime prevalence of psychological aggression, physical assault, injury perpetrated, and sexual coercion of their partner. As mentioned previously, lifetime prevalence scores on the CTS-2 are variety scores and were derived by summing responses across items as to whether a given behavior had ever occurred; thus, these scores cannot be compared to 6-month prevalence scores, which are based on actual frequencies of behaviors.

As can be seen in Table 6.2, results of a multivariate analysis of variance (MANOVA) analyzing CTS-2 scale scores for the preceding

Table 6.2

SELF-REPORTED VIOLENCE (CTS-2) IN PRECEDING 6 MONTHS AND LIFETIME AS A FUNCTION OF CLUSTER

SCALE	CLUSTER 1 ($N = 103$) MEAN (*SD*)	CLUSTER 2 ($N = 96$) MEAN (*SD*)	MULTIVARIATE *F*	UNIVARIATE *F*
Preceding 6 Months			2.39 *ns*	
Psychological Aggression	26.43 (23.34)	16.46 (23.11)		9.16**
Physical Assault	7.43 (11.08)	6.58 (18.92)		.15 *ns*
Injury	2.37 (3.26)	2.00 (6.03)		.28 *ns*
Sexual Coercion	3.42 (8.08)	3.03 (7.88)		.12 *ns*
Lifetime			8.14***	
Psychological Aggression	4.65 (1.69)	3.46 (1.96)		21.13***
Physical Assault	4.68 (2.79)	2.71 (2.54)		27.02***
Injury	1.96 (1.46)	1.12 (1.20)		19.21***
Sexual Coercion	.80 (1.21)	.46 (.96)		5.00*

Note. Lifetime prevalence is scored as to whether a specific behavior *ever* occurred. Psychological Aggression = CTS-2–Psychological Aggression Scale; Physical Assault = CTS-2–Physical Assault Scale; Injury = CTS-2 Injury Scale; Sexual Coercion = CTS-2 Sexual Coercion Scale.
*$p < .05$. **$p < .005$. ***$p < .001$.

6 months suggested that cluster 1 men self-reported only marginally higher rates of violence perpetrated against their partners than did cluster 2 men ($F[4, 194] = 2.39$, $p = .052$). In particular, they acknowledged significantly more psychological aggression against their partners ($F[1, 197] = 9.16$, $p = .003$). Results of a MANOVA analyzing self-reported lifetime perpetration of violence against their partners suggested that cluster 1 individuals self-reported significantly higher lifetime prevalence rates of violence than did cluster 2 individuals ($F[4, 194] = 8.14$, $p < .001$). Follow-up analyses of variance (ANOVAs) suggested that cluster 1 individuals acknowledged perpetrating significantly more psychological aggression ($F[1, 197] = 21.13$, $p < .001$), physical assault ($F[1, 197] = 27.02$, $p < .001$), injury ($F[1, 197] = 19.21$, $p < .001$), and sexual coercion ($F[1, 197] = 5.00$, $p < .03$) against their partners than did cluster 2 individuals.

Partner-Reported Violence

Because self-report measures do not allow us to ascertain whether cluster 1 members actually had perpetrated more violence or whether they were merely more likely to report that they had done so, it was necessary to compare the batterers' and the partners' reports on the CTS-2. However, not all partners had completed the initial CTS-2 scales. While an attempt is made at the APP to contact all partners of men enrolled in the batterer treatment program, the characteristics of batterers whose partners were successfully contacted ($N = 140$; 67%) were compared with the characteristics of those batterers whose partners were not able to be contacted ($N = 70$; 33%). To this end, ANOVAs and chi-squares were conducted on the basis of initial demographics and batterer self-report on the CTS-2 scales. As compared to batterers whose partners were contacted, batterers whose partners were not contacted were not found to differ on age ($F[1, 209] = .03$, ns), years of education ($F[1, 195] = .04$, ns), net monthly income ($F[1, 144] = .42$, ns), ethnicity ($\chi^2 = 5.12$, $df = 5$, ns), marital status ($\chi^2 = 1.77$, $df = 3$, ns), attrition ($\chi^2 = .98$, $df = 2$, ns), self-reported lifetime psychological aggression ($F[1, 204] = .44$, ns), self-reported lifetime physical aggression ($F[1, 203] = 1.19$, ns), self-reported lifetime injury ($F[1, 204] = .41$, ns), self-reported lifetime sexual coercion ($F[1, 203] = 1.14$, ns), depression ($F[1, 199] = .10$, ns), trait anxiety ($F[1, 206] = .08$, ns), internalizing anger ($F[1, 202] = .63$, ns), externalizing anger ($F[1, 206] = 1.35$, ns), trait anger ($F[1, 205] = 2.38$, ns), or anger control ($F[1, 206] = .01$, ns). There was, however, a tendency for batterers whose partners were contacted to be represented in cluster 1 rather than cluster 2 (χ^2 = 4.20, df = 1, p = .04).

Those batterers whose partners had completed the CTS-2 were selected in order to compare the batterers' and the partners' reports on the CTS-2 as a function of cluster. Results of MANOVAs suggested that, according to the partners, members of clusters 1 and 2 did not differ either in their level of violence perpetrated within the preceding 6 months ($F[4, 133]$ = .71, ns) or in their lifetime prevalence of violence perpetrated against their partners ($F[4, 133]$ = .41, ns) (see Table 6.3). Therefore, it appears that, contrary to differences in their self-report, members of clusters 1 and 2 do not differ with respect to their violent behavior, but instead seem to differ only with respect to their assessment of their violence.

Discrepancy Between Men's and Women's Reports of Violence

As can be seen in Table 6.4, the results of a series of paired comparison t tests between the men and their partners revealed that both cluster 1 and cluster 2 men significantly underestimated their lifetime prevalence of physical assault (cluster 1, $t[77]$ = 6.26, p < .001; cluster 2, $t[58]$ = 9.14, p < .001), injury perpetrated (cluster 1, $t[76]$ = 5.07, p < .001; cluster 2, $t[59]$ = 7.82, p < .001), and sexual coercion (cluster 1, $t[74]$ = 3.37, p = .001; cluster 2, $t[59]$ = 3.98, p < .001) as compared to their partners' reports. However, only cluster 2 men significantly underestimated their lifetime prevalence of psychological aggression as compared to their partners' reports (cluster 1, $t[76]$ = 1.69, p < .10; cluster 2, $t[59]$ = 5.82, p < .001). Moreover, the results of a MANOVA based on difference scores between the men's and women's reports on the CTS-2 scales demonstrated that cluster 2 individuals were significantly more likely to underestimate their lifetime perpetration of violence as compared to their partner's report than were cluster 1 members ($F[4, 129]$ = 4.54, p = .002), especially with respect to psychological aggression ($F[1, 132]$ = 11.46, p = .001), physical assault ($F[1, 132]$ = 9.46, p = .003), and injuries perpetrated ($F[1, 132]$ = 4.14, p = .044).

Self-Reported Distress and Problems With Anger

Results of a MANOVA suggested that cluster 1 individuals were significantly more likely than cluster 2 individuals to describe themselves as

Table 6.3

PARTNER-REPORTED VIOLENCE (CTS-2) IN PRECEDING 6 MONTHS AND LIFETIME AS A FUNCTION OF CLUSTER

SCALE	CLUSTER 1 (N = 77) MEAN (SD)	CLUSTER 2 (N = 61) MEAN (SD)	MULTIVARIATE F	UNIVARIATE F
Preceding 6 Months			.53 ns	
Psychological Aggression	51.49 (42.54)	46.70 (36.78)		.48 ns
Physical Assault	28.47 (43.58)	20.15 (33.16)		1.52 ns
Injury	9.12 (14.65)	6.39 (11.08)		1.46 ns
Sexual Coercion	6.81 (15.19)	7.36 (18.69)		.04 ns
Lifetime			1.00 ns	
Psychological Aggression	4.96 (1.78)	5.27 (1.76)		1.05 ns
Physical Assault	6.62 (2.69)	6.29 (2.97)		.44 ns
Injury	2.87 (1.41)	2.70 (1.49)		.50 ns
Sexual Coercion	1.62 (1.99)	1.43 (1.93)		.34 ns

Note. Lifetime prevalence is scored as to whether a specific behavior *ever* occurred. Psychological Aggression = CTS-2–Psychological Aggression Scale; Physical Assault = CTS-2–Physical Assault Scale; Injury = CTS-2 Injury Scale; Sexual Coercion = CTS-2 Sexual Coercion Scale.

distressed ($F[3, 164] = 5.72, p = .001$) (see Table 6.5). Follow-up univariate analyses suggested that cluster 1 individuals reported higher levels of depression ($F[1, 166] = 6.15, p = .014$), anxiety ($F[1, 166] = 10.10, p = .002$), and problems with alcohol ($F[1, 166] = 7.29, p = .008$). In addition, MANOVA results indicated that they described themselves as having significantly more problems with anger than did cluster 2 individuals ($F[4, 194] = 5.30, p < .001$). Follow-up univariate analyses of the STAXI revealed that their significant problems with anger included significantly

Table 6.4

COMPARISONS BETWEEN MEN'S AND WOMEN'S REPORTS OF LIFETIME VIOLENCE AS A FUNCTION OF CLUSTER

SCALE	MEN'S REPORTS MEAN (*SD*)	WOMEN'S REPORTS MEAN (*SD*)	PAIRED *t*-TESTS	F
Overall MANOVA				4.54**
Psychological Aggression				11.46**
Cluster 1	4.58 (1.67)	4.95 (1.79)	1.48 *ns*	
Cluster 2	3.52 (1.81)	5.24 (1.76)	5.82***	
Physical Assault				9.46**
Cluster 1	4.50 (2.62)	6.72 (2.74)	6.26***	
Cluster 2	2.32 (2.33)	6.22 (2.99)`	9.14***	
Injury				4.14*
Cluster 1	1.85 (1.45)	2.88 (1.40)	5.07***	
Cluster 2	1.05 (1.14)	2.69 (1.50)	7.82***	
Sexual Coercion				.16 *ns*
Cluster 1	0.73 (1.03)	1.57 (1.91)	3.37**	
Cluster 2	0.42 (1.02)	1.40 (1.93)	3.98***	

Note. MANOVA and ANOVA *F*s are based on difference scores between men's and women's reports.
*$p < .05$. **$p < .005$. ***$p < .001$.

more internalized anger ($F[1, 197] = 7.65$, $p = .006$), externalized anger ($F[1, 197] = 12.71$, $p < .001$), and trait anger ($F[1, 197] = 17.32$, $p < .001$). They also acknowledged having significantly more difficulty controlling their anger ($F[1, 197] = 9.73$, $p = .002$).

INITIAL DISTRESS AND ANGER AS A FUNCTION OF CLUSTER

SCALE	CLUSTER 1 MEAN (*SD*)	CLUSTER 2 MEAN (*SD*)	MULTIVARIATE *F*	UNIVARIATE *F*
Distress	(*N* = 87)	(*N* = 81)	5.72***	
BDI	12.01 (9.24)	8.62 (8.39)		6.15*
SMAST	16.20 (3.14)	15.06 (2.20)		7.29**
STAI	40.72 (9.65)	36.01 (9.53)		10.10***
Anger	(*N* = 101)	(*N* = 98)	5.30****	
STAXI-I	16.04 (3.90)	14.49 (3.98)		7.65**
STAXI-E	13.65 (3.56)	11.94 (3.20)		12.71****
STAXI-T	18.62 (5.33)	15.69 (4.55)		17.32****
STAXI-C	21.94 (4.84)	24.13 (5.06)		9.73***

Note. BDI = Beck Depression Inventory; SMAST = Short Michigan Alcohol Screening Test; STAI = State-Trait Anxiety Inventory; STAXI-I = State-Trait Anger Expression Inventory–Internalizing Anger; STAXI-E = State-Trait Anger Expression Inventory–Externalizing Anger; STAXI-T = State-Trait Anger Expression Inventory–Trait Anger; STAXI-C = State-Trait Anger Expression Inventory–Anger Control.
*$p < .05$. **$p < .01$. ***$p < .005$. ****$p < .001$.

Response to Treatment

By definition, those batterers who did not complete treatment did not complete posttreatment measures. Therefore, they were compared to successful completers on initial demographics and self-report on the CTS-2 scales. Completers (N = 127; 60%) did not differ from noncompleters (N = 83; 40%) on years of education ($F[1, 195]$ = .16, *ns*), net monthly income ($F[1, 144]$ = 2.42, *ns*), self-reported lifetime psychological aggression ($F[1, 204]$ = .16, *ns*), self-reported lifetime physical aggression ($F[1, 203]$ = .00, *ns*), self-reported lifetime injury ($F[1, 204]$ =

.38, *ns*), self-reported lifetime sexual coercion ($F[1, 203]$ = .03, *ns*), depression ($F[1, 199]$ = .36, *ns*), anxiety ($F[1, 206]$ = .30, *ns*), internalizing anger ($F[1, 202]$ = 2.85, *ns*), externalizing anger ($F[1, 206]$ = .91, *ns*), trait anger ($F[1, 205]$ = .29, *ns*), or anger control ($F[1, 206]$ = .45, *ns*). On the other hand, completers were significantly more likely to be older ($F[1, 209]$ = 4.52, p < .04), less likely to be African American (χ^2 = 13.51, df = 5, p < .02), and less likely to be either single or divorced (χ^2 = 16.64, df = 3, p = .001). Importantly, whether someone completed treatment (and therefore had posttreatment measures) was unrelated to the cluster to which he was assigned (χ^2 = .11, df = 1, *ns*).

A series of repeated-measures ANOVAs was conducted to determine whether clusters differed with respect to the amount of self-reported change in functioning over the course of the groups (see Table 6.6). With respect to depression, cluster 1 men reported significantly more improvement ($F[1, 112]$ = 23.10, p < .001) than did cluster 2 men. Similarly, cluster 1 men reported a significantly greater decrease in anxiety ($F[1, 114]$ = 9.38, p = .003) and a significantly greater increase in control over their anger ($F[1, 112]$ = 5.70, p = .019) than did cluster 2 men. On the other hand, the two clusters of men did not differ with respect to their change in internalizing anger ($F[1, 109]$ = 2.22, *ns*), externalizing anger ($F[1, 112]$ = 3.71, *ns*), or trait anger ($F[1, 113]$ = 3.69, *ns*). It is important to note, of course, that cluster 2 individuals did not acknowledge significant problems of distress or anger even at the beginning of treatment; therefore, it is difficult to interpret their lack of change over the course of treatment.

A new procedure of partner follow-up was begun at the APP toward the end of this study. The partners who were contacted were in no way different from previous partners who had not been contacted, but a change in the measures administered to clients at intake precluded further analyses. As mentioned previously, 15 partners were recontacted 6 months following the cessation of treatment, precluding any definitive analysis of the relationship of cluster to partner reports on improvement. However, even with this very small *N*, there was a tendency for a higher score on the URICA Action scale at pretreatment to be negatively correlated with the partner's report of injury posttreatment (r = –.66, p < .06), and a higher score on the URICA Precontemplation scale at pretreatment to be positively correlated with the partner's report of physical assault posttreatment (r = .59, p < .06). These results suggest that those individuals who were in a later stage of change at pretreatment actually did perpetrate less violence following the end of treatment than those

Table 6.6

CHANGE IN SYMPTOMS AS A FUNCTION OF CLUSTER

SCALE	PRETREATMENT MEAN (*SD*)	POSTTREATMENT MEAN (*SD*)	EFFECT OF TIME F	TIME X CLUSTER F
BDI			31.24***	23.10***
Cluster 1	12.40 (8.66)	5.41 (6.81)		
Cluster 2	7.76 (7.06)	7.23 (8.32)		
STAI			22.26***	9.38***
Cluster 1	41.21 (10.01)	33.84 (9.02)		
Cluster 2	34.96 (8.59)	33.39 (9.34)		
STAXI-I			3.57 *ns*	2.22 *ns*
Cluster 1	15.64 (3.73)	14.16 (3.80)		
Cluster 2	14.21 (4.11)	14.04 (3.81)		
STAXI-E			6.83**	3.71 *ns*
Cluster 1	13.99 (3.73)	12.16 (3.18)		
Cluster 2	12.19 (3.50)	11.91 (3.30)		
STAXI-T			.22 *ns*	3.69 *ns*
Cluster 1	18.68 (5.61)	17.14 (5.07)		
Cluster 2	15.74 (5.16)	16.68 (6.59)		
STAXI-C			5.67*	5.70*
Cluster 1	22.09 (4.88)	24.46 (4.04)		
Cluster 2	24.00 (5.37)	24.00 (4.81)		

Note: *$p < .05$. **$p < .01$. ***$p < .001$.

individuals who were presumably denying the severity of their violence at pretreatment.

DISCUSSION

This study demonstrates that it is possible to use the standard URICA (with reference to the specified behavior of IPV) to obtain apparently valid responses from men with respect to their stage of change in how they view their violent behavior. Evidence for the validity of these responses comes from several sources. First, men with a profile suggestive of an earlier stage of change (cluster 2) consistently reported fewer problems with anger on the STAXI and less abusive behavior on the CTS-2. However, as is consistent with a stages-of-change model, according to the partners, this apparent underreporting of anger and abuse is reflective of denial and minimization rather than an accurate description of their behavior. Indeed, while both clusters of IPV offenders in this study significantly underestimated the degree of their violent behavior, cluster 2 members underestimated it to a significantly greater degree. Second, men in an earlier stage of change (cluster 2) reported fewer symptoms of distress (depression, anxiety, and alcohol abuse) than did men with a profile suggestive of a later stage of change. Thus, the former men may have had less internal motivation to change because their behavior did not cause them any marked distress. Finally, preliminary predictive validity of the URICA with respect to intimate partner violence is evidenced by the differential response to treatment in the two clusters, with cluster 2 individuals demonstrating significantly less change on depression, anxiety, and anger control over the course of treatment. Exploratory analyses also tended to suggest that higher initial scores on Precontemplation were positively associated and that higher initial scores on Action were negatively associated with partner reports of violence 6 months following the end of treatment. This latter finding is similar to findings by Scott and Wolfe (2003) that partners of men in the Action stage report less victimization. Therefore, batterers do appear to differ with respect to their readiness to change. Moreover, this dimension of individual differences has implications both for the degree of validity of their self-reports and for their response to treatment.

It is, of course, not clear whether cluster 2 individuals were consciously denying both their anger and the distress that either precipitated their violence or followed from it or, alternatively, were either unaware of their feelings or were truly not experiencing them. Undoubtedly, each of these three possibilities may apply to different subgroups of cluster 2 batterers. For example, the public's stereotype of the batterer is that of someone who is denying his behavior (and perhaps any associated anger and distress) as an active and conscious attempt at impression management. While this view is an accurate portrayal of many batterers, there are also abusive men who, consistent with attachment theory's description of the dismissing individual, are not consciously aware of negative affect although they exhibit physiological arousal in response to perceived rejection by an attachment figure (Dozier & Kobak, 1992). Finally, another subgroup of cluster 2 batterers who deny anger and distress may conform more closely to psychopathic individuals who exhibit a fundamental disconnect between affect and cognition (Cleckley, 1982). In a review of physiological studies, Verona, Patrick, Curtin, Bradley, and Lang (2004) noted that psychopathic individuals evidence diminished reactivity to emotional stimuli of all types while exhibiting apparently normal verbal reports and overt facial expressions. Thus, these individuals' denial of negative affect is not a reflection of social desirability but rather an accurate report of their lack of response to emotional situations.

The question remains as to what to do with this presumably diverse group of resistant cluster 2 batterers. While it could be concluded that some of these batterers are not appropriate for treatment and should instead be jailed, the lack of demonstrated effectiveness in reducing recidivism through imprisonment casts doubt on the effectiveness of this strategy. On the other hand, Daniels and Murphy (1997) have presented a framework for group treatment that incorporates suggestions for engaging the client who is in an earlier stage of change. Namely, they emphasize interventions that focus on the goals of increasing awareness of the negative aspects of the problem, acknowledging the problem, and accurately evaluating oneself. They also note that a meaningful focus on the problem is more likely to occur when the client is able to find reasons to change that will meet his own needs rather than to simply avoid punishment. Thus, motivational discussions (encouraging the contemplation of change and promoting personal reasons for change) are particularly germane to batterers characterized by an earlier stage of change.

This focus on enhancing motivation in resistant individuals has been justified empirically by the evidence from substance-abusing populations demonstrating that even highly resistant individuals can benefit from treatment, using techniques such as motivational interviewing (cf. Miller & Rollnick, 2002). As applied to a population of intimate partner violence offenders, the goal of motivational interviewing would be to create a discrepancy or cognitive dissonance within the client as to the target behavior (i.e., the intimate partner violence) and other desired goals (such as seeing himself as manly or having a wife who cares about him). It should be noted that Rollnick and Miller's (1995) recommended therapist stance for working with unmotivated clients (namely, the use of reflective listening, expression of acceptance, affirmation of the client's freedom of choice and self-direction, and attention to the client's readiness to change) is quite discrepant from the use of confrontation typically espoused by the Duluth model (Gondolf, 1997a; Healey, Smith, & O'Sullivan, 1998) or the use of skills training and other behavioral interventions typically espoused by the cognitive-behavioral approach (Daniels & Murphy, 1997). While these treatment strategies may be effective for individuals in a later stage of change (i.e., cluster 1 individuals), it is quite clear, both empirically and theoretically, that they are not appropriate for individuals in an earlier stage of change. Thus, attention to the stage of change of the individual batterer would suggest the use of distinct strategies based on that readiness to change.

Limitations and Implications for Future Research

The results of this study must be interpreted within the context of its limitations. These limitations also suggest important areas of study in future research in this area. First and foremost, partner follow-up is essential to determine whether in fact these two clusters of individuals differ with respect to the most important indication of their response to treatment—namely, the perpetration of future violence. For example, both this study and the study by Scott and Wolfe (2003) are limited in their access to the partner's report at follow-up, with Scott and Wolfe (2003) contacting 17 partners at the end of treatment and this study contacting 15 partners at 6 months following the end of treatment. Second, these results can be generalized only to court-ordered batterers. While Begun and colleagues (2003) have assumed that men voluntarily seeking treatment for intimate partner violence are, by definition, more likely to be in a later stage of change and therefore more likely to benefit from standard treatments, Scott and Wolfe (2003) noted that men seeking treatment voluntarily were more likely to drop out of treatment. Therefore, future research is necessary to confirm this speculation. Third, it is possible and not altogether unlikely that cluster analyses conducted with different samples would derive different groups of individuals and different numbers of clusters. For example, Levesque and colleagues (2000) found that a cluster solution of seven clusters was most meaningful for their data. On the other hand, in this study, even three- and four-cluster solutions appeared to be characterized by small clusters of outliers. Moreover, in the short term, a two-cluster solution may be more useful clinically given limited numbers of individuals as well as the preliminary nature of our understanding of effective treatments for batterers. Ultimately, however, future cluster analyses of different samples need to be conducted to determine the most theoretically meaningful and practically useful number of clusters to consider.

It was suggested in the Discussion section that the cluster of men in the earlier stage of change was undoubtedly comprised of a diverse group, including men who were actively and consciously denying their behavior and associated emotions, who may have been dismissing of attachment, who acted "more normal than normal" (Crittenden, Partridge, & Claussen, 1991), who may not have been aware of their underlying arousal, and who may truly not have been experiencing any physiological arousal in response to negative affect. A measure of social desirability would be appropriate for the men in active denial and perhaps for those who are unaware of their underlying affect. On the other hand, social desirability is not applicable to psychopathic individuals and could even mask the actual positiveness with which they view themselves and their behavior. Perhaps because of the underlying diversity of cluster 2 individuals, social desirability is only inconsistently related to self-report in batterers (Scott & Wolfe, 2003). Therefore, a combination of additional measures of social desirability, dismissing attachment, and psychopathy would be helpful in making distinctions within this diverse cluster of batterers.

Finally, it is important to compare the stages-of-change conceptualization with that of other empirically and theoretically derived models of individual differences in batterers. The most well-known model is Holtzworth-Munroe and Stuart's (1994) typology of batterers, referring to the family-only batterer, the dysphoric or borderline batterer, and the generally violent or antisocial batterer. While Langhinrichsen-Rohling and colleagues (2000) have conducted preliminary research suggesting the utility of this model in predicting response to treatment, it is likely that both the transtheoretical model and Holtzworth-Munroe and Stuart's typology would benefit from a systematic comparison of these two conceptualizations. Stage of change may represent an additional significant factor or dimension to be considered in this ongoing development of a meaningful typology of abusers.

In conclusion, results of this study suggest that the transtheoretical model is indeed relevant to the perspectives, experiences, and behaviors of intimate partner violence offenders. Self-reports of distress, anger, and violent behavior, discrepancies with partners' reports, and differential response to treatment were all consistent in indicating the relevance of this model to the batterer population. The use of the stages-of-change model with another population frequently characterized by denial and minimization, namely, substance abusers, provides strong justification for the development of a treatment model for batterers based on their readiness to change. Finally, a comparison of this model with Holtzworth-Munroe and Stuart's (1994) typology of batterers would demonstrate the overlapping and unique characteristics of each model.

REFERENCES

Aldenderfer, M. S., & Blashfield, R. K. (1984). *Cluster analysis.* Newbury Park, CA: Sage.

Babcock, J. C., & LaTaillade, J. J. (2000). Evaluating interventions for men who batter. In J. Vincent & E. Jouriles (Eds.), *Domestic violence: Guidelines for research-informed practice* (pp. 37–77). Philadelphia: Jessica Kingsley.

Beck, A. T., Steer, R. A., & Brown, G. K. (1996). *Beck depression inventory B: Manual* (2nd ed.) San Antonio, TX: The Psychological Corporation.

Begun, A. L., Murphy, C., Bolt, D., Weinstein, B., Strodthoff, T., Short, L., et al. (2003). Characteristics of the safe at home instrument for assessing readiness to change intimate partner violence. *Research on Social Work Practice, 13,* 80–107.

Begun, A. L., Shelley, G., Strodthoff, T., & Short, L. (2002). Adopting a stages of change approach in intervention with individuals who are violent with their intimate partners. *Journal of Aggression, Maltreatment and Trauma, 5,* 105–127.

Cadsky, O., Hanson, R. K., Crawford, M. & Lalonde, C. (1996). Attrition from a male batterer treatment program: Client-treatment congruence and lifestyle instability. *Violence and Victims, 11,* 51–64.

Cleckley, H. M. (1982). *The mask of sanity* (6th ed.). St. Louis, MO: Mosby.

Crittenden, P. M., Partridge, M. F., & Claussen, A. H. (1991). Family patterns of relationship in normative and dysfunctional families. *Development and Psychopathology, 3,* 491–512.

Daniels, J. W., & Murphy, C. M. (1997). Stages and process of change in batterers' treatment. *Cognitive and Behavioral Practice, 4,* 123–145.

Davis, R. C., & Taylor, B. G. (1998). *Does batterer treatment reduce violence? A synthesis of the literature.* Report to the U.S. Department of Justice.

Dozier, M., & Kobak, R. (1992). Psychophysiology in attachment interviews: Converging evidence for deactivating strategies. *Child Development, 63,* 1473–1480.

Dunford, F. W. (2000). The San Diego Navy experiment: An assessment of interventions for men who assault their wives. *Journal of Consulting and Clinical Psychology, 68,* 468–476.

Eckhardt, C. I., Babcock, J. C., & Homack, S. (2004). Partner assaultive men and the stages and process of change. *Journal of Family Violence, 19,* 81–93.

Edleson, J. L., & Syers, M. (1990). Relative effectiveness of group treatments for men who batter. *Social Work Research and Abstracts, 26,* 10–17.

Feder, L., & Ford, D. (1999, July). *A test of the efficacy of court-mandated counseling for convicted misdemeanor domestic violence offenders: Results from the Broward County experiment.* Paper presented at the Sixth International Family Violence Research Conference, Durham, NH.

Fuqua, D. R., Leonard, E., Masters, M. A., & Smith, R. J., et al. (1991). A structural analysis of the state-trait anger expression inventory. *Educational and Psychological Measurement, 51,* 439–446.

Gondolf, E. W. (1997a). Batterer programs: What we know and need to know. *Journal of Interpersonal Violence, 12,* 83–98.

Gondolf, E. W. (1997b). A comparison of four batterer intervention systems: Do court referral, program length, and services matter? *Journal of Interpersonal Violence, 14,* 41–61.

Hamberger, L. K., Lohr, J. M., Bonge, D., & Tolin, D. F. (1996). A large sample empirical typology of male spouse abusers and its relationship to dimensions of abuse. *Violence and Victims, 11,* 277–292.

Harris, R., Savage, S., Jones, T., & Brooke, W. (1988). A comparison of treatments for abusive men and their partners within a family-service agency. *Canadian Journal of Community Mental Health, 7,* 147–155.

Healey, K., Smith, C., & O'Sullivan, C. (1998). *Batterer intervention: Program approaches and criminal justice strategies.* Report to the U.S. Department of Justice.

Holtzworth-Munroe, A., Meehan, J. C., Herron, K., Rehman, U., & Stuart, G. L. (2000). Testing the Holtzworth-Munroe and Stuart batterer typology. *Journal of Consulting and Clinical Psychology, 68,* 1000–1019.

Holtzworth-Munroe, A., & Stuart, G. L. (1994). Typologies of male batterers: Three subtypes and the differences among them. *Psychological Bulletin, 116,* 476–497.

Langhinrichsen-Rohling, J., Huss, M. T., & Ramsey, S. (2000). The clinical utility of the batterer typologies. *Journal of Family Violence, 15,* 37–53.

Levesque, D. A., Gelles, R. J., & Velicer, W. F. (2000). Development and validation of a stages of change measure for men in batterer treatment. *Cognitive Therapy and Research, 24,* 175–199.

Malloy, K. A., McCloskey, K. A., & Monford, T. M. (1999). A group treatment program for male batterers. In L. VandeCreek & T. L. Jackson (Eds.), *Innovations in clinical practice: A source book* (Vol. 17, pp. 377–395). Sarasota, FL: Professional Resource Press/Professional Resource Exchange.

McConnaughy, E. A., DiClemente, C. C., Prochaska, J. O., & Velicer, W. F. (1989). Stages of change in psychotherapy: A follow-up report. *Psychotherapy, 26,* 494–503.

Miller, W. R., & Rollnick, S. (2002). *Motivational interviewing: Preparing people for change* (2nd ed.). New York: Guilford Press.

Moffitt, T. E., Caspi, A., Krueger, R. F., Magdol, L., Margolin, G., Silva, P. A., et al. (1997). Do partners agree about abuse in their relationship? A psychometric evaluation of interpartner agreement. *Psychological Assessment, 9,* 47–56.

Pokorny, A. D., Miller, B. A., & Kaplan, H. B. (1972). The brief MAST: A shortened version of the Michigan Alcoholism Screening Test. *American Journal of Psychiatry, 129,* 342–345.

Prochaska, J. O., & DiClemente, C. C. (1984). *The transtheoretical approach: Crossing the traditional boundaries of therapy.* Homewood, IL: Dow Jones-Irwin.

Prochaska, J. O., DiClemente, C. C., & Norcross, J. C. (1992). In search of how people change: Applications to addictive behaviors. *American Psychologist, 47,* 1102–1114.

Rollnick, S., & Miller, W. R. (1995). What is motivational interviewing? *Behavioural and Cognitive Psychotherapy, 23,* 325–334.

Scalia, J. (1994). Psychoanalytic insights and the prevention of pseudosuccess in the cognitive-behavioral treatment of batterers. *Journal of Interpersonal Violence, 9,* 548–555.

Scott, K. L., & Wolfe, D. A. (2003). Readiness to change as a predictor of outcome in batterer treatment. *Journal of Consulting and Clinical Psychology, 71,* 879–889.

Selzer, M. L., Vinokur, A., & van Rooijen, M. A. (1975). A self-administered short Michigan alcohol screening test (SMAST). *Journal of Studies on Alcohol, 36,* 117–126.

Spielberger, C. D. (1988). *Manual for the state-trait anger expression inventory (STAXI).* Odessa, FL: Psychological Assessment Resources.

Spielberger, C. D., Gorsuch, R. L., & Lushene, R. (1970). *Manual for the state-trait anxiety inventory.* Palo Alto, CA: Consulting Psychologist Press.

Spielberger, C. D., & Sydeman, S. J. (1994). State-trait anxiety inventory and state-trait anger expression inventory. In M. E. Maruish (Ed.), *The use of psychological testing for treatment planning and outcome assessment* (pp. 292–321). Hillsdale, NJ: Lawrence Erlbaum Associates.

Straus, M. A., Hamby, S. L., Boney-McCoy, S., & Sugarman, D. B. (1996). The revised conflict tactics scales (CTS-2). *Journal of Family Issues, 7,* 283–316.

Verona, E., Patrick, C. J., Curtin, J. J., Bradley, M. M., & Lang, P. J. (2004). Psychopathy and physiological response to emotionally evocative sounds. *Journal of Abnormal Psychology, 113,* 99–108.

Waltz, J., Babcock, J. C., Jacobson, N. S., & Gottman, J. M. (2000). Testing a typology of batterers. *Journal of Consulting and Clinical Psychology, 68,* 658–669.

Ward, J. (1963). Hierarchical grouping to optimize an objective function. *Journal of the American Statistical Association, 58,* 236–244.

7

Does the Transtheoretical Model Predict Attrition in Domestic Violence Treatment Programs?

NORMAND BRODEUR, GILLES RONDEAU, SERGE BROCHU, JOCELYN LINDSAY, AND JASON PHELPS

Over the past 20 years, conjugal violence prevention in North America has evolved multilayered responses that include treatment programs mandated to help men cease their violent behavior toward their female partners. One issue of concern regarding the efficacy of these programs has been their particularly high dropout rates and the impact this has on ensuring the safety of the women and children in these men's lives. Men who end treatment prematurely have been shown to have higher rearrest rates for reassaulting their partners and are reported to be more controlling and psychologically abusive than men who complete (Gondolf, 1997).

THE PROBLEM OF ATTRITION

Attrition in intervention programs for domestically violent men ranges from 22% to 99% (for review, see Daly & Pelowski, 2000) and is considered to be a serious and enduring problem. The fact that most men who enter treatment programs terminate prematurely highlights the pressing need to identify program and client factors common to unsuccessful completion. Over the years, there have been a variety of studies intended to address this question, but results have been of limited utility for intervention planning. In their comprehensive review of 16 studies dealing specifically with dropout, Daly and Pelowski (2000) were able to identify the reoccurrence of several sociodemographic factors that predicted dropout but with only moderate accuracy. Specifically, early terminators were found more likely to be unmarried and/or childless, unemployed, have lower incomes, and less education than men who remained in treatment. Other variables that correlated with premature termination in the various studies included substance abuse, criminal history, marital status, psychopathology, and court or correctional services involvement. However, the latter variables presented less consistently and may be influenced by a combination of factors not yet identified. In a later study, Daly, Power, and Gondolf (2001) went beyond the dropout or completion dichotomy to identify how long clients with different sociodemographic characteristics actually stayed in treatment. In addition to confirming results from their earlier study, Daly and her colleagues were able to show that clients with low socioeconomic status (SES) and alcohol problems were not only dropping out but also terminating earlier than clients in other categories.

These results appear to mirror findings within the field of general psychotherapy that indicate that SES and lifestyle instability have a significant effect on treatment outcome (e.g., Garfield, 1994), especially when it comes to other serious public health issues like drinking and driving, substance abuse, and sexual assault (Gondolf, 1997). Although these findings can help service providers identify those clients that are at greater risk of dropping out, sociodemographic variables are generally static and unaffected by therapy, so they offer only limited insight into how interventions can be altered to meet client's needs best. For this reason, the identification of dynamic client factors that affect perseverance in treatment has been considered an essential building block to the creation of accurate prediction models that have therapeutic relevance and can guide program planning and design.

One recurring area of investigation into psychometric factors has focused on the relationship between men's motivation to change and their participation in treatment, the underlying assumption being that a man who is motivated to change his abusive behavior will also want to engage in therapy and stay until it is completed. The literature provides some support for this assumption. For example, De Maris (1989) asked abusive men how important it was for them to stop being violent with their partner and how hard they would try to avoid being violent in the future. Those whose responses indicated little interest in change were almost twice as likely to terminate treatment prematurely. Cadsky, Hanson, Crawford, and Lalonde (1996) attempted to identify attitudinal factors associated with men's participation in treatment and found that they were more likely to stay until the end when their motivation was congruent with treatment goals. More specifically, men who stayed in treatment were more likely to initiate treatment voluntarily and reported higher levels of marital discord, physical abuse, and indirect hostility. Rooney and Hanson (2001), using Hanson's Commitment to Change Scale, found that clients who chose not to begin treatment following initial assessment interviews had significantly lower motivation to change than program completers.

In their extensive review of attrition research, Daly and Pelowski (2000) also point to motivation as a promising direction to explore. They suggest that measuring clients' readiness to change can be used not only to predict perseverance but also to guide the development of stage-specific motivational enhancement strategies designed to help men progress and remain in treatment. Scott (2004) suggests that although encouraging, existing motivation research in domestic violence intervention lacks the support of a unifying theoretical framework and consistency in the operational definition of motivation and its measurement. Both of these studies point to the transtheoretical model of change (TTM; e.g., Prochaska & Norcross, 1999) for future investigation into client factors related to attrition. The purpose of this study is to explore the relationship between the TTM and the perseverance of men in treatment for domestic violence.

ATTRITION AND THE TTM

Over the past 20 years, James O. Prochaska and his colleagues at the University of Rhode Island have worked on developing the TTM as a promising tool for identifying specific client factors that influence treatment outcome (Prochaska & Norcross, 1999). Consistent with the broader common factors current in psychotherapy (e.g., Frank & Frank, 1991), they have advocated for a shift away from theory- or problem-driven models toward models that look for factors common to all effective therapy.

The most frequently discussed component of the TTM is its stages-of-change (SOC) construct. Stages-of-change articulates a progression in client attitudes and behavior through five stages: *Precontemplation* (not thinking of change), *Contemplation* (open to considering the possibility of change), *Preparation* (getting ready to commence change), *Action* (engaging in specific change-related behaviors), and *Maintenance* (relapse prevention strategies initiated once change has actually begun). Each stage is distinct and can be operationalized and measured using a variety of proposed instruments (e.g., the University of Rhode Island Change Assessment Scale [URICA]; McConnaughy, DiClemente, Prochaska, & Velicer, 1989). In addition to SOC, the TTM includes three other distinct constructs that are used to understand and measure how individuals approach change: (a) *processes of change* are defined as overt and covert activities and experiences that individuals engage in to change their behavior and explain how they move between stages, (b) *self-efficacy* measures clients' self-confidence in their ability to change and maintain results over time, and (c) the *decisional balance* looks at how a client views the pros and cons of changing.

The TTM developed in the areas of general psychotherapy (e.g., Prochaska, 1995) and smoking cessation (e.g., Prochaska, Velicer, DiClemente, & Fava, 1988). It has been applied to a wide range of other problematic behaviors, including substance abuse (Smyth, 1998). Recently, it has been tested for its applicability to the problem of treating male perpetrators of conjugal violence (Eckhardt, Babcock, & Homack, 2004; Levesque, Gelles, & Velicer, 2000; Scott, 2004).

The model's ability to predict program attrition has varied from study to study. Comparing the capacities of sociodemographic and TTM measures to predict client perseverance in general psychotherapy, Brogan, Prochaska, and Prochaska (1999) found that TTM measures were able to predict premature terminators by up to 92%. In a study on attrition in a smoke-free perinatal substance abuse treatment program (Haller, Miles, & Cropsey, 2004), women's smoking stage of change was associated with both length of stay and program completion. Women in Precontemplation withdrew sooner ($m = 42$ days) and were less likely to complete treatment successfully (9% completed) than those in Action ($m = 125.2$ days, 70% completed) or Maintenance stages ($m = 101$ days, 45% completed). However, other studies have been less successful. An SOC study done in the United Kingdom on psychotherapy outcome (Derisley & Reynolds, 2000) found no support for the hypothesis that clients with high Precontemplation scores would be more likely to drop out than those with lower scores. Using logistical regression analysis, only low Contemplation scores on the study's Stages of Change questionnaire were associated with an increased risk of premature termination.

Research into the application of the TTM to men in treatment programs for domestic violence has also produced mixed results. Bennett, Stoops, Flett, and Call (2005), using probation officer ratings of their client's SOC, found that participants in active stages of change were more likely to persist in treatment to the end (50% vs. 33%). Scott (2004) also found that counselor-rated SOC successfully predicted 72% of cases (98% of dropouts and 19% of completers) when combined with history of arrest and referral status as control variables. However, client-rated SOC did not predict attrition at all. Failure to predict was also an issue for Levesque and Chell (1999), who found that men's responses to SOC measures had no relationship with dropout.

Although these results indicate possible reliability problems with self-report data obtained by existing measures, more testing is needed. Other factors may be at play in the mixed results being obtained to date. Scott (2004) used a measure that has not been designed for men in treatment for domestic violence. She chose to use the general version of the URICA (McConnaughy et al., 1989) arguing that the social stigma of language related to abuse may bias the responses of men who are otherwise motivated to change (for discussion, see Scott & Wolfe, 2003). In contrast, Little and Girvin (2002) argue that the URICA measure is so general that it is difficult to ascertain what exactly is being measured and that problem-specific measures are needed for accurate assessment of attitudes toward change. Previous studies have also focused exclusively on SOC, which is only one component of the TTM. Prochaska and Velicer (1997) emphasize that the TTM is more complex and dynamic than a simple one-dimensional stage theory. In order to clarify the relationships between program attrition and the TTM more clearly, further testing is required on all constructs, including Decisional Balance, Processes of Change, and Self-Efficacy. Testing within diverse cultural contexts and with heterogeneous populations would also be necessary to explore the generalizability of the model.

OBJECTIVES AND HYPOTHESIS

This study was designed to verify if any of the core TTM constructs—Stages of Change, Processes of Change, Decisional Balance, and Self-Efficacy—could be used to improve prediction for (a) the decision of men who are referred to a domestic violence program to not participate in treatment after initial intake interviews, and (b) the decision of those who engage in group therapy to desist from treatment before the end. It was hypothesized that if all four TTM constructs were relevant, men who were at less advanced stages of change, had engaged in less processes of change, perceived less advantages in changing, and had more temptation to resort to violence would be less likely to participate in treatment after intake and less likely to complete the group.

METHODOLOGY

Participants

Participants were recruited from five treatment programs for male perpetrators of domestic violence in the province of Quebec, Canada.[1] Each program was distinct, and the number of sessions required to complete treatment varied from 14 to 25. A total of 578 men attended intake interviews at the five programs over a 13-month period. Of these men, 70 were immediately excluded from receiving the questionnaire for reasons related primarily to eligibility (domestic violence not primary reason for consultation, not appropriate for group treatment, could not read, and so on), 184 clients declined participation in the study (36% refusal), and eight questionnaires were excluded because they were incomplete. Of the 316 remaining questionnaires, 302 were completed in French and 14 in English. Only the French questionnaires were retained for data analysis because the English subsample was too small for a comparison of results based on language. The average age of these respondents was 37 years, 91% spoke French as a first language, 75% had a high school degree or less, 61% had gainful employment, 50% earned less than 20,000 Canadian dollars per year, 55% were living with their partner, 28% stated that they had a problem with either drugs or alcohol, 27% had already taken part in a program for conjugal violence, and 42% reported having a criminal record.

Procedures

Program counselors following standard intake interviews presented the questionnaire to all new clients requesting services. Those who accepted were asked to sign a consent form to take part in the study and then to complete a questionnaire and return it to their counselor or send it by mail in the postage-paid envelope provided. Those who were not returning their questionnaires were phoned by research personnel once to encourage them to do so. Respondents returning a completed questionnaire received a compensation of 15 Canadian dollars.

Attendance records were completed by program counselors and were collected after clients terminated or completed their participation in the program. In order to control for variances in program policies regarding attendance, clients were expected to complete the number of sessions agreed on during assessment interviews. If they stopped attending for more than 30 days without program dispensation, they were considered dropouts and were required to begin the program anew.

Measures

Data for this study were gathered through a self-report questionnaire designed to measure sociodemographic variables, social desirability, and core TTM constructs. The instruments measuring the latter were translated to French by the current investigators using a translation or back-translation procedure.

More specifically, the questionnaire included the following variables and instruments:

- *Sociodemographic Variables,* including SES and family composition; history of criminality, domestic violence, and alcohol or drug consumption; information related to any prior treatment received for the later two; and details related to the respondent's relationship with the abused partner.
- *Referral Status* was assessed by asking respondents whether their participation in the treatment program was mandated by the court and whether they were awaiting a court decision for a violence-related offense. The second question aimed to measure a more indirect form of coercion by the criminal justice system. Results from the two questions were combined to form a single dichotomous variable. Respondents were considered to be either coerced into treatment or seeking treatment voluntarily.
- *Social Desirability* was assessed using the M-C (20), a short version of Marlowe and Crowne's scale developed by Strahan and Gerbasi (1972). This instrument measures the respondent's tendency to answer in a socially desirable fashion by asking them 20 true or false questions. It was validated twice with university student samples (Fraboni & Cooper, 1989; Strahan & Gerbasi, 1972). The mean scores were, respectively, 9.1 and 10.0 (*SD* 3.9

and 4.3). It was also used in a previous study on dropout and completion among men who attend domestic violence treatment programs (Rondeau, Brodeur, Brochu, & Lemire, 2001).

- *Stages of Change* were measured with the URICA-DV2 (Levesque & Pro-Change, 2001d). The instrument has four scales (Precontemplation, Contemplation, Action, and Maintenance) and includes 20 items. Respondents answer on a 5-point Likert scale ranging from "strongly disagree" to "strongly agree" to questions such as "I'm beginning to see that the violence in my relationship is a problem."
- *Decisional Balance* was assessed using the Decisional Balance Scale for Domestic Violence (Levesque & Pro-Change, 2001a). This 12-item instrument is designed to measure a respondent's assessment of the various costs and benefits of change. It has three scales labeled "Pros General," "Pros Children" and "Cons."
- *Processes of Change* were assessed using the Processes of Change Questionnaire developed by Levesque and Pro-Change (2001b). This 49-item instrument measures 13 processes labeled "Stress Management," "Helping Relationships," "Counterconditioning," "Reinforcement Management," "Stimulus Control," "Self-Liberation," "Social Liberation," "Negative Self-Reevaluation," "Positive Self-Reevaluation," "Consciousness Raising," "Environment Reevaluation—Partner," "Environment Reevaluation—Children," and "Partner Collaboration."
- *Self-Efficacy* was measured with the Temptations Scale developed by Levesque and Pro-Change (2001c). Although the original instrument measures three different kinds of temptations (daily hassles, drug and alcohol use, and partner provocation), confirmatory factor analysis revealed that this structure did not replicate in the French translation. Thus, a one-factor scale was used in the study.

Table 7.1 shows reliability statistics, means, and standard deviations for each of the TTM subscales as well as how these are correlated with social desirability. Alphas ranged from fair to excellent, except for the Precontemplation subscale of the URICA-DV2, the cons subscale of the Decisional Balance Scale, and the Stress Management and the Consciousness Raising subscales of the Processes of Change questionnaire, which were below .60. A social desirability bias was found in the way respondents answered 9 of the 21 TTM subscales. These statistically

Table 7.1

PSYCHOMETRIC PROPERTIES OF TTM SUBSCALES (*N* = 302)

TTM SCALE	ALPHA	M	SD	SOCIAL DESIRABILITY
URICA-DV2				
Precontemplation	.53	9.325	3.491	.18[c]
Contemplation	.74	22.291	3.090	−.26[c]
Action	.69	22.614	2.565	.02
Maintenance	.68	17.644	3.986	−.33[c]
Decisional Balance				
Pros—general	.65	17.907	2.620	−.13[b]
Pros—children	.74	18.037	2.900	−.06
Cons	.55	7.270	3.132	−.12[b]
Self-efficacy				
Temptation to use violence	.88	28.4982	10.244	−.47[c]
Processes of Change[a]				
Stress management	.59	13.32	2.96	.09
Helping relationships	.71	9.15	3.34	−.10
Counter-conditioning	.63	11.89	3.06	.11
Reinforcement management	.72	7.17	2.59	.11
Stimulus control	.65	12.81	3.59	.07
Self-liberation	.64	14.60	2.94	.04
Social liberation	.65	11.76	3.45	.01
Negative self-reevaluation	.60	10.36	2.77	−.20[c]
Positive self-reevaluation	.62	10.08	2.26	.33[c]

(*Continued*)

Table 7.1

PSYCHOMETRIC PROPERTIES OF TTM SUBSCALES (N = 302) (Continued)

TTM SCALE	ALPHA	M	SD	SOCIAL DESIRABILITY
Consciousness raising	.52	10.66	2.90	–.06
Environment reevaluation—partner	.72	13.88	3.77	–.20[c]
Environment reevaluation—children	.79	13.99	4.08	.06
Partner collaboration	.84	11.58	4.16	–.04
Total use of processes	.91	151.26	24.63	.11

[a]N = 301. [b]The correlation is significant at the .05 level (two tailed). [c]The correlation is significant at the .01 level (two tailed).

significant correlations were weak, except for the Maintenance scale of the URICA-DV2 and the Temptations scale and the Positive Self-Reevaluation scale of the Processes of Change questionnaire, which were moderate. Respondents who scored high on social desirability were (a) more likely to evaluate themselves positively, (b) less likely to endorse the maintenance items, and (c) less likely to say that they were tempted to use violence toward their partner.

Data Analysis

Interpretation of URICA-DV2 scores followed similar procedures as Levesque and colleagues (2000). First, respondents' scores on each of the four subscales (Precontemplation, Contemplation, Action, and Maintenance) were standardized by converting them to t scores. Respondents were then randomly divided into two subgroups, and a cluster analysis was performed for each group. Squared Euclidean distance was used as the similarity or dissimilarity measure, and Ward's clustering method was used to pool respondents into clusters of similar response patterns. Clusters from each of the two subgroups were then compared and combined to form homogeneous categories of client profiles.

For the main analyses, chi-square was used to assess whether the empirically derived profiles were related to the decision to not participate in treatment following initial assessment interviews and/or the decision not to persist in treatment until the end; t tests were also performed to compare mean scores of the Temptations scale and on all subscales of the Decisional Balance and the Processes of Change questionnaire between men who decided to participate and those who did not as well as for those who dropped out and those who completed the programs.

RESULTS

Treatment Attendance

Of the clients for whom there were attendance records ($n = 296$), 32% decided not to participate in treatment after the initial intake interviews. Chi-square tests revealed that there were no significant differences between respondents who sought help voluntarily ($n = 165$) and those who were directly or indirectly coerced into treatment ($n = 131$). There was, however, a significant difference between treatment programs. In two of the programs, 75% or more respondents decided to participate in treatment. The rate was between 60% and 65% in two other programs and below 55% in the last one ($\chi^2 = 11.165$, $df = 4$, $p = .025$). No interaction effect was found between program and referral status that could have accounted for the respondents' decision.

Of the clients who participated in at least one group session ($n = 202$), 57% decided to withdraw from treatment prior to completion. Chi-square tests revealed that neither the treatment programs that the respondents attended nor their referral status was significantly associated with the decision to drop out or to complete.

Participant Cluster Analysis

The cluster analysis yielded five homogeneous groups presented here from least to most motivated:

- *Reluctant* ($n = 47$). Respondents in this group were above average in Precontemplation and below average in all other variables.
- *Immotive* ($n = 42$). Respondents in this group were above average in Precontemplation as well, but they were at average levels in all other variables.

- *Preparticipation* ($n = 72$). Respondents in this group were slightly below average in Precontemplation, higher in Contemplation and Maintenance, and average in Action.
- *Action—Low Fear of Relapse* ($n = 68$). Respondents in this group were average in Precontemplation and Contemplation, above average in Action, and below average in Maintenance.
- *Action—High Fear of Relapse* ($n = 73$). Respondents in this group were below average in Precontemplation and on a progressive incline above average through the other three variables.

These categories were inspired by the work of Levesque (Levesque, 2005; Levesque et al., 2000) with the exception of the two Action clusters. These clusters were identical in formation to the latter's Action–Low Relapse and Action–High Relapse clusters but were interpreted in a slightly different manner because the respondents' actual risk of relapse was not known. All that could be interpreted from the difference in Maintenance scores is that one cluster had more fear about returning to abusive behavior than the other. The Reluctant and Immotive clusters represent clients in the Precontemplation stage, the Preparticipation cluster represents clients in the Contemplation stage, and the final two clusters represent clients in the Action stage.

Chi-square and analyses of variance were conducted to check for differences between the five profiles on 16 sociodemographic variables. Men in the Reluctant profile stood out on six of these variables. They were more likely to have been born outside of Quebec, to not be living with their partners, and to be participating in the program nonvoluntarily. They were also less likely to have taken part in self-help groups for alcohol or drugs, to ever have received help with their violent behavior, or to have reported such behavior as existing more than 5 years prior to contacting the program. However, men in the Short-Term Action profile associated in the same way to each of these variables, with the exception that they were more likely to be living with their partner. Men in both of these profiles were more likely to answer the questionnaire with a social desirability bias. No relationships of significance were found between the other profiles and the sociodemographic variables tested.

Prediction of Decision Not to Participate

It was hypothesized that men in the Reluctant and Immotive clusters would be more likely not to participate after intake interviews. However, chi-square analyses indicated no significant differences between men from the various clusters. Nonparticipants were 35% in the Reluctant cluster, 39% in the Immotive cluster, 27% in the Preparticipation cluster, 30% in the Action–Low Fear of Relapse cluster, and 32% in the Action–High Fear of Relapse cluster ($\chi^2 = 2.077$, $df = 4$, $p = .722$).

To compare mean scores on the other TTM variables (Decisional Balance, Processes of Change, and Temptations) between respondents who entered treatment and those who did not, t tests were also conducted. None of these variables proved helpful in predicting which clients would not begin treatment following initial assessment interviews. Of the 17 subscales, 16 had p values larger than .106. The only exception was found in Reinforcement Management, which had a value of .058—approaching statistical significance but not reaching it.

Although TTM constructs did not help in predicting which clients would decide not to participate in treatment, four sociodemographic variables were found to be significant predictors. Respondents who were not married but cohabiting with their partners during the last incidence of domestic violence ($\chi^2 = 6.486$, $df = 1$, $p = .011$, $V = .148$), who had not previously received help to end their violent behavior ($\chi^2 = 4.678$, $df = 1$, $p = .050$; $V = .126$), who completed high school or less ($\chi^2 = 6.178$, $df = 1$, $p = .13$, $V = .144$), and who were not awaiting a court decision ($\chi^2 = 3.858$, $df = 1$, $p = .05$, $V = .144$) were less likely to decide to begin group treatment after an initial assessment interview. However, Cramer's V indicated a weak relationship between these variables and the respondents' decision.

Prediction of Withdrawal Prior to Completion

Among those who attended at least one group session, it was hypothesized that men in the low-motivation clusters would be more likely to withdraw from treatment prior to completion. As in the first hypothesis, there were no significant differences in perseverance between men from the various URICA-DV2 clusters. Noncompleters were 60% in the Reluctant cluster, 56% in the Immotive cluster, 58% in the Preparticipation cluster, 52% in the Action–Low Fear of Relapse cluster, and 61% in the Action–High Fear of Relapse cluster ($\chi^2 = .912$, $df = 4$, $p = .923$).

To compare mean scores between respondents who completed treatment and those who did not on the 17 subscales of the three other TTM measures (Decisional Balance, Processes of Change, and Temptations), t tests were also conducted. Only one significant difference was found. Men who did not complete treatment had a slightly lower score on the Consciousness Raising scale of the Processes of Change questionnaire than their counterparts who completed (M = 10.34 vs. M = 11.24; t = –2.089, df = 199, p = .038). The effect size for this difference was small (d = –.30). None of the other variables proved helpful in predicting which clients would drop out prior to completing the minimum number of sessions required by the program in which they were involved.

Because program durations differed, all previous analyses testing the relationship between TTM variables and dropout were repeated using 14 sessions as the standardized requirement for completion. No significant differences were found. The interaction that was noted previously between Consciousness Raising and dropout disappeared in this second wave of analyses.

Although TTM measures were not predictive of dropout, nine socio-demographic variables showed a capacity to predict which men would desist from treatment prior to completion. Dichotomous values for eight of these variables are presented in Table 7.2.

In addition to the variables listed in Table 7.2, men who dropped out were 4.3 years younger than those who persisted to the end (35.37 years vs. 39.65 years; t = –2.940, df = 200, p = .004, d = –.42). These results reflect similar findings as studies cited previously, showing that age, income, education, marital status, alcohol or drug use, and criminal history are all associated with the decision of men in treatment programs for domestic violence to withdraw prior to completion.

DISCUSSION

This study was conducted within the unique cultural context of the Canadian province of Quebec, which has a predominantly francophone population. In contrast to many other studies done on treatment programs for domestic violence, a relatively high proportion of subjects (55%) in this study were in treatment voluntarily. This reduces the sample bias that may result from having mostly court-mandated clients and introduces a greater variance in client motivation for requesting services.

The study set out to see if the TTM was effective in predicting the decision of men in domestic violence treatment programs to withdraw from treatment prior to completion. Self-report for the four TTM constructs (Stages of Change, Processes of Change, Self-Efficacy, and Decisional Balance) were included in questionnaires responded to by a sample of 302 men requesting services from five programs.

Table 7.2

RESULTS OF CHI-SQUARE TESTS COMPARING DROPOUTS (*N* = 116) AND COMPLETERS (*N* = 86) ON SOCIODEMOGRAPHIC VARIABLES

	DROPOUTS	COMPLETERS			
Sociodemographic variable	%	%	χ^{2a}	*p*	*V*
High school graduate or less	75.9	60.5	5.504	.019	.165
Annual income less than 20,000 Canadian dollars	52.6	38.4	4.010	.045	.141
Not currently married	82.8	65.1	8.253	.004	.202
Not currently living with partner	51.7	32.6	7.379	.007	.191
First domestic violence (DV) incident occurred less than 5 years ago	52.6	32.9	7.673	.006	.195
Participated in self-help group for drugs/alcohol	33.6	20.9	3.927	.048	.139
Believes currently has a drug/alcohol problem	33.6	18.6	5.620	.018	.167
Previously found guilty of a criminal offense	46.5	31.4	4.655	.031	.153

[a]*df* = 1.

Of the TTM variables that were tested, only the process of consciousness raising showed some capacity to predict who would desist from treatment prior to completion. This result should be interpreted with caution because of the low reliability coefficient of this scale, the small effect size that was computed for this variable, and the failure to replicate the results in a second analysis using 14 sessions as a standardized measure for completion of the programs. More research is needed to assess the role that consciousness raising may play in reducing dropout.

Overall, the TTM variables did not show much reliability in predicting desistence from the programs. However, this study did show that conventional sociodemographic variables like age, education, income, marital status, criminal history, and drug or alcohol consumption can be used to predict dropout with modest reliability. These results reproduce those of previous studies (e.g., Daly & Pelowski, 2000; Gondolf, 1997; Rondeau et al., 2001).

Two issues may have affected results in this study. First, the 36% client refusal to respond to the questionnaires may have had an impact on the sample and ability to test the initial hypotheses. Men who did not engage in the study may have been disproportionately in the Precontemplation stage and may simultaneously have accounted for many of the premature terminators, affecting the representativeness of the sample. If Precontemplators and dropouts were underrepresented, the study may not have captured the true relationship between SOC and dropout. Second, a social desirability bias was found in the way respondents answered half of the TTM scales. Of particular significance, those men who scored high in social desirability were less likely to endorse Maintenance items. This may have affected cluster formation because Maintenance was one of the four variables from which they were drawn. Processes of Change and Self-Efficacy variables were also influenced, as men scoring high in social desirability were more likely to self-evaluate positively and less likely to indicate that they would be tempted to use violence to resolve conflict with their partner. If some men did not accurately represent themselves and their motivation to engage in the change process, results from this study may not be accurately representing the relationship between the TTM and attrition.

This is the third study relying on self-report finding no relation between the TTM constructs and dropout, raising two questions in need of further exploration. First, one may ask whether self-reports are accurate measures with this population. Self-report measures can offer anonymity to clients and improve the cost-effectiveness of a study (Levesque & Chell, 1999). However, the viability of data obtained in this manner has been put into question in a number of studies. For example, Scott and Wolfe (2003) found significantly lower self-reported rates of violent behavior for men in the Precontemplation and Contemplation stages than those reported by their partners. They state that "there is now fairly consistent evidence that stage of change marks differential biases in the reporting of abusive men, with men in the Precontemplation stage showing the greatest bias" (p. 886). Self-reports of SOC may also not be accurate. There are at least some indications that men report themselves differently than others report them. Franks, Eckhardt, and Norlander (2001) found, in their study done with 40 domestic violence couples, that men placed themselves at a higher SOC than their partners. Scott

(2004) found only moderate agreement between client and clinician assessments of clients' SOC (varying from 40% to 55%). These differences between self- and third-party reports suggest that measuring SOC from various sources is warranted in further investigations of the TTM with this population. It may also be necessary to analyze how other self-report measures, such as the Safe-at-Home questionnaire (Begun et al., 2003), correlate with third-party sources, as SOC assessments done with an alcohol-dependent population entering treatment found agreement between client and clinician reports (Hodgins, 2001). The goal would be to determine if the bias rests primarily in the population being studied or in the TTM measures being used.

The second question involves a discussion of whether more motivation to change at intake necessarily relates to involvement in treatment for longer periods of time. This question can be looked at from three possible angles. First, perhaps in addition to clients' initial motivation to change, the capacity of programs to maintain that motivation should be measured as well. Some clients may be entering programs motivated to change but in-program factors are affecting them to the point of dropping out. This issue, for example, has been discussed extensively in addiction-related services and is marked most by the work of Miller (e.g., Miller, 1995; Miller & Rollnick, 2002) in the area of motivational enhancement. Miller discusses the limitations of focusing uniquely on client motivation as a static and voluntary trait of the individual instead of on program factors that may be impeding or limiting the arousal and maintenance of client motivation. An extreme example of negative program influence is discussed by Rooney and Hanson (2001), where one program had a high preprogram dropout rate (46% vs. 3%–13% for other programs), which they attributed to that program's 3-month waiting list. Some studies on men in treatment for intimate partner violence have shown improved retention rates through the addition of various attendance-enhancing procedures (Taft, Murphy, Elliot, & Morrel, 2001) and improved therapeutic alliance (Brown & O'Leary, 2000). Further investigations should measure motivation over the treatment span to see how it is influenced by program factors.

Second, participants who appear to have high motivation to change may be also presenting with lifestyle instability or facing social barriers to involvement in treatment over time. Recently, Levesque (personal communication, August 2005) found that men in her Action–High Relapse cluster were three times as likely to have prior arrests for violence outside the relationship and were twice as likely to report substance abuse problems. According to Levesque, while highly motivated for change, these men may need additional program support to remain in treatment. Corroboration for this idea has been found in other studies. In a recent publication, Stuart (2005), sighting research on the effect of problematic alcohol consumption and program retention, advocates for the integration of alcohol treatment, and conventional domestic violence interventions. Rooney and Hanson (2001) found a significant relationship between clients' verbal aptitude and program structure. Whereas 60% of participants with low verbal skills prematurely withdrew from unstructured treatment programs, only 30% withdrew from more structured ones. This, Rooney and Hanson argue, indicates that more structured programming may improve retention of clients with less education. Cadsky and colleagues (1996) discuss the use of crisis intervention strategies and extended services such as home visits and arranged transportation for clients characterized by severe lifestyle instability.

Third, clients with high motivation may terminate treatment because they find other sources of support in their community. As discussed by Turcotte, Damant, and Lindsay (1995), men who are violent with their partners employ a variety of help-seeking patterns that do not necessarily follow the path prescribed by conventional domestic violence treatment programs. In making their decision, men will often consider the costs of various options and choose the solution that is the least threatening and least guilt inducing and that demands the least reciprocity from them in return. For example, they may consult a professional only after exhausting their own social support network of friends and family. Support for these ideas has been found in other studies. In a recent clinical trial, Levesque (personal communication, August 2005) found that clients following up several months after treatment used several strategies, including talking to their partner, talking to friends or family, talking to a medical professional, or reading self-help books. These strategies were used at higher rates by clients in the Action stages, as would be expected. Rondeau, Brochu, Lemire, and Brodeur (1999) also found that some premature terminators were still seeking help after dropping out of their treatment program. About one-third of participants of that study indicated in follow-up interviews that they were trying to find services that responded to their expectations more closely. Such findings indicate the importance of including pretreatment and posttreatment assessments of broader help-seeking patterns as a way of more accurately assessing motivation to change as it relates to clients' actual engagement in the change process.

CONCLUSION

This study suggests that sociodemographic variables are still the most reliable predictors of attrition for men in domestic violence treatment programs. Because they are not easily affected by psychosocial intervention, it was hoped that the TTM would be at least as helpful in addressing the issue. This did not occur in this study. However, this does not mean the model should be discarded. Future studies may improve results by (a) controlling for social desirability bias, (b) monitoring how TTM measures interplay with program factors, and (c) accounting for broader help-seeking patterns instead of focusing exclusively on program attrition.

NOTE

1. Pro-Gam (Montreal), Caho (Joliette), Option (Montreal), Gapi (Quebec City), and Via L'Anse (Valleyfield).

ACKNOWLEDGMENT

The research on which this chapter is based was funded by the Fonds québécois de la recherche sur la société et la culture (FQRSC) [Quebec Fund for research on society and culture].

REFERENCES

Begun, A. L., Murphy, C., Bolt, D., Weinstein, B., Strodthoff, T., Short, L., et al. (2003). Characteristics of the safe at home instrument for assessing readiness to change in intimate partner violence. *Research on Social Work Practice, 13,* 80–107.

Bennett, L., Stoops, C., Flett, H., & Call, C. (2005, July). *Program completion and re-arrest in a batterer intervention system.* Paper presented at the Ninth International Conference on Family Violence Research, Portsmouth, NH.

Brogan, M. M., Prochaska, J. O., & Prochaska, J. M. (1999). Predicting termination and continuation status in psychotherapy using the transtheoretical model. *Psychotherapy, 36,* 105–113.

Brown, P. D., & O'Leary, D. O. (2000). Therapeutic alliance: Predicting continuance and success in group treatment for spouse abuse. *Journal of Consulting and Clinical Psychology, 68,* 340–345.

Cadsky, O., Hanson, K., Crawford, M., & Lalonde, C. (1996). Attrition from a male batterer treatment program: Client treatment congruence and lifestyle instability. *Violence and Victims, 11,* 51–64.

Daly, J. E., & Pelowski, S. (2000). Predictors of dropout among men who batter: A review of studies with implications for research and practice. *Violence and Victims, 15,* 137–160.

Daly, J. E., Power, T. G., & Gondolf, E. G. (2001). Predictors of batterer program attendance. *Journal of Interpersonal Violence, 16,* 971–991.

De Maris, A. (1989). Attrition in batterers' counselling: The role of social and demographic factors. *Social Service Review, 63,* 142–154.

Derisley, J., & Reynolds, S. (2000). The transtheoretical stages of change as a predictor of premature termination, attendance and alliance in psychotherapy. *British Journal of Clinical Psychology, 39,* 371–382.

Eckhardt, C. I., Babcock, J., & Homack, S. (2004). Partner assaultive men and the stages and processes of change. *Journal of Family Violence, 19,* 81–93.

Fraboni, M., & Cooper, D. (1989). Further validation of the short forms of the Marlowe-Crowne scale of social desirability. *Psychological Reports, 65,* 595–600.

Frank, J. D., & Frank, J. B. (1991). *Persuasion and healing: A comparative study of psychotherapy.* Baltimore: Johns Hopkins University Press.

Franks, E., Eckhardt, C., & Norlander, B. (2001, July). *The utility of intimate partner reports in validation of batterer's self-reported stages and processes of change.* Paper presented at the Seventh International Family Violence Research Conference, Portsmouth, NH.

Garfield, S. L. (1994). Research on client variables in psychotherapy. In A. E. Bergin & S. L. Garfield (Eds.), *Handbook of psychotherapy and behavior change* (4th ed., pp. 190–228). New York: Wiley.

Gondolf, E. W. (1997). Patterns of reassault in batterer programs. *Violence and Victims, 12,* 373–387.

Haller, D. L., Miles, D. R., & Cropsey, K. L. (2004). Smoking stage of change is associated with retention in a smoke-free residential drug treatment program for women. *Addictive Behaviors, 29,* 1265–1270.

Hodgins, D. C. (2001). Stages of change assessments in alcohol problems: Agreement across self and clinician-reports. *Substance Abuse, 22,* 87–96.

Levesque, D. (2005, August). *URICA-DV2. Measure norming, subtype analysis, and external validity.* Unpublished manuscript. Pro-Change Behavior Systems Inc., Kingston, RI.

Levesque, D., & Chell, D. (1999, November). *Stage of change and attrition from batterer treatment.* Paper presented at the 51st meeting of the American Society of Criminology, Toronto.

Levesque, D., Gelles, R. J., & Velicer, W. F. (2000). Development and validation of a stages of change measure for men in batterer treatment. *Cognitive Therapy and Research, 24,* 175–199.

Levesque, D., & Pro-Change. (2001a). *Decisional balance scale for domestic violence.* Kingston, RI: Pro-Change Behavior Systems Inc.

Levesque, D., & Pro-Change. (2001b). *Processes of change questionnaire.* Kingston, RI: Pro-Change Behavior Systems Inc.

Levesque, D., & Pro-Change. (2001c). *Temptations scale.* Kingston, RI: Pro-Change Behavior Systems Inc.

Levesque, D., & Pro-Change. (2001d). *University of Rhode Island change assessment scale–domestic violence (URICA-DV2).* Kingston, RI: Pro-Change Behavior Systems Inc.

Little, J. H., & Girvin, H. (2002). Stages of change: A critique. *Behavior Modification, 26,* 223–273.

McConnaughy, E. A., DiClemente, C. C., Prochaska, J. O., & Velicer, W. F. (1989). Stages of change in psychotherapy: A follow-up report. *Psychotherapy, 26,* 494–503.

Miller, W. R. (1995). Increasing motivation for change. In R. K. Hester (Ed.), *Handbook of alcoholism treatment approaches: Effective alternatives* (2nd ed., pp. 89–104). Boston: Allyn and Bacon.

Miller, W. R., & Rollnick, S. (2002). *Motivational interviewing: Preparing people to change addictive behavior* (2nd ed.). New York: Guilford Press.

Prochaska, J. O. (1995). An eclectic and integrative approach: Transtheoretical therapy. In A. S. E. Gurman & S. B. E. Messer (Eds.), *Essential psychotherapies: Theory and practice* (pp. 403–440). New York: Guilford Press.

Prochaska, J. O., & Norcross, J. C. (1999). *Systems of psychotherapy: A transtheoretical analysis* (4th ed.). Pacific Grove, CA: Brooks/Cole.

Prochaska, J. O., & Velicer, W. F. (1997). Response: Misinterpretations and misapplications of the transtheoretical model. *Health Promotion, 12,* 11–12.

Prochaska, J. O., Velicer, W. F., DiClemente, C. C., & Fava, J. (1988). Measuring processes of change: Applications to the cessation of smoking. *Journal of Consulting and Clinical Psychology, 56,* 520–528.

Rondeau, G., Brochu, S., Lemire, G., & Brodeur, N. (1999). *La persévérance des conjoints violents dans les programmes de traitement qui leur sont proposés* [Domestically violent men's perseverance in the treatment programs that are offered to them]. Montréal: Centre de Recherche Interdisciplinaire sur la Violence Familiale et la Violence Faite aux Femmes (CRI-VIFF).

Rondeau, G., Brodeur, N., Brochu, S., & Lemire, G. (2001). Dropout and completion of treatment among spouse abusers. *Violence and Victims, 16,* 127–143.

Rooney, J., & Hanson, K. (2001). Predicting attrition from treatment programs for abusive men. *Journal of Family Violence, 16,* 131–149.

Scott, K. (2004). Stage of change as a predictor of attrition among men in a batterer treatment program. *Journal of Family Violence, 19,* 37–47.

Scott, K., & Wolfe, D. (2003). Readiness to change as a predictor of outcome in batterer treatment. *Journal of Consulting and Clinical Psychology, 71,* 879–889.

Smyth, N. J. (1998). Substance abuse. In J. S. Wodarski & B. A. Thyer (Eds.), *Handbook of empirical social work practice* (Vol. 2, pp. 123–153). New York: Wiley.

Strahan, R., & Gerbasi, K. C. (1972). Short, homogeneous versions of the Marlowe-Crowne social desirability scale. *Journal of Clinical Psychology, 28,* 191–193.

Stuart, G. L. (2005). Improving violence intervention outcomes by integrating alcohol treatment. *Journal of Interpersonal Violence, 20,* 388–393.

Taft, C. T., Murphy, C. M., Elliot, J. D., & Morrel, T. M. (2001). Attendance enhancing procedures in group counselling for domestic abusers. *Journal of Counselling Psychology, 48,* 51–60.

Turcotte, D., Damant, D., & Lindsay, J. (1995). Pour une compréhension de la démarche de recherche d'aide des conjoints violents [Understanding the help-seeking strategies of domestically violent men]. *Service Social, 44,* 91–110.

8

Motivating Substance-Involved Perpetrators of Intimate Partner Violence to Seek Treatment: A Focus on Fathers

LYUNGAI MBILINYI, DENISE WALKER, CLAYTON NEIGHBORS, ROGER ROFFMAN, JOAN ZEGREE, AND JEFFREY EDLESON

Intimate partner violence (IPV) is a common and serious public health problem, adversely impacting millions of adult victims and children who are exposed to the violence. The majority of victims (85%) identify their abuser as male (Tjaden & Thoennes, 2000). For nearly three decades, programs for IPV perpetrators (typically men) have offered weekly groups ranging in duration from 12 to 52 weeks with one or two facilitators (Austin & Dankwort, 1999; Maiuro & Eberle, 2008). Studies have largely focused on mandated populations. The effectiveness of these programs, however, has been questioned. At best, the few evaluation studies utilizing experimental designs have found them to have modest positive effects (Babcock, Green, & Robie, 2004; Bennett & Williams, 2001; Davis & Taylor, 1999; Feder & Wilson, 2005). One consistent finding across most studies is that IPV treatment is effective with some individuals, particularly program completers, those who are not abusing or dependent on substances, and those high in motivation.

A surge of new theories and intervention models has emerged to address the mixed results of treatment programs, a heavy reliance on the criminal justice response that reaches only a minority of perpetrators, and a lack of focus on prevention or early intervention. Years of intervention research in the substance abuse field have led some in the IPV field to incorporate and adapt the transtheoretical model of change (TTM) (i.e., Stages of Change) and Motivational Interviewing when working with victims and perpetrators (see below) (Roffman, Edleson, Neighbors, Mbilinyi, & Walker, 2008).

The IPV field has also begun to develop programs addressing multiple issues facing their clients, including substance abuse (SA) and parenting. Considerable evidence suggests that many IPV perpetrators concurrently abuse alcohol or other drugs, and points to the importance of including a focus on SA in interventions for perpetrators (Holtzworth-Munroe & Meehan, 2004; Thompson & Kingree, 2006).

The overlap of IPV and child abuse (Edleson, 1999a), the adverse and enduring effects of exposure to IPV by children (Edleson, 1999b; Fantuzzo & Mohr, 1999), the manipulative use of children by the IPV perpetrator against the nonabusive parent (Bancroft & Silverman, 2002; Edleson, Mbilinyi, Beeman, & Hagemeister, 2003; Edleson, Mbilinyi, & Shetty, 2003), and the likelihood that even after divorce the perpetrator will continue to have a relationship with the children, have led to the development of programs targeting perpetrators who are fathers. Examples of such programs include the Men's Parenting Program of the Amherst H. Wilder Foundation's Violence Prevention and Intervention Services (formerly known as the Community Assistance Program), the EVOLVE program, Men Overcoming Violence for Equality (MOVE), and Caring Dads (www.caringdadsprogram.com). (For a detailed description of these programs and a comprehensive discussion of parenting in the context of IPV, see Edleson, Mbilinyi, & Shetty, 2003.) These programs are still somewhat new and are currently being replicated and evaluated in different settings. Development and evaluation of new programs are crucial, given that many perpetrators will continue to be involved with their children. In addition, a focus on fatherhood provides a *back-door* entry to address IPV issues for some men (Baker, Perilla, & Norris, 2001). The use of motivational interviewing with IPV perpetrators in discussing fatherhood and the impact of their behavior on their children has the potential to increase discrepancy, resolve ambivalence, and increase motivation for change.

In this chapter, we first discuss the overlap of IPV and SA and perpetrators' experience with batterer intervention programs (BIPs). We then describe the concept of Stages of Change and discuss a motivational enhancement intervention (a check-up) to be used as a catalyst for entering treatment. We describe the design of such a model (the Men's Domestic Abuse Check-Up—MDACU) and share key outcome findings for substance-using, IPV-perpetrating fathers and men without children.

INTIMATE PARTNER VIOLENCE AND SUBSTANCE ABUSE

Alcohol use increases the risk of intimate partner violence (Fals-Stewart, 2003; Fals-Stewart, Leonard, & Birchler, 2005). Thompson and Kingree (2006) found that women whose partners had been drinking at the time of assault were significantly more likely to be injured than were women whose partners had not been drinking. Brown and his colleagues (1999) found up to a 92% lifetime diagnosis of substance abuse or dependence among IPV perpetrators in their sample. The high level of co-occurrence led Goldkamp, Weiland, Collins, and White (1996) to design and pilot test one of the few integrated interventions aimed at ending both SA and IPV among a group of men who were court ordered to treatment and found greater retention (79%) in the integrated program compared to the traditional program (55%) after 1 month of services. Easton and Sinha's (2002) evaluation of Yale's Substance Abuse Treatment Unit's Substance Abuse–Domestic Violence integrated approach has preliminarily found that the model increased participants' motivation to engage in positive behavior change (IPV and SA) and improved their compliance with treatment. Following a 12-week integrated treatment group with alcohol-dependent men who were arrested for IPV, Easton and colleagues (2007) found these participants had significantly decreased IPV behaviors from pre- to posttreatment.

TREATMENT ENTRY, ENGAGEMENT, AND PROGRAM COMPLETION AMONG IPV PERPETRATORS

Most IPV perpetrators are nonadjudicated and untreated and enter treatment only after they have injured a partner or family member *and* have been arrested (Gondolf, 2002). Many abusers in treatment drop out, with rates ranging from 22% to 99% (Daly & Pelowski, 2000). Low motivation and SA are often found to be predictors of dropout. Yet, program completers are more likely to be nonviolent than are the non-completers. Gondolf (2004) found a 50% greater overall reduction in recidivism among program completers in his four-city study that included 840 court-ordered IPV perpetrators. More recent studies have found that program completion reduces the probability of IPV reassaults by 40% to 60% (Bennett, Stoops, Call, & Flett, 2007; Jones, D'Agostino, Gondolf, & Heckert, 2004). These findings make a compelling case for developing interventions that promote motivation for treatment, voluntary treatment entry, and retention.

THE STAGES OF CHANGE MODEL

A paradigm of change that has had considerable heuristic influence on the design of behavioral interventions in recent years was first articulated with reference to smoking cessation. Prochaska and DiClemente (1983) hypothesized that before smokers ultimately succeed in quitting, they've likely experienced earlier stages of readiness to change, one of which involves ambivalence, that is, having the goal of quitting and being unready to commit to the steps necessary for its achievement. They referred to this phase in a continuum of readiness as the contemplation stage, and noted that having an opportunity to explore these ambivalent feelings and reflect on one's personal dissatisfaction with being a smoker would likely be helpful in tipping the scales toward readiness to make an abstinence commitment.

In the field of IPV, the need for interventions tailored for individuals who are experiencing ambivalence and are contemplating change is beginning to be discussed (Brown, 1997; Daniels & Murphy, 1997; Murphy & Baxter, 1997; Murphy & Eckhardt, 2005; Roffman et al., 2008). The ultimate objective is to facilitate voluntary treatment entry and improve outcomes.

MOTIVATIONAL ENHANCEMENT THERAPY (MET)

At about the same time that the stages-of-change model was beginning to appear in the literature, an intervention model that came to be known as motivational enhancement therapy was being developed. Its first iteration, a brief intervention called "The Drinkers' Check-Up" (Miller, Benefield, & Tonigan, 1993; Miller & Sovereign, 1989), involved an assessment interview and a subsequent feedback session, with the provider using an empathic style of counseling called motivational interviewing (Miller & Rollnick, 2002). Advertised as a chance to take stock of one's drinking with no pressure to commit to changing, the DCU intervention reached individuals who met diagnostic criteria for alcohol dependence. Moreover, when followed up several months later, many were found to have self-initiated change or entered treatment. In sum, this new modality was tailored for individuals who were not yet making the change and, in succeeding at facilitating the voluntary participation of clearly alcohol-impaired individuals, challenged the prevailing notion that alcoholics had to hit bottom and be confronted before they would be ready to change.

MET WITH UNTREATED, NONADJUDICATED SUBSTANCE-ABUSING IPV PERPETRATORS

Defense dynamics attributed to IPV perpetrators are similar to individuals with addictive disorders, such as minimizing the severity of consequences, blaming others for causing the behavior, and making excuses for one's actions (see Murphy & O'Farrell, 1997; Roffman et al., 2008). Motivational enhancement therapy has demonstrated efficacy among individuals with these characteristics (Karno & Longabaugh, 2004; Project MATCH Research Group, 1997).

Motivational interviewing (MI), a counseling style within MET, includes resistance reduction strategies that are particularly relevant in enhancing motivation for change in individuals with abusive behaviors. Intimate partner violence perpetrators have been found to show remorse and ambivalence regarding their behavior, suggesting compatibility with MI principles. A study at the University of Washington, the Men's Domestic Abuse Check-Up, adapted and tested motivational enhancement therapy for men engaging in both IPV and SA and who are precontemplative and contemplative about their behaviors.

THE MEN'S DOMESTIC ABUSE CHECK-UP (MDACU)

The MDACU was a federally funded, randomized controlled trial conducted by researchers with the University of Washington and the University of Minnesota Schools of Social Work. Adapted from the DCU, the MDACU targeted adult men who were ambivalent or concerned about their IPV and SA behaviors, and in the precontemplation or contemplation stage of change. A telephone-delivered, brief intervention, the MDACU was developed to reach and motivate untreated and nonadjudicated substance-using IPV perpetrators to self-refer into treatment.

The marketing for this project had to be universal as IPV perpetrators represent all socioeconomic, racial, ethnic, and religious backgrounds. Due to continued stigma linked with domestic violence and the broad target population, developing a universal recruitment campaign presented a substantial challenge. The research team contracted with an advertising agency, worked closely with IPV perpetrator and victim treatment providers, as well as adult men who had successfully completed IPV treatment in designing a recruitment plan. Through this collaboration, a marketing campaign was designed to be nonjudgmental, engaging, and appealing to men from diverse backgrounds who are in the precontemplation and contemplation stages of change. In order to increase desirability and lower barriers to the potential participant, the check-up was described in advertising as brief, by telephone, a *taking stock* experience rather than treatment, and offering the assurance of privacy including anonymity.

The MDACU recruited participants through feature or news stories in mainstream press, radio, and television; display ads in mainstream and culturally specific newspapers; radio ads; and project flyers at social, health, workplace, and law enforcement establishments (see Mbilinyi et al., 2008, for a detailed description of the marketing development process). Figure 8.1 is an example of marketing materials developed for this project. Another manuscript documenting the effectiveness of the recruitment strategies is currently underway.

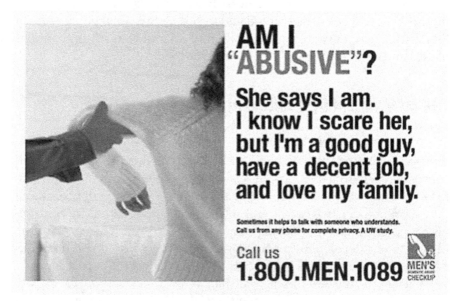

Figure 8.1 Display advertisement—Partner print ad.

One hundred twenty-four eligible men were recruited from the community and were randomly assigned to receive a telephone-delivered, individual feedback session (MET condition) or were mailed educational materials on IPV and SA (education condition). Participants in the education condition were offered the individual feedback session after the final follow-up assessment.

THE EXPERIMENTAL (MET) AND COMPARISON (MAILED EDUCATIONAL MATERIALS) CONDITIONS

The MET session consisted of one individual, 60-to-90-minute session by phone with a counselor using motivational interviewing techniques. After affirming the participant for calling, the counselor asked him his reasons for responding to the study advertisements, and what he was interested in getting out of the session. The counselor then introduced the Personal Feedback Report (PFR), summarizing the topics that would be discussed. The PFR, constructed from data collected in the assessment interviews, was comprised of the following sections: history of perpetrator's abusive behavior, IPV normative data, consequences to the perpetrator of his IPV, family history of IPV, exposure to IPV by children, current alcohol use patterns, alcohol normative data, estimated blood alcohol concentrations, risk factors for developing an alcohol problem, alcohol use consequences, current drug use patterns, drug normative data, and consequences related to drug use.

The Comparison Condition consisted of an educational brochure on the definitions and prevalence of IPV and SA, as well as their social, legal, and health consequences on the individual, family, and society.

THE OPTIONAL LEARNING SESSION (OLS): LEARNING ABOUT AND CONSIDERING OPTIONS IN THE COMMUNITY

The OLS was a 20-to-45-minute in-person session, focused on providing detailed information about treatment resources such as length, format, fees, and location. Attendance at the OLS served as an outcome measure indicating increased readiness to change behavior. Each participant was invited to the OLS, which was delivered in a case management and didactic style.

Screening, Assessment, and Follow-Up

The MDACU's phone line was open Monday through Friday, from 9 a.m. to 7 p.m. All participants were assessed by phone during two screening interviews and one baseline interview prior to the intervention, and at 1-week and 1-month follow-up. Callers who were ineligible, seeking other services, or in crisis were referred to relevant community resources (see Mbilinyi et al., 2008, and Roffman et al., 2008, for a detailed description of the screening process).

Summary of Findings

The MDACU demonstrated the feasibility of recruiting, enrolling, assessing, offering feedback, and reassessing current substance-using IPV male perpetrators who are neither being treated nor adjudicated. The project attracted a demographically diverse community sample of IPV perpetrators, the majority of whom had been exposed to IPV in their families of origin. Virtually all reported committing psychological violence and at least minimal physical violence directed at the partner, and half reported using severe physical violence such as kicking on one or more occasions. At baseline, most *were not* taking steps toward IPV (84%) or SA (92%) treatment. A manuscript documenting findings of our key outcomes is currently underway. Briefly, we found the MDACU to be a promising approach for motivating men to take steps in the direction of treatment and to at least temporarily reduce the frequency and severity of their abusive behavior. Below, we present outcome findings comparing fathers and men without children in our sample, which were analyzed specifically for this chapter and not included in the primary outcomes paper.

MDACU Findings: IPV-Perpetrating Fathers and Men Without Children

Of the 124 enrolled participants, 92 (74.2%) were fathers and 32 (25.8%) were not. Table 8.1 presents demographic information as a function of fatherhood. The two groups did not differ significantly with respect to race, $\chi^2(6) = 3.31$, $p = ns$, or ethnicity, $\chi^2(1) = .51$, $p = ns$. Fathers, however, were older, $t(122) = 2.96$, $p < .01$, and more likely to be married, $\chi^2(1) = 6.78$, $p < .01$.

Table 8.1

DEMOGRAPHICS

	FATHERS (*N* = 92)	MEN WITHOUT CHILDREN (*N* = 32)
Married	69.6%	43.8%
Ethnicity-Hispanic	6.5%	3.1%
Race		
White	62.0%	71.9%
Black/African American	18.5%	12.5%
Asian	1.1%	3.1%
American Indian/Alaska Native	4.3%	3.1%
Hawaiian/Pacific Islander	1.3%	0.0%
Other	9.8%	9.4%
	Mean (*SD*)	Mean (*SD*)
Age	41.10 (10.07)	34.47 (13.14)

DIFFERENCES IN BASELINE CHARACTERISTICS

Intimate Partner Violence

Intimate partner violence was assessed by the Conflict Tactics Scale–Revised (CTS-2). At baseline, fathers reported using an average of 13.27 (*SD* = 25.29) incidents of psychological violence during the past 90 days in comparison to 14.80 (*SD* = 36.06) incidents reported by men without children. Fathers reported using an average of 5.41 (*SD* = 3.56) incidents of physical violence or injurious behaviors in comparison to an average of 4.19 (*SD* = 3.39) incidents reported by men without children. Fathers reported using an average of 1.65 (*SD* = 9.67) acts of sexual violence in comparison with .41 (*SD* = 1.21) acts reported by men without children. Results of generalized linear models where outcomes were modeled using negative binomial distributions revealed no significant differences between fathers and men without children on psychological violence, $B = .08$, $\chi^2(1) = .51$, $p = ns$, or physical violence or injurious behaviors, $B = .26$, $\chi^2(1) = 1.28$, $p = ns$. In contrast, fathers reported committing significantly more sexual violence, $B = 1.40$, $\chi^2(1) = 15.67$,

$p < .001$. This result remained significant when we controlled for differences in marital status.

Alcohol and Drug Use

Fathers reported consuming an average of 8.68 (SD = 12.01) alcoholic drinks and using other drugs on an average of 13.40 (SD = 11.52) days during the past 90 days at baseline. In comparison, men without children reported consuming an average of 14.28 (SD = 16.37) drinks and using other drugs on an average of 18.09 (SD = 12.03) days during the past 90 days. Results of generalized linear models using negative binomial distributions indicated that fathers consumed significantly less alcohol at baseline, $B = -.50$, $\chi^2(1) = 5.42$, $p < .01$, but the difference in other drug use was not statistically significant, $B = -.30$, $\chi^2(1) = 2.02$, $p = .15$.

Readiness to Change

Readiness to change domestic violence, alcohol, and drug use were examined in separate general linear models using a modification of the Brief Readiness to Change questionnaire. Results indicated that fathers did not differ from men without children in terms of their readiness to change domestic violence, $B = -.10$, $t(122) = -.28$, $p = ns$, or drug use, $B = -.11$, $t(122) = -.08$, $p = ns$. Fathers' scores on readiness to change drinking behavior were somewhat lower, although not significantly so, $B = -1.26$, $t(122) = 1.31$, $p = .19$. This difference in readiness to change drinking probably reflects the fact that fathers drank less than men without children.

Treatment Seeking

Treatment-seeking behaviors included inquiries to treatment agencies by phone or in person, requesting materials from a treatment agency, or attending an intake session or a session of treatment. At baseline, 16.3% of fathers reported having engaged in one or more treatment-seeking behaviors for domestic violence during the past 90 days in comparison to 12.5% of men without children. This difference did not approach statistical significance, $\chi^2(1) = .26$, $p = ns$. With respect to treatment seeking for alcohol or other substance abuse, at baseline only 4.3% of fathers reported any treatment-seeking behavior in comparison to 15.6% of men without children, $\chi^2(1) = 4.49$, $p < .05$. Thus, while they did not differ with respect to prior treatment seeking for domestic violence, fathers were less likely to have engaged in treatment seeking for alcohol or other substance use. This latter finding probably reflects lower, alcohol and somewhat lower drug use among fathers to begin with. Indeed, when we statistically controlled for prior alcohol and other substance use there was no significant difference in treatment seeking between fathers and men without children.

Summary of Baseline Characteristics

The fathers in our sample were older and more likely to be married. The pattern of differences in baseline characteristics suggests two primary differences between these two groups. First, although both groups used similar levels of psychological, physical, and injurious violence, fathers were more likely to report having used sexual violence. Second, fathers reported lower rates of substance use, alcohol in particular. Lower substance use, and hence less need to change, appeared to translate into lower readiness to change substance use among fathers in comparison to men without children.

Intervention Effects Among Fathers

For this chapter we looked at follow-up outcomes for fathers only, examining change as a function of intervention among fathers by evaluating differences in follow-up outcomes controlling for baseline outcomes (reported above). The relatively small number of men without children, when divided by intervention group at follow-up, precluded our ability to more comprehensively evaluate whether intervention effects at follow-up assessments varied as a function of fatherhood (e.g., we had only eight men without children in the control group at 30-day follow-up). In a larger study we would evaluate interactions between fatherhood and intervention condition on follow-up outcomes. However the present sample size did not provide sufficient power for us to do this in a meaningful way.

Optional Learning Session Attendance

Attendance at the OLS was a primary outcome of MDACU. Overall, the OLS was attended by 32.6% of fathers. In the intervention group, 36.1% of fathers attended the OLS whereas in the control group 30.4%

of fathers attended. Moreover, fathers in the intervention group were not significantly more likely to attend the OLS in comparison to fathers in the control condition, $\chi^2(1) = .33$, $p = ns$.

Intimate Partner Violence

At 30-day follow-up, fathers in the intervention group reported an average of 1.01 ($SD = 1.21$) incidents of psychological violence during the past month in comparison to 3.04 ($SD = 8.73$) incidents reported by fathers in the control group. Fathers in the intervention group reported an average of .21 ($SD = .68$) incidents of physical violence or injurious behaviors during the past 90 days in comparison to an average of .85 ($SD = 2.83$) incidents reported by fathers in the control group. Results of generalized linear models using negative binomial distributions indicated that controlling for baseline CTS-2 scores, fathers in the intervention condition reported using somewhat fewer acts of psychological violence, $B = -.44$, $\chi^2(1) = 3.04$, $p = .08$, and significantly fewer acts of physical or injurious violence, $B = -1.40$, $\chi^2(1) = 7.24$, $p < .01$. At the 30-day follow-up, only five fathers reported having used any sexual violence during the past month. All five of these fathers were in the control group.

Alcohol and Drug Use

At the 30-day follow-up, fathers in the intervention group reported having consumed an average of 9.66 ($SD = 11.34$) drinks per week in the past month and having used other drugs on an average of 16.33 ($SD = 11.40$) days. In comparison, fathers in the control group reported having consumed 8.04 ($SD = 12.48$) drinks and having used drugs on 11.52 ($SD = 11.29$) days. Results of generalized linear models using negative binomial distributions indicated that, controlling for baseline use, differences between fathers in the intervention group versus fathers in the control group did not approach statistical significance for drinking, $B = .30$, $\chi^2(1) = 1.23$, $p = ns$, or drug use, $B = -.09$, $\chi^2(1) = .11$, $p = ns$.

Readiness to Change

Readiness to change domestic violence, alcohol, and drug use at 30-day follow-up were examined among fathers as a function of intervention condition controlling for baseline readiness in separate general linear models. No differences between fathers in the intervention condition versus those in the control group approached significance for domestic violence, $B = .23, t(74) = .77, p = ns$, alcohol use, $B = .54, t(74) = .68, p = ns$, or drug use, $B = -.50, t(74) = -.32, p = ns$.

Treatment Seeking

At the 30-day follow-up, 13.9% of fathers in the intervention condition reported having engaged in any treatment-seeking behaviors in the prior 30 days in comparison to 17.9% of fathers in the control condition. A logistic regression evaluating likelihood of engaging in treatment seeking for domestic violence, controlling for baseline treatment seeking, indicated that the difference between intervention fathers and control fathers did not approach significance, $B = -.72, \chi^2(1) = 1.43, p = ns$. Only four fathers reported engaging in any treatment-seeking behaviors for substance use during the previous 30 days at the 30-day follow-up assessment. The relative infrequency of treatment seeking for alcohol and other substance use during this period precluded statistical evaluation. Three of the four fathers who reported treatment seeking for alcohol and other substance abuse were in the intervention condition.

Summary of Intervention Effects Among Fathers

Overall, the intervention effects specifically among fathers mirror the preliminary primary outcomes summarized above. This is noteworthy because the sample size is smaller when only examining fathers. Results indicated that, controlling for baseline outcomes, fathers in the intervention condition committed fewer acts of intimate partner violence at the 30-day follow-up in comparison to fathers in the control group. We did not find evidence for other intervention differences among fathers, although it is interesting to note that three of the four fathers who engaged in treatment seeking during the 30-day period following baseline were in the intervention condition.

DISCUSSION

Preliminary data from our pilot trial indicate that substance-using IPV perpetrators who are not involved in court procedures or treatment can be attracted to participate in an experience with a counselor to discuss their IPV behaviors. This alone is encouraging, given the infrequency of self-referral to IPV treatment and suggests that men who are engaging in IPV are concerned about their behaviors. Further research is needed to explore how best to capitalize on this experience and encourage more of these men to enter a formal treatment program.

The majority of our participants were fathers, who said that being a good dad and setting a good example were important values for them. Thus the role of fatherhood offers potential value as an intrinsic motivator with men who are abusive to the other parent. Aspects of the Personal Feedback Report specifically targeted fathers to encourage a thoughtful discussion about how their IPV behavior may be affecting their children. Participants were asked if they had witnessed IPV in their home growing up. They were also asked if they had children living in their home. Information was provided on how men who have witnessed IPV in the home are at risk for perpetrating IPV in adulthood and the negative effects IPV can have on children.

Preliminary data suggest that fathers reduced their violence more when exposed to the MET intervention than the control condition. However, treatment seeking did not differ between the two groups. While the reduction of violence is encouraging, there may be significant barriers to treatment seeking with this population. A father may feel that entering treatment for IPV is an admission of guilt or of being an unfit parent leading to the loss of his children. Specific reasons fathers had for not entering treatment were not evaluated in the current study, but would be fruitful to explore in the future. Also, the sample size was too small to investigate potential differences between fathers who currently had children living in their home versus those who did not. Fathers may have children who are grown and out of the home, or children outside the home whom they have little contact with. The age of the children, access to, and living situation may all be interesting factors to explore in the future with regard to this population, and may provide further insight into how to work with fathers to motivate them to stop their IPV behavior as a pretreatment or treatment intervention. Overall, in the MDACU, many fathers were attracted to voluntarily talk with someone about their violence in the home and reduce their abusive behaviors. Further work should continue to explore ways to attract and engage abusive fathers into intervention services.

REFERENCES

Austin, J. B., & Dankwort, J. (1999). Standards for batterer intervention programs: A review and analysis. *Journal of Interpersonal Violence, 14,* 152–168.

Babcock, J. C., Green, C. E., & Robie, C. (2004). Does batterers' treatment work? A meta-analytic review of domestic violence treatment. *Clinical Psychology Review, 23,* 1023–1053.

Baker, C. K., Perilla, J. L., & Norris, F. H. (2001). Parenting stress and parenting competence among Latino men who batter. *Journal of Interpersonal Violence, 16*(11), 1139–1157.

Bancroft, L., & Silverman, J. (2002). *The batterer as parent.* Thousand Oaks, CA: Sage.

Bennett, L., Stoops, C., Call, C., & Flett, H. (2007). Program completion and re-arrest in a batterer intervention system. *Research on Social Work Practice, 17*(1), 42–54.

Bennett, L., & Williams, O. J. (2001). *Controversies and recent studies of batterer intervention effectiveness.* Harrisburg, PA: National Electronic Network on Violence Against Women (VAWnet, PCADV/NRCDV). Retrieved June 21, 2007, from http://www.vawnet.org

Brown, J. (1997). Working toward freedom from violence: The process of change in battered women. *Violence Against Women, 3,* 5–26.

Brown, T. G., Werk, A., Caplan, T., & Seraganian, P. (1999). Violent substance abusers in domestic violence treatment. *Violence and Victims, 14,* 179–190.

Daly, J., & Pelowski, S. (2000). Predictors of dropout among men who batter: A review of studies with implications for research and practice. *Violence and Victims, 15,* 137–160.

Daniels, J. W., & Murphy, C. M. (1997). Stages and processes of change in batterers' treatment. *Cognitive and Behavioral Practice, 4,* 123–145.

Davis, R. C., & Taylor, B. G. (1999) Does batterer treatment reduce violence? A synthesis of the literature. *Women & Criminal Justice, 10*(2), 69–93.

Easton, C. J., Mandel, D., Babuscio, T., Rounsaville, B. J., & Carroll, K. M. (2007). Differences in treatment outcome between male alcohol dependent offenders of domestic violence with and without positive drug screens. *Addictive Behaviors, 32*(10), 2151–2163.

Easton, C. J., & Sinha, R. (2002). Treating the addicted male batterer: Promising directions for dual-focused programming. In C. Wekerle & A. Wall (Eds.), *The violence and addiction equation: Theoretical and clinical issues in substance abuse and relationship violence* (pp. 275–292). New York: Brunner-Routledge.

Edleson, J. L. (1999a). The overlap between child maltreatment and woman battering. *Violence Against Women, 5*(2), 134–154.

Edleson, J. L. (1999b). Children's witnessing of adult domestic violence. *Journal of Interpersonal Violence, 14*(8), 839–870.

Edleson, J., Mbilinyi, L., Beeman, S. K., & Hagemeister, A. K. (2003). Children's exposure and involvement with domestic violence: A four-city study. *Journal of Interpersonal Violence, 18*(1), 18–32.

Edleson, J. L., Mbilinyi, L. F., & Shetty, S. (2003). *Parenting in the context of domestic violence.* San Francisco: Judicial Council of California.

Fals-Stewart, W. (2003). The occurrence of partner physical aggression on days of alcohol consumption: A longitudinal diary study. *Journal of Consulting and Clinical Psychology, 71,* 41–52.

Fals-Stewart, W., Leonard, K. E., & Birchler, G. R. (2005). The occurrence of male-to-female intimate partner violence on days of men's drinking: The moderating effect of antisocial personality disorder. *Journal of Consulting and Clinical Psychology, 73*(2), 239–248.

Fantuzzo, J. W., & Mohr, W. K. (1999). Prevalence and effects of child exposure to domestic violence. *The Future of Children, 9,* 21–32.

Feder, L., & Wilson, D. B. (2005). A meta-analytic review of court-mandated batterer intervention programs: Can courts affect abusers' behavior? *Journal of Experimental Criminology, 1,* 239–262.

Goldkamp, J. S., Weiland, D., Collins, M., & White, M. (1996). *The role of drug and alcohol abuse in domestic violence and its treatment: Dade County's domestic violence court experience: Final report.* Philadelphia, PA: Crime and Justice Research Institute.

Gondolf, E. W. (2002). *Batterer intervention systems: Issues, outcomes, and recommendations.* Thousand Oaks, CA: Sage.

Gondolf, E. W. (2004). Evaluating batterer counseling programs. *Aggression and Violent Behavior, 9,* 605–631.

Holtzworth-Munroe, A., & Meehan, J. C. (2004).Typologies of men who are martially violent. *Journal of Interpersonal Violence, 19*(12), 1369–1389.

Jones, A. S., D'Agostino, R. B., Jr., Gondolf, E. W., & Heckert, A. (2004). Assessing the effect of batterer program completion on reassault using propensity scores. *Journal of Interpersonal Violence, 19,* 1002–1020.

Karno, M. P., & Longabaugh, R. (2004). What do we know? Process analysis and the search for a better understanding of Project MATCH's anger-by-treatment matching effect. *Journal of Studies on Alcohol, 65,* 501–512.

Maiuro, R. D., & Eberle, J. A. (2008). State standards for domestic violence perpetrator treatment: Current status, trends, and recommendations. *Violence and Victims, 23,* 133–155.

Mbilinyi, L. F., Zegree, J., Roffman, R. A., Walker, D., Neighbors, C., & Edleson, J. (2008). Development of a marketing campaign to recruit non-adjudicated and untreated abusive men for a brief telephone intervention. *Journal of Family Violence, 23*(5), 343–351.

Miller, W. R., Benefield, G. S., & Tonigan, G. S. (1993). Enhancing motivation for change in problem drinking: A controlled comparison of two therapist styles. *Journal of Consulting and Clinical Psychology, 61,* 455–461.

Miller, W. R., & Rollnick, S. (2002). *Motivational interviewing* (2nd ed.). New York: Guilford.

Miller, W. R., & Sovereign, R. G. (1989). The check-up: A model for early intervention in addictive behaviors. In T. Loberg, W. R. Miller, P. E. Nathan, & G. A. Marlatt (Eds.), *Addictive behaviors: Prevention and early intervention* (pp. 219–231). Amsterdam: Swets & Zeitlinger.

Murphy, C. M., & Baxter, V. A. (1997). Motivating batterers to change in the treatment context. *Journal of Interpersonal Violence, 12,* 607–619.

Murphy, C. M., & Eckhardt, C. I. (2005). *Treating the abusive partner: An individualized cognitive behavioral approach.* New York: Guilford Press.

Murphy, C. M., & O'Farrell, T. J. (1997). Couple communication patterns of martially aggressive and nonaggressive male alcoholics. *Journal of Studies on Alcohol, 58,* 83–90.

Prochaska, J. O., & DiClemente, C. C. (1983). Stages and processes of self-change of smoking: Toward an integrative model of change. *Journal of Consulting and Clinical Psychology, 51,* 390–395.

Project MATCH Research Group. (1997). Project MATCH secondary a priori hypotheses. *Addiction, 92,* 1671–1698.

Roffman, R., Edleson, J., Neighbors, C., Mbilinyi, L., & Walker, D. (2008). The men's domestic abuse check-up: A protocol for reaching the non-adjudicated and untreated man who batters and abuses substances. *Journal of Violence Against Women, 14*(5), 589–605.

Thompson, M. P., & Kingree, J. P. (2006). The roles of victim and perpetrator alcohol use in intimate partner violence outcomes. *Journal of Interpersonal Violence, 21*(2), 163–177.

Tjaden, P., & Thoennes, N. (2000). *Full report of the prevalence, incidence, and consequences of violence against women.* Washington, DC: Office of Justice Programs, U.S. Department of Justice.

The Revised Safe At Home Instrument for Assessing Readiness to Change Intimate Partner Violence

AUDREY L. BEGUN, MICHAEL J. BRONDINO, DANIEL BOLT,
BENJAMIN WEINSTEIN, TERRI STRODTHOFF,
AND GENE SHELLEY

The transtheoretical model of behavior change (TTM) has been offered as an innovation in assessing individuals' readiness to change their intimate partner violence (IPV) behavior as well as a means of evaluating treatment effectiveness (Begun, Shelley, Strodthoff, & Short, 2001; Daniels & Murphy, 1997; Levesque, Gelles, & Velicer, 2000). The model delineates the processes by which individuals attempt to change health-related behaviors both with and without supportive therapeutic intervention (Connors, Donovan, & DiClemente, 2001; DiClemente et al., 1991; Littell & Girvin, 2002; Prochaska & DiClemente, 1983). The readiness-to-change approach of the TTM was adopted by the Safe At Home project prior to published controversy about its applicability (Sutton, 1996). It was adopted because it offers practitioners an opportunity to elucidate the actual change process itself, in addition to observing intervention outcomes, and because of its empirically demonstrated clinical utility with a wide variety of behavioral change efforts (Begun et al., 2001; Connors et al., 2001; Heather, Rollnick, & Bell, 1993; Prochaska et al., 1994; Prochaska & Velicer, 1997).

The stages-of-change elements of the TTM are based on repeated observations that intentional behavior change efforts can be understood within an empirically supported, multistage, sequential model (Petrocelli, 2002). This model attends to the developmental nature of change processes, emphasizes the naturally occurring self-change processes, addresses the vertical spiral nature of change, and acknowledges that change occurs within, without, and between therapeutic interventions (DiClemente et al., 1991; Prochaska, DiClemente, & Norcross, 1992). The five recognized stages through which individuals progress (and regress) during the change process include Precontemplation, Contemplation, Preparation, Action, and Maintenance (Prochaska & DiClemente, 1992). The stages are characterized by specific beliefs, thoughts, feelings, behaviors, and efforts with particular processes prevailing during particular stages (Prochaska & DiClemente, 1982, 1984; Prochaska et al., 1992; Prochaska & Norcross, 2001).

Specifically, the stage of *Precontemplation* is characterized by a lack of intention to change. This may result from any combination of not perceiving that a problem exists and/or a strong belief that sufficient efficacy for change does not exist. *Contemplation* is evidenced by recognition that a problem exists, feeling the need for significant change, and awareness that the relative costs and benefits associated with changing or not changing the behaviors must be weighed. It is also characterized by an absence of concrete, specific, and decisive actions for change and/or a lack of firm commitment to take actions necessary for change. *Preparation* is presumably a period in which initial baby steps are taken as evidence of a decision to change. But this stage is empirically elusive—it appears in cluster analyses, not through factor analyses in most staging instruments. Specifically, individuals at this stage endorse both Contemplation and Action statements. Preparation may appear behaviorally through self-monitoring of the problematic behavior and in seeking out information and role models for change. *Action* is characterized by actually exhibiting concrete, specific change efforts as well as by a decisional balance that emphasizes the costs of not changing and the benefits of changing. There is an emphasis on skill building, implementation of plans, and imposing environmental controls to support the change effort. *Maintenance* involves definitive efforts to sustain the changes that have been achieved during a concentrated period of action (often defined as 6 months), acknowledgment of the tremendous efforts involved in the change process, awareness of the factors that may lead to a recurrence, a sense of self-efficacy and mastery of the problem, and the adoption of strategies to avoid relapse. The duration of maintenance may be measured in years—termination as a completed change process, with no temptation to relapse, may or may not eventually be accomplished.

Access to appropriate measures related to changing IPV is crucial to the application of this approach in treatment and prevention. First, appropriate assessment can provide a conceptual basis for effective client–treatment matching (Holtzworth-Munroe & Stuart, 1994; Levesque et al., 2000; Prochaska, DiClemente, Velicer, & Rossi, 1993; Prochaska & Norcross, 2001). For example, applying motivational strategies for batterers engaged in Precontemplation processes may assist in moving them to Contemplation; for other health behaviors, when this movement occurs during the first month of intervention, the probability of progressing to Action doubles (Prochaska & Norcross, 2001). According to Weinstein, Rothman, and Sutton (1998), stage-based interventions are only as good as the ability to accurately and efficiently identify stages. Second, a promising intervention strategy for promoting the change process involves providing personally salient feedback and test interpretation (Martin, Prupas, & Sugarman, 1998). The ability to therapeutically employ this type of motivational feedback depends on the availability of accurate and accessible measures. Third, accurate measures are helpful in predicting treatment process and treatment outcomes (Prochaska & Norcross, 2001; Taft, Murphy, Musser, & Remington, 2004). Fourth, the ability to assess progress through the change stages allows for program evaluation that is sensitive to program impact on process, not only on final outcomes (Begun et al., 2001, 2003).

Until recently, published instruments specifically designed to assess readiness to change violence toward an intimate partner did not exist. At least two instruments related to readiness to change IPV have emerged. One such instrument is the University of Rhode Island Change Assessment–Domestic Violence (URICA-DV; described by Levesque et al., 2000). Designed as a measure to assess men's readiness to end the use of physical violence in their relationships, the URICA-DV is based on the generic URICA instrument for staging psychotherapy patients' readiness to address an unspecified problem. The difficulties in applying the generic URICA to domestic violence include (a) the lack of a consistent referent in questions about the problem and (b) norms based on middle-class, White samples that may not be representative of the population entering batterer treatment.

Item content for the URICA-DV was generated through an intensive, qualitative focus group process that employed the five-stage model to guide generation of the scales. Validation efforts involved 258 men at various points in the counseling process, and subtype cluster analysis was conducted. The instrument was cross-validated using measures of social desirability, use of strategies for ending relationship violence, the Modified Conflict Tactics Scale, attribution of blame for the violence, and a Decisional Balance Inventory (for instrument specifics, see Levesque et al., 2000). While described as a brief measure, the 240-item URICA-DV required approximately 50 to 60 minutes to complete (Levesque et al., 2000). This presents a significant drawback to field use in batterer intervention programs that face acute restrictions because of space, time, staff, and competing intake demands. Furthermore, field friendliness is limited by complexity of scoring the measure and other costs associated with its use.

The other available measure is the original 35-item Safe At Home Stages of Change Instrument (Begun et al., 2003). Like the URICA-DV, the original Safe At Home instrument is a self-administered questionnaire that asks respondents to rate their level of agreement with statements using a 5-point scale—coding is adjusted so that higher values indicate greater agreement with the statement. Item content was developed by employing experienced batterer treatment professionals as the key informants. There were two reasons for adopting this strategy. The first was to economize in the degree of effort involved in creating the item content, while the second was to create items worded in terms that are in common usage by the widely diverse target population.

Initial Exploratory Factor Analysis results (Begun et al., 2003) on intake data ($n = 829$ batterers) determined that a three-factor solution was superior to either the two- or the four-factor solution, and the results were explicable with concepts in the TTM stages of change. The three derived factors—Precontemplation, Contemplation, and Preparation/Action—were reasonably uncorrelated with one another. An overall, continuous Readiness to Change estimate could be provided by summing scores for the latter two stages and subtracting Precontemplation scores.

Validity of the original instrument was assessed by comparing scores to other conceptually related variables (concurrent validity) and through its ability to predict outcomes (predictive validity). The instrument's concurrent validity was supported, at least in part, by its significant negative correlation between Precontemplation and personal assumption of responsibility for abusive behavior and by significant positive correlations between personal assumption of responsibility and both Contemplation and overall Readiness to Change scores (Begun et al., 2003). Additionally, minimization of both physical assault and psychological aggression were negatively correlated at a significant level with Contemplation scores, and the tendency to minimize psychological aggression was negatively correlated with the overall Readiness to Change scores, though this was not true for minimization of physical aggression. Furthermore, scores on self-efficacy for abstaining from verbal or psychological aggression were correlated with Preparation/Action scores, although there was not a significant correlation with this variable and self-efficacy for abstaining from physical aggression.

In general, the scale scores on the original instrument were unrelated to social desirability response bias, as measured on the Beck Index of Depression Revised Impression Management scale (see Begun et al., 2003). Further concurrent validity for the original measure is derived from the observation that self-referred participants, compared to court-ordered individuals, had significantly higher average Contemplation scores and higher overall Readiness to Change scores. However, these two groups did not differ significantly on Precontemplation or Preparation/Action. Finally, it is important to note that no significant or systematic differences were observed in relation to demographic or socioeconomic variables in the sample (e.g., age, education, or income).

In terms of predictive validity, intake scores on the original instrument did predict certain posttreatment outcome variables as indicators of change. Overall Readiness to Change scores predicted self-reported use of negotiation as an alternative to abusive behavior, self-efficacy for abstaining from verbal aggression, and self-efficacy for abstaining from physical aggression. Readiness to change at intake also predicted partner reports of the batterers' posttreatment use of negation as an alternative behavior (Begun et al., 2003). Results of a second study that employed the original instrument also provide some predictive validity evidence. Motivational readiness to change was a strong predictor of the working alliance established in cognitive-behavioral therapy groups for partner violent men (Taft et al., 2004). Motivational readiness was correlated at .43 ($p < .01$) with early client working alliance as well as being correlated (.42) with late client working alliance ($p < .01$). Positive working alliance in treatment for partner violence is, in turn, associated with reductions in abusive behavior (Taft et al., 2004).

Usefulness of the original instrument lay in its ease of application in the field and ease of hand scoring (since the batterer treatment programs involved in its development did not have access to computers for analysis). As a public domain instrument, there is no cost associated with its use, and it requires less than 20 minutes for administration. One limitation of the original Safe At Home instrument was

Table 9.1

INSTRUMENT CONTENTS LISTED BY CFA STANDARDIZED FACTOR LOADING ESTIMATES AND STANDARD ERRORS COMPUTED FOR *N* = 281 AT INTAKE

ITEM CONTENT (ITEM NUMBER)	PRECONTEMPLATION	CONTEMPLATION	PREPARATION/ACTION	MAINTENANCE
It's no big deal if I lose my temper from time to time. (5)	.47 (.08)			
I'll come to groups but I won't talk. (11)	.49 (.07)			
There's nothing wrong with the way I handle situations but I get into trouble for it anyway. (14)	.62 (.08)			
It'll cost me plenty to get help. (18)	.53 (.08)			
If my partner doesn't like the way I act, it's just too bad. (20)	.46 (.09)			
It's my partner's fault that I act this way. (26)	.58 (.07)			
I'd get help if I had more free time. (29)	.41 (.07)			
I need to control my partner.[a]	.47 (.07)			
The last time I lost control of myself, I realized that I have a problem. (1)		.84 (.07)		

It feels good to finally face how I've been messing up my life. (4)	.80 (.07)
I want to do something about my problem with conflict. (9)	.80 (.06)
I want help with my temper. (10)	1.0 (.06)
I need to change before it's too late. (13)	.95 (.06)
I guess I need help with the way I handle things. (17)	.87 (.06)
It's time for me to listen to the people telling me that I need help. (32)	.81 (.06)
Some of what I see and hear about people being abusive seems to apply to me.[a]	.73 (.07)
I'm sick of screwing up my life.[a]	.80 (.06)
I try to listen carefully to others so that I don't get into conflicts anymore. (3)	.33 (.06)

(Continued)

Table 9.1

INSTRUMENT CONTENTS LISTED BY CFA STANDARDIZED FACTOR LOADING ESTIMATES AND STANDARD ERRORS COMPUTED FOR N = 281 AT INTAKE (*Continued*)

ITEM CONTENT (ITEM NUMBER)	PRECONTEMPLATION	CONTEMPLATION	PREPARATION/ACTION	MAINTENANCE
Even though I get angry I know ways to avoid losing control of myself. (15)			.69 (.05)	
When I feel myself getting upset I have ways to keep myself from getting into trouble. (22)			.61 (.06)	
It's becoming more natural for me to be in control of myself. (28)			.60 (.05)	
I have a plan for what to do when I feel upset. (30)			.62 (.05)	
I handle it safely when people get angry with me.[a]			.54 (.06)	
I am actively keeping my cool when my partner(s) and I have conflicts.[a]			.51 (.06)	
I really am different now than I was when conflicts were a problem for me. (16)				.69 (.05)

I try to talk things out with others so that I don't get into conflicts anymore. (24)	.49 (.05)
I know the early cues for when I'm losing control. (33)	.52 (.05)
I do not believe that I will return to my old ways of losing control.[a]	.43 (.07)
I have been successful at keeping myself from going back to my old ways of acting when I have conflicts with my partner.[a]	.69 (.05)
I am sure that I will never return to my old ways of treating my partner(s).[a]	.61 (.06)
Anyone can talk about changing old ways of acting in relationships. I am actually doing it.[a]	.54 (.05)

ITEMS INCLUDED ON REVISED INSTRUMENT, DELETED FROM ANALYSES

I have a problem with losing control of myself. (8)

It's okay that I got into trouble because it means that now I'm getting help. (27)

Sometimes I find that it is still very hard for me to avoid my old ways of treating my partner.[a]

Recent changes that I have made probably won't last.[a]

(Continued)

Table 9.1

INSTRUMENT CONTENTS LISTED BY CFA STANDARDIZED FACTOR LOADING ESTIMATES AND STANDARD ERRORS COMPUTED FOR $N = 281$ AT INTAKE (*Continued*)

ITEMS FROM ORIGINAL INSTRUMENT, DELETED FROM REVISED VERSION

(2): If it was up to me, I wouldn't be here.

(6): In the future, I know I will get some help before I hurt myself or others.

(7): No one "makes" me act the way I do.

(12): I believe that others can learn from my past mistakes.

(19): It's important for me to keep practicing what I've learned about controlling myself.

(25): There may be some things I need to change about myself.

(31): There's nothing wrong with me.

(34): Getting help would be a waste of my time.

(35): I've been thinking a lot about how to change the way I act.

Note. Numbers in parentheses reflect item numbers from original instrument.
[a]These items are new to the revised version.

that an important stage in the change process, Maintenance, did not emerge as easily discernible; it is a stage that has elements resembling Precontemplation (i.e., statements that a problem with IPV does not presently exist) and Action (i.e., statements that the individual is actively engaged in violence prevention efforts). This is not a significant problem when the instrument is being used as an intake assessment tool or for evaluating change between Precontemplation through Action phases of the model. This becomes a notable limitation when an attempt is made to include Maintenance as an aspect of program evaluation or as a means of documenting an individual's change progress beyond the stage of Preparation/Action. In order to address this concern, nine new items reflecting Maintenance-type statements were developed and added to the measure through consultation with batterer treatment providers.

A second concern was the gendered language used in a few of the items, limiting the instrument's utility for same-sex partnerships and women in batterer treatment. Gendered language was addressed by editing item content to become gender neutral.

Finally, efforts to enhance Precontemplation and Action involved adding one item each. Nine items from the original instrument did not contribute to factor loadings; therefore, they were eliminated to maintain brevity of the instrument (Begun et al., 2003). Table 9.1 presents the list of items in the revised measure. The following is a discussion of the revised form of the Safe At Home instrument. Confirmatory factor analysis was employed to assess the new instrument's factor structure, based on the original instrument factors and the presumed existence of a new Maintenance factor.

METHOD

Participants

Data were derived from the Milwaukee Safe At Home project. A total of 286 individuals completed the Revised Safe At Home instrument at intake to one of two batterers' intervention programs: Batterers Anonymous/Beyond Abuse and Task Force on Family Violence. This total represents all individuals at intake who provided consent for their data to be shared with program evaluators (94% of 304 consented). Subsequently, data were eliminated for five women batterers enrolling in treatment.

This is a unique sample of participants, independent of participants involved in analysis of the original instrument.

The remaining 281 individuals ranged in age from 18 to 64 years (M = 33 years, SD = 8.9 years); 79% were referred by court or probation officers (though not all were court ordered), 21% were self-referred or referred by family or friends, 54% were currently involved in a relationship with the same partner toward whom the violence had been directed, and the time lag between the IPV incident and intake averaged 37 weeks or 9 months (range = 1 week to 10 years, SD = 59 weeks, median = 16 weeks or 4 months). The self-reported racial and ethnic distribution of the participants was as follows: 55% African American, 34% White, 8% Latino or Hispanic, and 3% Combined or Other (including Asian or Asian American, and Native American). Participants were not compensated for participation. Information was collected as part of the routine clinical intake assessment, and clients were asked for their informed consent to have these materials coded and analyzed by the research team. The university's institutional review board for the involvement of human subjects approved the project.

Instruments

Demographics and History

Standard demographic data were part of the intake process (e.g., age, race, referral, employment, and education), along with relationship, substance use, criminal justice, and relationship history questions.

The Revised Safe At Home Instrument

This instrument (see Figure 9.1) was administered to participants, during intake and again at program completion. The instrument was developed through modifying content in the original Safe At Home instrument (Begun et al., 2003). The nine items with low factor loadings were eliminated from the original instrument. ("If it was up to me, I wouldn't be here." "In the future, I know I will get some help before I hurt myself or others." "I've been thinking a lot about how to change the way I act." "It's important for me to keep practicing what I've learned about controlling myself." "There may be some things I need to change about myself." "There's nothing wrong with me." "I believe that others can learn from my past mistakes." "Getting help would be a waste of my time." "No one 'makes' me act the way I do.") A total of seven new items

Instructions: Please circle the number that best describes how much you agree or disagree with each statement in the list below.

Num-ber	Item Statement	I strongly agree	I agree	I don't agree or disagree	I disagree	I strongly disagree
1	The last time I lost control of myself, I realized that I have a problem.	1	2	3	4	5
2	I do not believe that I will return to my old ways of losing control.	1	2	3	4	5
3	I try to listen carefully to others so that I don't get into conflicts anymore.	1	2	3	4	5
4	It feels good to finally face how I've been messing up my life.	1	2	3	4	5
5	It's no big deal if I lose my temper from time to time.	1	2	3	4	5
6	I handle it safely when people get angry with me.	1	2	3	4	5
7	Sometimes I find that it is still very hard for me to avoid my old ways of treating my partner.	1	2	3	4	5
8	I have a problem with losing control of myself.	1	2	3	4	5
9	I want to do something about my problem with conflict.	1	2	3	4	5
10	I want help with my temper.	1	2	3	4	5
11	I'll come to groups but I won't talk.	1	2	3	4	5
12	I am actively keeping my cool when my partner(s) and I have conflicts.	1	2	3	4	5
13	I need to change before it's too late.	1	2	3	4	5
14	There's nothing wrong with the way I handle situations but I get into trouble for it anyway.	1	2	3	4	5
15	Even though I get angry I know ways to avoid losing control of myself.	1	2	3	4	5
16	I really am different now than I was when conflicts were a problem for me.	1	2	3	4	5
17	I guess I need help with the way I handle things.	1	2	3	4	5
18	It'll cost me plenty to get help.	1	2	3	4	5
19	I have been successful at keeping myself from going back to my old ways of acting when I have conflicts with my partner.	1	2	3	4	5
20	If my partner doesn't like the way I act, it's just too bad.	1	2	3	4	5
21	Some of what I see and hear about people being abusive seems to apply to me.	1	2	3	4	5
22	When I feel myself getting upset I have ways to keep myself from getting into trouble.	1	2	3	4	5
23	I'm sick of screwing up my life.	1	2	3	4	5
24	I try to talk things out with others so that I don't get into conflicts anymore.	1	2	3	4	5
25	I am sure that I will never return to my old ways of treating my partner(s).	1	2	3	4	5
26	It's my partner's fault that I act this way.	1	2	3	4	5
27	It's okay that I got into trouble because it means that now I'm getting help.	1	2	3	4	5
28	It's becoming more natural for me to be in control of myself.	1	2	3	4	5
29	I'd get help if I had more free time.	1	2	3	4	5
30	I have a plan for what to do when I feel upset.	1	2	3	4	5
31	Recent changes that I have made probably won't last.	1	2	3	4	5
32	It's time for me to listen to the people telling me that I need help.	1	2	3	4	5
33	I know the early cues for when I'm losing control.	1	2	3	4	5
34	I need to control my partner.	1	2	3	4	5
35	Anyone can talk about changing old ways of acting in relationships. I am actually doing it.	1	2	3	4	5

Figure 9.1 Recommended structure for revised instrument.

were constructed through consultation with batterer treatment providers to reflect maintenance-type statements. In addition, one new item to enhance Precontemplation and two to enhance Contemplation were developed.

In addition to factor content issues, the instrument developers identified limitations in the original instrument derived from reliance on some gendered items (Begun et al., 2003). Thus, item content revisions involved rendering the one remaining gendered item gender neutral ("It's my partner's fault that I act this way"). Three of the original items also had some ambiguity that was edited in the new version. For example, "If my partner doesn't like the way I act, she can leave" was intended to imply that "it's just too bad." However, it is possible that batterers might misinterpret the phrase "she can leave," particularly if asserting control over their partner is part of the pattern of abuse. This item was reworded to indicate more clearly the intended meaning. The ambiguity of two other items also relates to who is being controlled. The item "I have a problem with losing control" was intended to refer to a person's self-control, not control exerted over a partner. This item was modified to indicate more clearly the intended meaning. Similarly, the item "Even though I get angry, I know ways to avoid losing control" was modified to indicate self-control. The recommended 5-point scale of degree of agreement with each statement was utilized, where 1 = strongly disagree to 5 = strongly agree (Begun et al., 2003).

RESULTS

Confirmatory Factor Analysis

Confirmatory factor analysis (CFA) was used to evaluate the structure of the revised instrument with respect to a four-factor model of behavior change. The initial tested factor structure was based on (a) an 8-item Precontemplation scale, (b) an 11-item Contemplation scale, (c) a 7-item Action scale, and (d) a 9-item Maintenance scale. These scales were postulated on the basis of recommendations for the original instrument (Begun et al., 2003) and the specific objectives associated with each item revision. The CFAs were performed on sample covariance matrices computed from intake data using maximum likelihood estimation and the Mplus software package (version 2.13; Muthén & Muthén, 2001). Because of the presence of a small amount of missing data, the MISSING option was specified in Mplus, instructing the software to estimate model variances and covariances by means of the EM algorithm, thereby using all available information in the input data set for the analysis.

Fit of the model, with latent variances set to 1.0, was assessed using several goodness-of-fit indices. These included chi-square, root mean square error of approximation (RMSEA; Steiger, 1990), the comparative fit index (CFI; Bentler, 1990), and the Tucker and Lewis index (TLI; Tucker & Lewis, 1973). Following the convention for CFA, all factors were allowed to correlate. For the initial model (model 1), applied to all 35 items, the index values for the CFA (N = 281) were as follows:

χ^2 (model 1) (df = 554) = 1,235.62, p < .001; RMSEA = .066; CFI = .80; and TLI = .79. The RMSEA values of .05 or lower indicate a very close fit of the model to the data, while values of around .08 are considered reasonably good fit (Browne & Cudeck, 1993). For the CFI and TLI, values range between 0 (lack of fit) and 1 (perfect fit), with values near .90 considered satisfactory. Taken together, the fit indices for model 1 suggested that further refinements were needed to improve the overall model fit. Examination of the model 1 output indicated that items 8, 27, 43, and 47 were associated with high to moderate loadings on multiple factors, leading to the conclusion that the items added little discriminatory power to the measure. When these items were dropped and the data re-analyzed in a second CFA, now with 31 items, overall fit improved significantly over model 1: χ^2 (model 2) (df = 428) = 803.57, p < .001; RMSEA = .056; CFI = .87; and TLI = .86. The factor loadings and standard errors for model 2 are presented in Table 9.1 and the interfactor correlations in Table 9.2. The four factors accounted for an estimated 6.7%, 20.9%, 7.4%, and 7.6% of the variance, respectively, for a total of 42.6% of the total variation.

With the exception of the loading for item 3 on the Preparation/Action subscale (.33), the factor loadings were all in the moderate to high range (.40–1.0). Interfactor correlations were also low, with the exception of the .89 correlation between Preparation/Action and Maintenance. This high correlation left open the possibility that the two factors

Table 9.2

FACTOR CORRELATION MATRIX: FOUR-FACTOR MODEL ON N = 281 AT INTAKE

	PRECONTEM-PLATION	CONTEM-PLATION	PREPARATION/ACTION	MAINTE-NANCE
Precontemplation	1.00			
Contemplation	0.08	1.00		
Preparation/Action	0.19*	−0.24*	1.00	
Maintenance	0.26*	0.09	0.89*	1.00

*p < .05.

might be better represented as a single factor in the model. To test this possibility, a third CFA was run in which the correlation between the Preparation/Action and Maintenance factors was constrained to 1.0 and the correlations between these factors and the factors representing Precontemplation and Contemplation were constrained to be equal. The difference in chi-square between this third model and model 2 was significant ($\Delta\chi^2[df = 3] = 60.21$, $p < .01$), indicating an unwanted decrease in fit if Maintenance was not treated as a separate factor.

Scale Reliability

Cronbach's alpha was calculated as a lower-bound estimate of the subscale reliability for each factor represented in the final CFA (model 2) using SPSS for Windows version 11.0.1. For the eight-item Precontemplation subscale, $\alpha = .69$ (Hotelling's $t^2 = 137.71$, $F[7, 244] = 19.2$, $p < .001$) and α level with any one item deleted ranged from .64 to .69. For the nine items making up the Contemplation subscale, $\alpha = .90$ (Hotelling's $t^2 = 381.44$, $F[9, 242] = 41.03$, $p < .001$), and the α level with any one item deleted, ranged from .88 to .91. Reliability of the seven-item Preparation/Action subscale was estimated as $\alpha = .77$ (Hotelling's $t^2 = 53.17$, $F[6, 258] = 8.69$, $p < .001$). The α range after deleting any one item was .71 to .79. Finally, for the new seven-item Maintenance factor, $\alpha = .79$ (Hotelling's $t^2 = 74.38$, $F[6, 257] = 12.16$, $p < .001$), and the α level with any one item deleted, ranged from .75 to .80. The best reliability was achieved by deleting item 41 ("I do not believe that I will return to my old ways of losing control"). This item's loading in the factor analysis also was less when compared to the other items associated with the Maintenance factor.

As a result of these observations, it is recommended that all 35 items be administered but that scale scores be computed using 31 items as follows:

1. Precontemplation scores are the mean of eight items—5, 11, 14, 18, 20, 26, 29, and 48. In this sample, the scale mean was 20.15, and the standard deviation was 4.92.
2. Contemplation scores are the mean of nine items—1, 4, 9, 10, 13, 17, 21, 23, and 32. Item 27 ("It's okay that I got in trouble because it means that now I'm getting help") was associated with a low item-total correlation, with the result that reliabil-

ity improved to .91 by dropping this item. This item's poor performance is probably related to its "double-barreled" nature (a stage of change measurement concern raised by Jefferson, 1991, as cited by Littell & Girvin, 2002). In this sample, the scale mean was 34.45, and the standard deviation was 8.48 for the nine recommended variables.

3. Preparation/Action scores are the mean of seven items—3, 15, 22, 28, 30, 42, and 44. In this sample, the scale mean was 26.23, and the standard deviation was 4.42.

4. Maintenance scores could be computed as the mean of seven items—16, 24, 33, 41, 45, 46, and 49. The sample mean of the scale and standard deviation were 26.40 and 4.48, respectively.

This recommendation is based on the rationale that administration of a 31-item array has not been systematically tested at this time and could conceivably lead to different results and response patterns being elicited from respondents.

Additional Analyses

As a preliminary assessment of concurrent and predictive validity associated with the revised instrument, several additional analyses were conducted. First, analyses were run to examine the relationships between the four scale scores and the variables age, educational level, attendance at first intervention session, and completion of treatment. With the exception of age and Precontemplation, which correlated weakly ($r = .15$, $p = .01$), none of the scale scores correlated significantly with the demographic variables of age or educational level. This is as would be hoped if the instrument is free from demographic bias and was observed in the original instrument (Begun et al., 2003). Binary logistic regression analyses showed that none of the scale scores at intake predicted whether the individual attended the first treatment group session or completed treatment, as would have been hoped if the instrument had this sort of predictive validity.

In a second set of analyses, the scale scores for court-referred versus non-court-referred clients were compared using one-way analysis of variance. The mean Precontemplation scores for 218 court-referred batterers ($M = 20.1$) was not significantly different from scores for 56 non-court-referred clients ($M = 19.9$; $F[1, 273] = .062$, $p > .05$).

Contemplation scores were significantly higher $(F[1, 272] = 11.58, p = .001)$ for the non-court-referred individuals $(M = 35.13)$ compared to court-referred individuals $(M = 31.09)$, as might be expected if the instrument is assessing readiness-to-change factors. The Preparation/Action and Maintenance scores were significantly different between the court-referred and non-court-referred groups but in the opposite direction: court-referred men were higher on Preparation/Action than non-court-referred men $(M = 26.4$ and $M = 24.61$, respectively; $F[1, 274] = 7.61, p < .01)$ and were also higher on Maintenance $(M = 26.59$ and $M = 24.89; F[1, 275] = 6.48, p = .01)$. Given these results, it is not surprising that there was not a significant difference in the overall Readiness to Change score detected since this score is comprised of these components with conflicting results $(M = 37.2$ vs. $M = 39.87; F[1, 267] = 3.65, p > .05)$.

A similar pattern of relationships was observed for Pearson correlations run between the four scale scores and the variables number of weeks since the incident leading to intake, self-reported physical aggression, and self-reported verbal or emotional aggression. Nonsignificant correlations were found between weeks since the incident, Precontemplation scores $(r = .05, p > .05; n = 260)$, and overall Readiness to Change scores $(r = -.066, p > .05; n = 255)$. A weak negative correlation was found between weeks since the incident and Contemplation scores $(r = -.14, p < .05)$ and weak positive correlations between weeks since the incident and scores on the Preparation/Action $(r = .21, p = .001)$ and Maintenance $(r = .17, p < .01)$ scales. Precontemplation, Maintenance, and overall Readiness to Change failed to correlate significantly with self-reported physical aggression (calculated as the sum of physical aggression items on the Duluth questionnaire). Contemplation was significantly correlated to self-reported physical aggression $(r = .43, p < .001)$, and Preparation/Action was negatively correlated $(r = -.38, p < .001)$. Self-reported verbal or emotional aggression was weakly but significantly correlated with Precontemplation scores $(r = .24, p < .05)$, somewhat more strongly correlated with Contemplation scores $(r = .38, p < .001)$, negatively correlated with Preparation/Action scores $(r = -.25, p = .01)$, and not correlated with Maintenance or overall Readiness to Change scores.

The observed pattern of relationships between the scale scores and variables used to validate the scores suggested that the Preparation/Action and Maintenance scales might be affected by a self-presentational bias. To determine if such an interpretation could be supported, a discriminant function analysis was run, predicting self-reported history of domestic violence in relationships (coded as 1 = no history or no current domestic violence relationships reported, 2 = only one violent relationship reported, or 3 = history of more than one domestic violence relationship reported) from the four-scale scores. This analysis resulted in two significant discriminant functions, the data for which are presented in Table 9.3. The classification means and structure coefficients on the first discriminant function ($L^2[5] = 20.30$, $p < .001$) indicated that the group reporting a history of domestically violent relationships scored higher on Contemplation but lower on Preparation/Action and Maintenance than the other groups, with the group reporting no history of domestic violence (including no violence in the relationship for which the referral was made) being lowest on the function and the group reporting a history of more than one such relationship being highest. The second discriminant function ($L^2[3] = 9.97$, $p < .02$) indicated that the groups reporting a history of domestic violence (one or more relationships) scored higher on Precontemplation and Maintenance than the group reporting no history of domestic violence. Together with the analyses presented earlier, these results suggest that the measure may be useful in appropriately discriminating between persons who vary in their readiness to change, but that such decisions may need to be made on the basis of profiles eventually formed across scales.

Table 9.3

DISCRIMINANT FUNCTION STRUCTURE MATRIX AND CLASSIFICATION MEANS

STRUCTURE MATRIX	DF1	DF2
Precontemplation	.10	.53
Contemplation	.80	−.08
Preparation/Action	−.69	−.10
Maintenance	−.41	.49
CLASSIFICATION MEANS		
No history or current domestic violence reported	−.32	−.97
One domestic violence relationship reported	−.12	.06
History of >1 domestic violence relationship reported	.63	−.06

DISCUSSION AND APPLICATIONS FOR PRACTICE

The goal of the current project was to evaluate the appropriateness of revisions to the Safe At Home instrument for assessing batterer readiness to change. The aims in revising the instrument, guided by recommendations associated with the original instrument (Begun et al., 2003), were (a) enhancing the measurement of the Maintenance, Precontemplation, and Contemplation factors; (b) achieving gender neutrality in all item content; and (c) reducing content ambiguity. The numbering of items on the revised instrument was generated here for ease of presentation. In reality, the items on the questionnaires completed by study participants were numbered from 1 to 35 since the new items were inserted sequentially into the spaces left vacant when the old items were dropped. As a result, the revised instrument provides a more randomized sequencing of stage content than it would seem from simply examining Table 9.1.

CFA supported the adequacy of a four-scale interpretation for 31 items of the 35-item Revised Safe At Home instrument, consistent with the full continuum described in the TTM—Precontemplation, Contemplation, Preparation/Action, and Maintenance. Although the chi-square value associated with the 31-item model was significant, the remaining fit indices (RMSEA, CFI, and TLI) were within acceptable ranges, indicating that the modifications had moved the scale in the proper direction. In addition, scale reliability was reasonably good for all four factors at intake. While these results are promising, it is clear that additional work is necessary in order to further improve the measure. Recommendations for scoring the revised instrument include limiting the scoring to 31 of the 35 items, using an equal weighting approach.

Stage categories for readiness in intentionally changing behavior may be represented in one of two ways. The first is a set of mutually exclusive and exhaustive dichotomous variables (i.e., yes-or-no responses to questions about current behavior, future intentions, and past attempts to change). The second is the more subtle approach of creating scales comprised of ordinal stage of change variables (Littell & Girvin, 2002). Prochaska and DiClemente (1998) recommend the latter approach. The Revised Safe At Home instrument, like the original, is based on the ordinal scale approach. It appears to be a useful tool in assessing readiness to change, with potential applications for predesign and postdesign program evaluation. However, it is most useful for programs with a curricular emphasis on anger management and self-control—it is less sensitive to questions of change in other domains of abusive behavior toward intimate partners. This instrument is an improvement over the original instrument in terms of having gender-neutral content that is more appropriate for same-sex partners and for use with either men or women in batterer treatment. Gender neutrality was achieved without loss of instrument integrity compared to the original instrument. The instrument has not yet been tested for validity with women batterers or same-sex partnerships.

Overall, the tentative validity analyses conducted with the revised instrument parallel those described in relation to the more complete analyses permissible with the original instrument. The results of analyses related to the scales and variables, such as voluntary or involuntary intake to batterer treatment and length of time elapsing between an incident of IPV and intake, are complicated in this particular sample. There are many factors that influenced timing of intake for the present sample, only one set of which might reflect motivation and readiness features—for example, periods of incarceration prevent help seeking from community-based agencies, and impending court dates may lead to referrals regardless of readiness status. It is unclear what kind of readiness-to-change distinctions exists in terms of "voluntary" and "nonvoluntary" intake related to court-ordered versus court-referred or court-recommended treatment as well. It is notable that Contemplation and Preparation/Action were correlated with self-reported acts of IPV in the ways that they were. Individuals who are recognizing the problematic nature of their abusive behaviors (higher on Contemplation) are also ready to acknowledge that they are aggressing physically and emotionally against their partner(s). Furthermore, individuals who report that they are taking actions to change their IPV behavior report less physical and emotional aggression than individuals who are lower on Preparation/Action.

Limitations

Like the URICA-DV, this instrument is limited by having been developed and evaluated with men who actually participate in intake to a batterer intervention program. Thus, the instrument is applicable primarily to this treatment-seeking population. Little can be inferred concerning its applicability to the broader population of individuals who engage in IPV. More specifically, there is little known about the responses that would be generated from men who are never arrested, those who are arrested but not referred, or those referred who do not show up for intake. This concern is underscored by the observation that one item loading on Precontemplation actually contains content that is more reflective of Contemplation. This item (29: "I'd get help if I had more free time") may reflect the transitional nature of the sample population—these respondents may no longer consistently endorse only items associated with a pure Precontemplation stage.

Similarly, little is known about the men who have achieved Maintenance, as few are likely to be at this point at intake and the participating treatment programs are not sufficient in duration to ensure movement from Action to Maintenance stages. Furthermore, in the present study, the sample of 79 program completers was not sufficient to permit reassessment of the factor structure given the number of parameters to be estimated (31 loadings, 31 error variances, and 6 correlations). In theory, the dimensionality of responses to Maintenance items should persist regardless of sample type (Levesque et al., 2000, cite Thurstone, 1947, concerning this assumption of factorial invariance). However, the result of assessing the instrument with this more restricted sample is a compression of the range and distribution of observed scores as well as limits on the range of cluster types that emerge.

Future Directions

Future research should address the continuing need for tests of this instrument with individuals likely to be functioning at both the earliest and the latest phases of the change cycle. More specifically, we need to understand the difference in responding by individuals prior to intake into a treatment program (e.g., at arrest, time of referral, or case disposition), as the Precontemplation response patterns seen here may actually reflect a transition between stages since the individuals did make and attend an intake appointment. Similarly, the Action and Maintenance response patterns seen here may not reflect those of individuals who have completed a treatment program and extended their successful change efforts into a follow-up period.

In addition, future research efforts should be directed toward developing batterer typologies that include readiness-to-change variables. Study designs should include latent profile analysis along with data collection on measures and outcome variables that are useful in validating such typologies. Such research would help address questions concerning

the appropriateness of applying the stages-of-change model to the problem of IPV, and help develop empirically supported protocols for effectively matching different types of intervention with specific individuals
by including readiness-to-change variables.

ACKNOWLEDGMENTS

This work and related research have been supported by the Centers for Disease
Control and Prevention grant #U50/CCU511248–01 to the Milwaukee Safe At Home
collaboration between the Milwaukee Women's Center, Sojourner Truth House, Asha
Family Services, and the University of Wisconsin–Milwaukee School of Social Welfare/
Center for Addiction and Behavioral Health Research and a Jane Bradley Pettit Founda-
tion grant to Milwaukee's Task Force on Family Violence.

REFERENCES

Begun, A. L., Murphy, C., Bolt, D., Weinstein, B., Strodthoff, T., Short, L., et al. (2003).
Characteristics of the Safe At Home instrument for assessing readiness to change
intimate partner violence. *Research on Social Work Practice, 13,* 80–107.

Begun, A. L., Shelley, G., Strodthoff, T., & Short, L. (2001). Adopting a stages of change
approach in intervention with individuals who are violent with their intimate partners. *Journal of Aggression, Maltreatment and Trauma, 5,* 105–127.

Bentler, P. M. (1990). Comparative fit indices in structural models. *Psychological Bulletin, 107,* 238–246.

Browne, M. W., & Cudeck, R. (1993). Alternative ways of assessing model fit. In K. A.
Bollen & J. S. Long (Eds.), *Testing structural equation models* (pp. 136–162). Newbury Park, CA: Sage.

Connors, G. J., Donovan, D. M., & DiClemente, C. C. (2001). *Substance abuse treatment and the stages of change: Selecting and planning interventions.* New York: Guilford Press.

Daniels, W., & Murphy, C. (1997). Stages and processes of change in batterers' treatment. *Cognitive and Behavioral Practice, 4,* 123–145.

DiClemente, C. C., Prochaska, J. O., Fairhurst, S. K., Velicer, W. F., Velasquez, M. M., &
Rossi, J. S. (1991). The process of smoking cessation: An analysis of precontempla-
tion, contemplation, and preparation stages of change. *Journal of Consulting and
Clinical Psychology, 59,* 295–304.

Heather, N., Rollnick, S., & Bell, A. (1993). Predictive validity of the readiness to change
questionnaire. *Addiction, 88,* 1667–1677.

Holtzworth-Munroe, A., & Stuart, G. L. (1994). Typologies of male batterers: Three
subtypes and differences among them. *Psychological Bulletin, 116,* 476–497.

Levesque, D. A., Gelles, R. J., & Velicer, W. F. (2000). Development and validation of
a stages of change measure for men in batterer treatment. *Cognitive Therapy and
Research, 24,* 175–200.

Littell, J. H., & Girvin, H. (2002). Stages of change: A critique. *Behavior Modification, 26,* 223–273.

Martin, J., Prupas, L., & Sugarman, J. (1998). Test interpretation as the social-cognitive construction of therapeutic change. In J. W. Lichtenberg & R. K. Goodyear (Eds.), *Scientist-practitioner perspectives on test interpretation* (pp. 132–150). Boston: Allyn and Bacon.

Muthén, L. K., & Muthén, B. O. (2001). *Mplus user's guide* (2nd ed.). Los Angeles: Muthén & Muthén.

Petrocelli, J. V. (2002). Processes and stages of change: Counseling with the transtheoretical model of change. *Journal of Counseling and Development, 80,* 22–30.

Prochaska, J. O., & DiClemente, C. C. (1982). Transtheoretical therapy: Toward a more integrative model of change. *Psychotherapy: Theory, Research and Practice, 19,* 276–288.

Prochaska, J. O., & DiClemente, C. C. (1983). Stages and process of self-change of smoking: Toward an integrative model of change. *Journal of Consulting and Clinical Psychology, 51,* 390–395.

Prochaska, J. O., & DiClemente, C. C. (1984). *The transtheoretical approach: Crossing the traditional boundaries of therapy.* Malabar, FL: Krieger.

Prochaska, J. O., & DiClemente, C. C. (1992). Stages of change in the modification of problem behaviors. In M. Herson, R. M. Eisler, & P. M. Miller (Eds.), *Progress in behavior modification* (Vol. 28, pp. 183–218). Sycamore, IL: Sycamore Publishing.

Prochaska, J. O., & DiClemente, C. C. (1998). Comments, criteria, and creating better models: In response to Davidson. In W. R. Miller & N. Heather (Eds.), *Treating addictive behaviors* (2nd ed., pp. 39–45). New York: Plenum Press.

Prochaska, J. O., DiClemente, C. C., & Norcross, J. C. (1992). In search of how people change: Applications to addictive behaviors. *American Psychologist, 47,* 1102–1114.

Prochaska, J. O., DiClemente, C. C., Velicer, W. F., & Rossi, J. S. (1993). Standardized, individualized, interactive, and personalized self-help programs for smoking cessation. *Health Psychology, 13,* 39–46.

Prochaska, J. O., & Norcross, J. C. (2001). Stages of change. *Psychotherapy, 38,* 443–448.

Prochaska, J. O., & Velicer, W. F. (1997). Misinterpretations and misapplications of the transtheoretical model. *American Journal of Health Promotion, 12,* 11–12.

Prochaska, J. O., Velicer, W. F., Rossi, J. S., Goldstein, M. G., Marcus, B. H., Rakowski, W., et al. (1994). Stages of change and decisional balance for 12 problem behaviors. *Health Psychology, 13,* 39–46.

Steiger, J. H. (1990). Structural model evaluation and modification: An interval estimation approach. *Multivariate Behavioral Research, 25,* 173–180.

Sutton, S. (1996). Can "stages of change" provide guidance in the treatment of addictions? A critical examination of Prochaska and DiClemente's model. In G. Edwards & C. Dare (Eds.), *Psychotherapy, psychological treatments and the addictions* (pp. 189–205). Cambridge, UK: Cambridge University Press.

Taft, C. T., Murphy, C. M., Musser, P. H., & Remington, N. A. (2004). Personality, interpersonal, and motivational predictors of the working alliance in group cognitive-behavioral therapy for partner violent men. *Journal of Consulting and Clinical Psychology, 72,* 349–354.

Thurstone, L. L. (1947). *Multiple factor analysis.* Chicago: University of Chicago Press.
Tucker, L. R., & Lewis, C. (1973). A reliability coefficient for maximum likelihood factor analysis. *Psychometrika, 38,* 1–10.
Weinstein, N. D., Rothman, A. J., & Sutton, S. R. (1998). Stage theories of health behavior: Conceptual and methodological issues. *Health Psychology, 17,* 290–299.

Working With Victims

10

A Comparison of Women Versus Men Charged With Intimate Partner Violence: General Risk Factors, Attitudes Regarding Using Violence, and Readiness to Change

CATHERINE A. SIMMONS, PETER LEHMANN, AND NORMAN COBB

The increasing number of women arrested for charges related to intimate partner violence (IPV) presents challenges to professionals working in the domestic violence treatment arena. It is speculated that men and women IPV arrestees differ in their reasons for using violence, as well as in their overall risk for using violence in the future. Some have suggested that many, if not most, of the women arrested for IPV are victims of abuse who may have been acting in self-defense and are therefore at lower risk for recidivism (e.g., Hamberger & Potente, 1994; Miller, 2001; Saunders, 1995). These reasons and risk are different from male IPV offenders whose violence has been associated with power and control issues (Dobash & Dobash, 1979) or concerns about abandonment (Dutton, 1999) and are therefore at a higher risk for recidivism. Although a growing body of research is developing tangible information about women arrested for partner violence and how they differ from men arrested for partner violence (e.g., Bible, Dasgupta, & Osthoff, 2002; Carney & Buttell, 2005; Dasgupta, Osthoff, & Bible, 2002, 2003; Frieze & McHugh, 2005; Hamberger, 2005; McHugh & Frieze, 2005), a great deal is yet to be explored concerning this population. From this increased interest in the professional literature, tangible information about women's use of partner violence and how it is different from and similar to men's use of partner violence is helping to build a better understanding about the overarching problem of family violence. The current descriptive study explores topics related to general risk factors, justification for using violence, and readiness to change in a sample of women enrolled in a domestic violence diversion program and compares these findings to a sample of men enrolled in the same program.

LITERATURE REVIEW

In recent years the number of women arrested in the United States has risen. Of note is the 46.2% increase of women arrested for aggravated assaults between 1991 and 2000 (Federal Bureau of Investigation, 2001). Women's use of IPV has also increased, with women representing 15% of all domestic violence arrests in the United States (Rennison, 2002). The increase may be the result of mandatory pro-arrest laws designed to protect women (Mignon & Holmes, 1995; Victim Services Agency, 1989). For many in the domestic violence field, however, the increase in female arrests has been unexpected (Martin, 1997; Saunders, 1995; State of California, 1999), as it is contrary to the common perception that women are not typically violent aggressors (Pearson, 1997).

From the increase of female IPV-related arrests and the relative absence of understanding about the phenomenon, a sudden increase of theoretical and empirical investigation into this topic has occurred. For example, although relatively few articles were published on women IPV aggressors before 2002, multiple special editions of domestic violence and criminal justice journals have been published since that time (e.g., Bible et al., 2002; Carney & Buttell, 2005; Dasgupta et al., 2002, 2003; Frieze & McHugh, 2005; Hamberger, 2005; McHugh & Frieze, 2005). Of particular interest to the current work are findings that women IPV arrestees (a) have lower risk factors than men IPV arrestees (Henning & Feder, 2004), and (b) are at similar stages in their readiness to change as men IPV arrestees (Babcock, Canady, Senior, & Eckhardt, 2005). From these works, questions remain regarding the attitudes of these women toward when using violence is justified and how this relates to risk for recidivism.

Risk Factors

A few recent manuscripts have addressed the relative risk factors presented by women IPV arrestees. In their study of 2,254 men and 281 women arrested for assaulting their partner, Henning, Jones, and Holdford (2003) found that men were more likely than women to have prior arrests on record and to have a substance abuse problem, whereas women were more likely to have personality dysfunction and/or a mood disorder. In a similar work, Henning and Feder (2004) compared 20 risk factors for recidivism of 5,578 men and 1,126 women IPV offenders using the risk measures Spousal Assault Risk Assessment (SARA), the Violence Risk Appraisal Guide (VRAG), and the Danger Assessment Scale (DAS). In this study, men IPV offenders scored higher than women IPV offenders on 13 of the 20 assessed items including escalation in conflict frequency or severity, threats to kill victim or self, victims rating of risk or threat, ending of relationship or ongoing conflict, severity of prior physical assaults, extrafamilial violence, nonviolent arrests, violations of protection orders, substance abuse, antisocial peer group, access to a gun, and involvement of children in domestic violence (Henning & Feder, 2004). Women scored higher than men on 3 of the 20 items, however, including the severity of offense index, unemployment or employment problems, and younger age (Henning & Feder, 2004). Also, the two groups scored similarly on four of the risk factor items, including severity of psychological abuse, unmarried, family of origin violence, and arrests before age 16 (Henning & Feder, 2004). Likewise, victims of 41.8% of the men arrestees and 24.4% of the women arrestees felt the offender was a serious threat (Henning & Feder, 2004). What is interesting about these findings is that although men arrested for partner assault appear to present the greater threat compared to women arrested for partner assault, women still appear to present a threat. Therefore it is important to understand more about situations when they believe it is acceptable to use violence against their partner.

ATTITUDES TOWARD USING VIOLENCE

In addition to the increase in risk factor research, a number of articles have been published addressing the reasons women use violence in their intimate relationship. Clinical studies based on shelter data, hospital records, police reports, homicide data, and victimization surveys repeatedly find that women are disproportionately the users of domestic violence victim services and when they use violence, they do so while "fighting back" (e.g., Cascardi & Vivian, 1995; Hamberger & Potente, 1994; McMahon & Pence, 2003; Tjaden & Theonnes, 2000). From these works, it has been speculated that the majority of women arrested for domestic violence are acting in self-defense; therefore their use of violence is justified (e.g., Hamberger & Potente, 1994; Saunders, 1995). There is growing consensus, however, that, at least in some instances, women are not simply fighting back (e.g., Busch & Rosenberg, 2004; Dutton, Nicholls, & Spidel, 2005; McNeely, Cook, & Torres, 2001; Swan & Snow, 2002). For this reason it is important to examine the spectrum of reasons for using violence presented by this group of women.

Attributions of blame and their levels of socially desirable responding have been explored to explain women IPV arrestees' reasons for using violence. In their study of 52 women referred to a treatment agency, Babcock, Miller, and Siard (2003) differentiated women participants into two groups based on whether they were considered generally violent (i.e., used instrumental violence to exert control over their partner) or partner-only violent (i.e., used reactive violence to partner threat). In their work, there was no significant difference between the two groups in their motivation for using violence, with self-defense (28.3%) being the most common response and anger or frustration (20%) also being highly common (Babcock et al., 2003). In assessing attributions of blame, minimization, denial, and socially desirable responding, Henning, Jones, and Holdford (2005) compared 1,267 men and 159 women convicted of IPV-related charges. Their findings suggest that both men and women attribute greater blame to their spouse or partner than they take for themselves, engage in socially desirable responding, and either deny the incident or minimize the severity of the offense (Henning et al., 2005). Even the title of their article "I didn't do it but if I did I had a good reason" implies that their participants felt highly justified in using violence against their partner (Henning et al., 2005).

Even though findings from previous studies of women's reasons for using violence suggest that women feel justified when they do so, no work specifically addresses women's attitudes regarding when it is acceptable to use violence against their partner. Because the primary mission of most domestic violence treatment programs is to prevent future incidents of domestic violence from occurring (Holtzworth-Munroe & Stuart, 1994), it is important to explore these attitudes. Based on findings that women generally use violence in self-defense, minimize their use of violence, and tend to respond in a socially desirable manner, understanding how this group determines when using violence is justified can help treatment workers by providing insight that can then be used to guide treatment options and safety planning.

Readiness to Change Behavior

In addition to general risk factors and attitude toward using violence, women IPV arrestees' readiness to change their behavior is an important component of treatment evaluation that needs additional exploration. To date, only one published study examines this group's readiness to change the behaviors that led to their using violence and subsequent arrest. In their study of 52 women and 68 men in a domestic violence treatment program, Babcock and colleagues (2005) used the University of Rhode Island Change Assessment–Domestic Violence (URICA-DV) to explore how the transtheoretical model (TTM; Prochaska, DiClemente, & Norcross, 1992) of behavior change applies to women. The TTM suggests that as people change their behavior, they move through the following five stages:

1. Precontemplative—the person has no intention of changing behavior.
2. Contemplative—the person becomes aware that a problem exists and is interested in making a change, but has not yet made a commitment to do so.
3. Preparation—the person intends to change behavior immediately and is making decisions regarding what course of action to take to make these changes.
4. Action—the person is actively modifying or changing behavior.
5. Maintenance—the person has successfully changed behavior and is actively working to prevent relapse to old behaviors (Prochaska, 1995).

ᐧ Although the order of the stages are invariant, individuals spiral through them at varying rates, often returning to an earlier stage then progressing to the next stage numerous times before actual behavior change occurs. Data investigating the TTM with various populations suggest that offering stage-matched intervention has a greater effect than one-size-fits-all types of programs (Levesque, Gelles, & Velicer, 2000). For example, individuals in the contemplative stage might start treatment by attending orientation and information sessions, whereas individuals in the preparation or action stage might benefit from going directly into traditional mixed groups. Indeed, the TTM-based URICA-DV has successfully been used with the male batterer population for just such reasons (e.g., Eckhardt, Babcock, & Homack, 2004; Levesque et al., 2000). Although Babcock and colleagues (2005) found the TTM to be relevant for both men and women IPV offenders and that both groups present to treatment programs at similar stages of readiness for change, their work has yet to be replicated with a population of women IPV arrestees.

Purpose of the Current Study

Even though some findings indicate that women IPV arrestees are at lower risk for recidivism than men IPV arrestees (Henning & Feder, 2004) and both women and men IPV arrestees present to domestic violence treatment programs at similar stages in their readiness to change (Babcock et al., 2005), the evidence related to these topics is preliminary and not yet replicated. Also, studies that examine the attitudes of women IPV arrestees about when using violence is acceptable have not been published. Therefore, in an effort to gain a better understanding of this population, the current study addresses the following questions:

1. What risk factors do women IPV arrestees endorse?
2. What attitudes do women have toward when it is acceptable to use violence in their relationship?
3. What stage of change do women IPV offenders endorse when they present to treatment?
4. What (if any) are the differences between men and women IPV arrestees in these three areas?

METHODS

Participants

Participants in this study were 78 female court-ordered clients of a domestic violence diversion program located in a large north Texas city who were seen between 1999 and 2003. Inclusion in this particular domestic violence diversion program predicates on the referring incident being the individual's first domestic violence arrest and their willingness to both admit guilt and participate in a 1-year treatment program. A comparison sample of 78 men was selected from the 646 male court-ordered clients of the same program. Participants were matched on ethnicity (50% White, 25% African American, 20% Hispanic, 2.5% Asian, and 2.5% other), age (mean age = 30.44 years), and income (mean income between $20,000 and $29,999 a year) to control for ethnic, age, and income variables related to domestic violence. Also, comparison of the police reports, victim statements, and offender statements indicated the two groups are similar in the type of incident that brought them to treatment (83% of the women and 83% of the men were the only aggressors, 2% of the women and 0% of the men were involved in mutual incidents where both they and their partner were arrested, and 15% of the women and 17% of the men were involved in mutual incidents where their intimate partner was not arrested). A total of 4 of the women and 12 of the men reported their victim defended themselves during the incident. Finally, consent to release information forms were signed by all of the participants before selection for this study.

Measurement Instruments

It is important to note that none of the currently available assessment instruments measuring the topics explored in this study have tested validity with women arrested on IPV-related charges. Therefore, selecting appropriate instruments for this project was predicated on the only knowledge available—that of the male batterer population. Because of this limitation, four different instruments were selected that look at different aspects of attitudes and risk factors associated with domestic violence recidivism. Despite the limitations found in selecting measurement instruments, the following four were selected because of their versatility: (a) Spousal Assault Risk Assessment (SARA), (b) Propensity to Abuse Scale (PAS), (c) Abusive Attitudes Toward Marriage (AAM), and (d) the University of Rhode Island Change Assessment–Domestic Violence (URICA-DV). Of the instruments selected, two had previously been used with the female IPV arrestee population: the SARA (Henning & Feder, 2004) and the URICA-DV (Babcock et al., 2005). To enhance comparability of the two groups, thereby adding to the validity of the current work, coefficient alpha scores for both women and men were calculated for the scale-based instruments: the PAS, the AAM, and the URICA-DV.

Because the SARA is a checklist and not a scale, reliability assessment was not conducted for this instrument. By looking at this topic from three perspectives, using two instruments previously used with this population, and comparing answer pattern reliability within the two samples, greater generalizability and validity may be ascertained even though caution is still noted.

Spousal Assault Risk Assessment

The Spousal Assault Risk Assessment (SARA) is a 20-item clinician-completed paper–pencil checklist that is designed to assess risk factors in individuals being treated for spousal assault (Kropp & Hart, 2000). Using six samples of adult male offenders (N = 2,681), convergent and discriminant validity was determined with respect to other risk for violent criminal behavior (Kropp & Hart, 2000). The SARA is grouped into five areas including criminal history, psychosocial adjustment, spouse abuse history, current offense history, and other. Predictive variables include spousal assault, criminal history, psychosocial adjustment, and alleged most recent offense (Kropp, Hart, Webster, & Eaves, 1999). Designed to be completed by the clinician after all other psychosocial and criminal history has been collected, the SARA describes individual items that are critical to risk for domestic violence (Kropp et al., 1999).

Propensity for Abusiveness Scale

The Propensity for Abusiveness Scale (PAS) is a 29-item, 5-subscale self-report perpetrator profile measure that assesses batterers' predisposition to be abusive in their relationships (Dutton, Landolt, Starzomski, & Bodnarchuk, 2001). The five subscales include identity diffusion and primitive defenses, presence of trauma symptoms, parental rejection, attachment style, and anger. Answers to each item per subscale are scored using different versions of a Likert scale, which are then added into one sum score. Risk may also be determined by scoring individual subscale scores. Using the answers provided by 144 men in treatment for partner abuse and 44 demographically matched controls, the PAS correlated significantly with partner reports of abusiveness and correctly classified men 82.2% of the time (Dutton, 1995). Since the original validation study, the PAS has also been validated using male outpatients, homosexual males, male college students, and a group of male spousal assaulters (Dutton et al., 2001). Both the PAS total score and individual subscale scores are used to assess risk (Dutton, 1995). Coefficient alpha scores for the data sets used in the current study were similar, indicating comparable response patterns (.9157 women; .8927 men).

Attitudes About Marriage Index

The Attitudes About Marriage index (AAM) is a 25-item scale that assesses approval of aggression toward one's spouse in specific circumstances (Margolin & Foo, 1992, as cited in Garcia-O'Hearn & Margolin, 2000). The scale includes three labels (justifiable, somewhat justifiable, and not justifiable), anchored on a 7-point Likert scale. Respondent answers are totaled into one sum score. Using the answers provided by 47 men recruited from temporary employment agencies, predictive validity was correlated with both attitudes toward aggression and history of exposure to domestic violence (Garcia-O'Hearn & Margolin, 2000). The original version of the AAM uses gender-specific language. For example, "a husband slaps or hits his wife if . . . she. . . ." For the current study, the language was altered for the female participants to read "a wife slaps or hits her husband if . . . he. . . ." The original version was used for the comparison group of men. Coefficient alpha scores for the data sets used in the current study were similar indicating comparable response patterns (.9042 women; .9238 men).

University of Rhode Island Change Assessment–Domestic Violence (URICA-DV)

Based on the transtheoretical model of change, the University of Rhode Island Change Assessment–Domestic Violence (URICA-DV) is a 20-item 4-dimensional stage instrument measuring a profile of scores along a continuum to determine respondent's attitudes about being ready to end their violence (Levesque et al., 2000). Respondents indicate the extent to which they agree to each of the items on a 5-point Likert scale (1 = strongly disagree to 5 = strongly agree). The items are then summed into a single score by adding each of the four subscales. Using the responses of 250 batterers in treatment at two Rhode Island agencies, the authors found preliminary construct validity of the URICA-DV and coefficient alphas ranging from .68 for Maintenance scale to .81 for Action scale. Predictor variables include attitudes toward change (Levesque et al., 2000). Although the Babcock et al. (2005) study is the only work published to date using the URICA-DV with women IPV offenders, TTM-based

URICA(s) have been successfully applied to a number of other female populations including (a) battered women living in a shelter (Schifrin, 2004), (b) women in treatment for eating disorders (Hasler, Delsignore, & Milos, 2004), and (c) women in substance abuse treatment (El-Bassel, Schilling, & Ivanoff, 1998). Coefficient alpha scores for the data sets used in the current study were similar indicating comparable response patterns (total score: .7984 women, .7974 men; precontemplative: .4065 women, .4513 men; contemplative: .7854 women, .7370 men; action: .8408 women, .7868 men; maintenance: .7519 women, .8073 men).

Data Analysis

In response to the first research question, *what risk factors do women IPV arrestees endorse,* women participant profile means and percentages were calculated for the risk factors endorsed on the SARA, the PAS, and the respective PAS subscales (Table 10.1). Results of the SARA indicated that 89.7% (70) of the women participants indicate at least 1 risk factor and 64.1% (50) indicate 2 or more risk factors. By excluding the two items that women are more likely than men to endorse, namely child present and current unemployment, findings decreased to 57.2% (40) and 32.0% (25), respectively. Results of the propensity to abuse scale (PAS) showed some of the women in the study were at high risk for continued use of intimate partner violence, whereas others were not [total score $M = 55.8$, $SD = 18.36$; 51.2% (40) score > 50; 39.7% (31) score > 60; 19.2% (15) score > 70]. Of note is the relatively high PAS standard deviation and extreme differential in percentages noted in both the SARA and the PAS indicating heterogeneity of responses within the study participants.

In response to the second research question, *what attitudes do women have toward when it is acceptable to use violence in their relationship,* descriptive statistics were calculated for the total score and for each question (see Tables 10.1 and 10.2). Descriptive statistics for women's responses to the Attitudes About Marriage (AAM) scale resemble those found in the work of Garcia-O'Hearn and Margolin (2000) that addresses validity with a male IPV offender sample. The women participants' scores were congruent with a moderate to high feeling of justifiability for their use of violence as measured by the Attitudes About Marriage index (AAM) [$M = 19.51$; $SD = 19.37$; 35.8% (28) score > 20; 26.9% (21) score > 30]. The incidents where women felt most justified by their use of violence included the following: (a) he comes at her with

Table 10.1

GENDER COMPARISONS FOR VIOLENCE SCALES

	MEAN MALES	SD MALE	MEAN FEMALE	SD FEMALE	2-WAY t TEST	p FOR t TEST
SARA	2.85	2.30	3.70	2.06	-2.401	.018*
AAM	11.24	17.23	19.51	19.37	-2.789	.006*
PAS	49.04	14.58	55.08	18.37	-2.251	.026*
PAS anger subscale	5.69	2.63	5.44	2.53	.613	ns
PAS identity diffusion subscale	10.72	4.00	11.32	4.21	-.904	ns
PAS attachment subscale	5.81	2.81	6.96	3.29	-2.313	.022*
PAS trauma symptom subscale	3.37	3.65	4.61	3.89	-2.185	.030*
PAS paternal warmth and rejection subscale	10.41	6.14	11.61	8.84	-1.078	ns
PAS maternal warmth and rejection subscale	11.94	4.54	13.27	6.55	-2.070	.040*
URICA-DV precontemplation	6.34	2.36	5.95	1.94	1.126	ns

(*Continued*)

GENDER COMPARISONS FOR VIOLENCE SCALES (*Continued*)

	MEAN MALES	SD MALE	MEAN FEMALE	SD FEMALE	2-WAY *t* TEST	*p* FOR *t* TEST
URICA-DV contemplation	18.57	4.75	18.03	5.09	.678	*ns*
URICA-DV action	21.17	4.31	19.90	5.10	1.670	*ns*
URICA-DV maintenance	12.71	5.31	10.71	4.41	2.522	.013*

Note. SARA = Spousal Assault Risk Assessment (Kropp & Hart, 2000); AAM = Attitudes About Marriage Index (Margolin & Foo, 1992, as cited in Garcia-O'Hearn & Margolin, 2000); PAS = Propensity for Abusiveness Scale (Dutton, 1995); URICA-DV = University of Rhode Island Change Assessment–Domestic Violence (Levesque, Gelles, & Velicer, 2000).
*   *p* < .05.

Table 10.1

Table 10.2

WOMEN PARTICIPANTS' RESPONSES ON THE ATTITUDES ABOUT MARRIAGE (*N* = 78)

A WIFE SLAPS OR HITS HER HUSBAND IF . . .	MEAN (*SD*) JUSTIFICATION RATING	PERCENT ENDORSEMENT		
		UNJUSTIFIABLE (0)	SOMEWHAT JUSTIFIABLE (1–4)	JUSTIFIABLE (5–6)
He comes at her with a knife	3.01 (2.61)	33.8%	24.7%	41.5%
He physically abuses their child	3.09 (2.65)	33.8%	22.1%	44.1%
In an argument, he hits her first	2.18 (2.41)	41.5%	29.9%	28.6%
She catches him in bed with another woman	1.90 (2.35)	50.6%	27.3%	22.1%
She learns that he is having an affair	1.44 (2.02)	54.5%	32.5%	13.0%
He terrorizes and abuses her pet	1.08 (1.72)	62.3%	31.1%	6.5%
He uncontrollably smashes her belongings	.66 (1.40)	74.0%	27.3%	2.6%
He screams hysterically	.26 (.70)	83.1%	16.9%	0.0%
At a party he flirts with another woman in front of her and her friends	.48 (1.14)	77.9%	20.8%	1.3%

(*Continued*)

Table 10.2

WOMEN PARTICIPANTS' RESPONSES ON THE ATTITUDES ABOUT MARRIAGE (*N* = 78) (*Continued*)

A WIFE SLAPS OR HITS HER HUSBAND IF . . .	MEAN (*SD*) JUSTIFICATION RATING	PERCENT ENDORSEMENT		
		UNJUSTIFIABLE (0)	SOMEWHAT JUSTIFIABLE (1–4)	JUSTIFIABLE (5–6)
He threatens verbally to get his gun	.95 (1.72)	66.2%	26.0%	7.8%
He is drunk, belligerent, and acting crazy	.68 (1.33)	72.7%	24.7%	2.6%
He calls her "stupid" over and over again	.43 (1.03)	79.2%	20.8%	0.0%
He calls her mother nasty names all the time	.45 (1.12)	79.2%	19.5%	1.3%
She is drunk and out of control	.66 (1.50)	76.6%	16.9%	6.5%
He accuses her of being an incompetent and insensitive human being	.32 (.83)	83.1%	16.9%	0.0%
He makes her look like a fool in front of her family and friends	.39 (.93)	81.8%	18.2%	0.0%
She overhears him talking on the phone with his ex-girlfriend	.23 (.58)	83.1%	16.9%	0.0%

(Continued)

Table 10.2

WOMEN PARTICIPANTS' RESPONSES ON THE ATTITUDES ABOUT MARRIAGE (*N* = 78) (*Continued*)

A WIFE SLAPS OR HITS HER HUSBAND IF . . .	MEAN (*SD*) JUSTIFICATION RATING	PERCENT ENDORSEMENT		
		UNJUSTIFIABLE (0)	SOMEWHAT JUSTIFIABLE (1–4)	JUSTIFIABLE (5–6)
He refuses to let her enroll in college courses	.17 (.52)	88.3%	11.7%	0.0%
She is upset about losing her job	.16 (.61)	92.2%	7.8%	0.0%
He insults her best friend	.14 (.53)	90.9%	9.1%	0.0%
He refuses to have sex with her	.19 (.63)	88.3%	11.7%	0.0%
He refuses to let her go out for an evening with her friends	.12 (.46)	92.2%	7.8%	0.0%
She is angry because she got a speeding ticket	.10 (.45)	93.5%	6.5%	0.0%
He tells her he should have divorced her a long time ago	.21 (.64)	87.0%	13.0%	0.0%
He threatens to move out in the middle of an argument	.17 (.52)	88.3%	11.7%	0.0%

Note. Questions adapted from Margolin and Foo (1992), as cited in Garcia-O'Hearn and Margolin (2000).

a knife [M = 3.01; SD = 2.61; unjustified = 33.8%, somewhat justified = 24.7%, justified = 41.5%]; (b) he physically abuses their child [M = 3.09; SD = 2.65; unjustified = 33.8%, somewhat justified = 22.1%, justified = 44.1%]; (c) in an argument, he hits her first [M = 2.18; SD = 2.41; unjustified = 41.5%, somewhat justified = 29.9%, justified = 28.6%]; (d) she catches him in bed with another woman [M = 1.90; SD = 2.35; unjustified = 50.6%, somewhat justified = 27.3%, justified = 22.1%]; (e) she learns that he is having an affair [M = 1.44; SD = 2.02; unjustified = 54.5%, somewhat justified = 32.5%, justified = 13.0%]; (f) he terrorizes and abuses her pet [M = 1.08; SD = 1.72; unjustified = 62.3%, somewhat justified = 31.1%, justified = 6.5%]. Like the SARA and the PAS, the large standard deviation found in the AAM results indicates heterogeneity of responses within the participants of this study.

In response to the third research question, *what stage of change do women IPV offenders endorse when they present to treatment*, URICA-DV raw-score means were calculated and interpreted into the various stages of change (see Table 10.1). Participant responses indicate URICA-DV profiles representative of individuals in the contemplative and action stage in their readiness to change (precontemplative M = 5.95, SD = 1.94, t = 40; contemplation M = 18.03, SD = 5.09, t = 50; action M = 19.90, SD = 5.10, t = 45; maintenance M = 10.71, SD = 4.41, t = 40).

In response to the fourth research question, *what (if any) are the differences between men and women IPV arrestees on these three areas*, comparisons were made between men and women participants on both the overall scores and the individual subscales of each instrument (see Table 10.1). Results of the SARA showed a significant difference between men and women participants in 3 of the 12 items assessed by the SARA. The women participants were more likely to have prior arrests (t = –2.226, df = 152, p > .05) and be unemployed (t = –2.610, df = 152, p > .01), whereas male respondents were more likely to have a restraining order against them at the time of their arrest (t = 2.003, df = 152, p > .05). Significance, however, is not met in the additional nine SARA items: (a) prior nondomestic violence convictions, (b) prior domestic violence treatment, (c) prior drug or alcohol treatment, (d) history of domestic violence-related restraining orders, (e) history of violation(s) of domestic violence restraining orders, (f) evidence of object used as weapon in commission of a crime, (g) children present during the domestic violence incident, (h) has victim separated from defendant within the last 8 months, and (i) was defendant under any form of community supervision (probation, etc.) at the time of the offense.

Female participants demonstrated the presence of abusive personality characteristics as measured by the total score on the PAS (men M = 49.04, men SD = 14.58, women M = 55.08, women SD = 18.37; t = -2.254, df = 144.366, p > .05). Also, three of the six PAS subscales were higher for women participants than for men participants including attachment subscale (men M = 5.81, men SD = 2.81, women M = 6.96, women SD = 3.29; t = -2.313, df = 147.99, p > .05), the trauma symptom subscale (men M = 3.25, men SD = 3.65, women M = 4.61, women SD = 3.89; t = -2,185, df = 150.616, p > .05), and the maternal warmth and rejection subscale (men M = 11.57, men SD = 4.54, women M = 13.46, women SD = 6.55; t = -2.070, df = 151, p > .05). There were no gender differences on the remaining three subscales: identity diffusion, anger, and paternal warmth and rejection subscale.

Women participants endorsed a significantly higher level of acceptable violence usage than men participants as measured by the AAM (men M = 11.24, men SD = 17.23, women M = 19.51, women SD = 19.37; t = -2.791, df = 149.391, p > .01). The higher scores reported on the AAM, the PAS total score, and the three PAS subscales indicate that women participants appear to be more at risk for continued use of violence in their relationship than men participants. Also, the lack of significant difference in the remaining three PAS subscales indicates the women participants are at the same risk for continued use of violence as the men participants.

Finally, no significant differences were found between the men participants and the women participants on the first three of the four readiness to change subscales (precontemplation, contemplation, and action) as measured by the URICA-DV. The two groups, however, did demonstrate a significant difference in the readiness to change stage maintenance, with men participants reporting to be more inclined to maintain nonviolence in their relationship than the women participants (men M = 12.71, men SD = 5.31, women M = 10.71, women SD = 4.11; t = 2.522, df = 149, p < .05).

DISCUSSION

Based on the findings of the two research questions, the current study supports four key points that have significant implications for professionals working with women in domestic violence treatment programs. First, data analysis suggests that women arrested for intimate partner violence are not a homogeneous group. Second, some of the women in domestic violence treatment programs may exhibit risk factors that indicate an elevated likelihood that they will continue to use violence in their intimate relationship. Third, many of the women included in this study showed an increased level of tolerance for using violence in their relationship. Finally, women who find themselves in domestic violence treatment programs may be amenable to treatment opportunities. From these findings the importance of providing suitable treatment options for women charged with intimate partner violence and furthering research with this population is addressed in each area.

Women Arrested for Intimate Partner Violence Are Not a Homogeneous Group

One of the most important findings of the current study is that women arrested for domestic violence may not be a homogeneous group. The large standard deviations found in the results suggest that some of the women in the study score very high, but others score quite low. Results of this nature suggest that the mean scores are relevant for some (but not all) of the respondents (Rosenthal, 2000). Babcock, Miller, and Siard (2003) propose that two distinct subgroups exist within the population of women who use violence: (1) partner-only and (2) generally violent. For the partner-only group, violence is a reaction, for example, as a method of self-defense (Babcock et al., 2003). For the generally violent group, violence is more instrumental, for example, to exert control over another person (Babcock et al., 2003). Unfortunately, differentiation of these two subgroups requires answers to questions not asked of the participants and is therefore outside the scope of the current study. The idea of heterogeneity in the population of women arrested for domestic assault, however, is an interesting area for further research and should be considered by those working in the treatment setting.

Risk Factors

A second important finding is that some (but not all) of the women are showing elevated scores in their risk level for violence as measured by the SARA and their overall propensity to use violence as a coping mechanism as measured by the PAS. Responses on the SARA indicate that the women were more likely to have prior arrests and be unemployed than men, but the men were more likely to have a restraining order against them at the time of their arrest. Still, what is truly interesting about these findings is that the two groups showed similarity in response patterns on the remaining nine SARA items. These findings suggest that the risk factors of men and women domestic violence offenders may not be as different as once thought. Likewise, women scored higher than men on the overall PAS score and on three of the six subscales (attachment, trauma symptoms, and maternal warmth and rejection) and the same on the remaining three subscales (identity diffusion, anger, and paternal warmth and rejection). From these findings it can be concluded that the women participants in this study could be at a greater risk for continued use of violence than their men counterparts; however, the two groups showed more similarities in reported risk factors than differences.

In the domestic violence treatment setting, risk factors are important to address since the primary concern of most domestic violence treatment programs is to prevent future incidents (Holtzworth-Munroe & Stuart, 1994). Finding that some of the women are scoring relatively high on both the SARA and the PAS demonstrates that treating all women arrested for domestic violence as the secondary victims may miss important aspects of this mission. Instead, it seems more appropriate to use risk assessment instruments to differentiate among those women who need victim services, those who need offender treatment, and those who need a combination of the two. Unfortunately, treatment options are outside the scope of the current study and little empirical evidence is available on this topic. It is apparent that more research in this area is needed.

Justifiable Use of Violence

A third interesting finding is the level of justifiable use of violence that many of the women participants reported on the AAM (moderate to high). These findings were evident both when comparing the women's responses to the men's and when looking at the women's scores independently. Although causes of these findings are outside the scope of the current study, it is likely that women offenders' higher level of justifiable violence use is environmental, learned, and/or contextual. It is likely that women who use violence in their intimate relationships may be exposed to violence in their daily lives or may have histories of past violence as perpetrators or survivors (Mills, 2003). Mills has stated, "people who are exposed to violence are more likely to absorb pro-violence norms and values, which, in turn, makes them more violence prone" (p. 88). Using this position, it could be that the women in the current study have been exposed to many levels of violence, giving them greater reason for its use. Unfortunately, this may also put them at greater risk for both victimization and recidivism. Individuals who believe it is justified to use violence in their relationships may have both a higher tolerance for others who use violence against them and be at higher risk for retaliation. Furthermore, women who feel that it is acceptable to use violence are more likely to do so in the future, regardless of whether their violence is used in self-defense or as a means to express their feelings and/or exert their will. Consequently, it is important that domestic violence treatment programs assess both their female client's use of violence and attitudes toward this use. From the client's responses to this assessment, treatment options and safety planning can be improved.

Amenability to Treatment

The final point for discussion is related to amenability to treatment. Both the men and the women participants in this study endorsed relatively high levels of readiness to change their abusive relationship as measured by the URICA-DV. Even though people move in and out of the stages of change (Levesque et al., 2000), from a treatment perspective these findings are important. Clients who indicate a greater affinity toward the action stage are more likely to be amenable to treatment methods that they otherwise may not be ready for (Levesque et al., 2000). Therefore, identifying effective treatment options for this population becomes even more important as an increasing number of women use treatment resources.

Limitations

It is important to highlight three of the main limitations of the current study. First, there is the possibility that a continuum of female domestic violence aggressors exists, with the current sample representing only an outlying portion, not the entire population. Those arrested for and subsequently admitting to have harmed their partner may be the women who are found to be the "most obvious" sole perpetrators by the police officers responding to domestic violence calls and proven to be the highly "at risk" in court. It is likely that without unquestionable evidence that a woman is the primary perpetrator, the male partner is more likely to be arrested and convicted for a domestic violence incident that may have been mutually violent (Pearson, 1997). Likewise, participants in the current study included only those without prior domestic violence arrest histories and their past nonarrest-related use of violence was not directly measured. Therefore, the current sample may not be indicative of all women who use violence in their interpersonal relationships, but rather those who are arrested and admit to their actions.

A second limitation of the current research is related to the potential perpetrators have for minimizing in the treatment setting. Mainstream feminists hold that men who batter have a chronic pattern of minimizing symptoms of their abusive behavior (Mills, 2003). These beliefs are supported by research that indicates male intimate partner violence offenders report they participate in lower levels of violence and inflict fewer injuries than their female partners report (Browning & Dutton, 1986). More recent findings, however, show that women who use violence in their intimate relationships also minimize their actions. Archer (1999) found that both men and women underreport their own acts of aggression toward their partner. Likewise, Henning and colleagues (2003) found that both male and female domestic violence offenders "tended to respond in ways that made them look favorable" (p. 852). Therefore, caution should be taken with regard to both women's response patterns and comparisons between men and women.

Third, validity of the four measures used in the current study was not tested with a population of women arrested for domestic violence. As addressed in the *Measurement Instruments* section of this chapter, studies currently available measuring attitudes toward violence or risk factors have not been validated on women. That is why four different instruments were selected, two of which were previously used with a female IPV arrestee sample (Babcock et al., 2005; Henning & Feder, 2003). Also, coefficient alphas were conducted on the response patterns of both groups indicating both (a) moderate to high reliability and (b) comparability of samples. By using multiple methods, a greater generalizability and validity may be ascertained from the current findings. It is also likely that even though the measures used were validated on men, this study can demonstrate the use of such instruments as relevant for women as well. Nevertheless, caution should still be used when interpreting the findings of this work.

CONCLUSION

Despite the limitations of the current study to the overall population of women who use violence in their intimate relationships, the findings are representative of many of the women who find themselves in domestic violence treatment programs and should therefore be treated accordingly. It appears that women who use violence in their intimate relationships are a heterogeneous population for which the one-size-fits-all treatment options available may not be sufficient. Caution should be taken when selecting treatment options for this population, as their high tolerance for using violence may put them at higher risk for both victimization and recidivism. Similarly, because these women are likely to present to treatment programs in the contemplative and readiness stages of change, using these strengths in determining treatment options is likely to be beneficial. Of final importance is the clear need for additional research on the population of women who are arrested for domestic assault.

REFERENCES

Archer, J. (1999). Assessment of the reliability of the conflict tactics scales: A meta-analytic review. *Journal of Interpersonal Violence, 14*(12), 1263–1289.

Babcock, J. C., Canady, B. E., Senior, A., & Eckhardt, C. I. (2005). Applying the transtheoretical model to female and male perpetrators of intimate partner violence: Gender differences in stages and processes of change. *Violence and Victims, 20*(2), 235–250.

Babcock, J. C., Miller, S. A., & Siard, C. (2003). Toward a typology of abusive women: Differences between partner-only and generally violent in the use of violence. *Psychology of Women Quarterly, 27*, 153–161.

Bible, A., Dasgupta, S. D., & Osthoff, S. (Eds.). (2002). Women's use of violence in intimate relationships, Part 1 [Special Issue]. *Violence Against Women, 8*(11).

Browning, J., & Dutton, D. (1986). Assessment of wife assault with the conflict tactics scale: Using couple data to quantify the differential reporting effect. *Journal of Marriage and the Family, 48*(2), 375–379.

Busch, A. L., & Rosenberg, M. S. (2004). Comparing women and men arrested for domestic violence: A preliminary report. *Journal of Family Violence, 19*(1), 49–57.

Carney, M. M., & Buttell, F. P. (Eds.). (2005). Women who perpetrate relationship violence: Moving beyond political correctness [Special Issue]. *Journal of Offender Rehabilitation, 41*(4).

Cascardi, M., & Vivian, D. (1995). Context for specific episodes of marital violence: Gender and severity of violence differences. *Journal of Family Violence, 10*(3), 265–293.

Dasgupta, S. D., Osthoff, S., & Bible, A. (Eds.). (2002). Women's use of violence in intimate relationships, Part 2 [Special Issue]. *Violence Against Women, 8*(12).

Dasgupta, S. D., Osthoff, S., & Bible, A. (Eds.). (2003). Women's use of violence in intimate relationships, Part 3 [Special Issue]. *Violence Against Women, 9*(1).

Dobash, R., & Dobash, R. E. (1979). *Violence against wives: A case against patriarchy.* New York: Free Press.

Dutton, D. G. (1995). A scale for measuring propensity for abusiveness. *Journal of Family Violence, 10*(2), 203–221.

Dutton, D. G. (1999). The traumatic origins of intimate rage. *Aggression and Violent Behavior,* 4(4), 431–448.

Dutton, D. G., Landolt, M. A., Starzomski, A., & Bodnarchuk, M. (2001). Validation of the propensity for abusiveness scale. *Journal of Family Violence,* 16(1), 59–73.

Dutton, D. G., Nicholls, T. L., & Spidel, A. (2005). Female perpetrators of intimate violence. *Journal of Offender Rehabilitation,* 41(4), 1–32.

Eckhardt, C. I., Babcock, J., & Homack, S. (2004). Partner assaultive men and the stages and processes of change. *Journal of Family Violence,* 19(2), 81–93.

El-Bassel, N., Schilling, R. F., & Ivanoff, A. (1998). Stages of change profiles among incarcerated drug-using women. *Addictive Behaviors,* 23(3), 389–394.

Federal Bureau of Investigation. (2001). *Crime in the United States 2000.* Washington, DC: U.S. Department of Justice.

Frieze, I., & McHugh, M. C. (Eds.). (2005). Female violence against intimate partners [Special Issue]. *Psychology of Women Quarterly,* 29(3).

Garcia-O'Hearn, H., & Margolin, G. (2000). Men's attitudes condoning marital aggression: A moderator between family of origin abuse and aggression against female partners. *Cognitive Therapy and Research,* 24(2), 159–174.

Hamberger, K. (Ed.). (2005). Women's and men's use of interpersonal violence [Special Issue]. *Violence and Victims,* 20(3).

Hamberger, K., & Potente, T. (1994). Counseling heterosexual women arrested for domestic violence: Implications for theory and practice. *Violence and Victims,* 9(2), 125–137.

Hasler, G., Delsignore, A., & Milos, G. (2004). Application of Prochaska's transtheoretical model of change to patients with eating disorders. *Journal of Psychosomatic Research,* 57(1), 67–72.

Henning, K., & Feder, L. (2004). A comparison between men and women arrested for domestic violence: Who presents the greater threat? *Journal of Family Violence,* 19(2), 69–81.

Henning, K., Jones, A., & Holdford, R. (2003). Treatment needs of women arrested for domestic violence: A comparison with male offenders. *Journal of Interpersonal Violence,* 18(8), 839–856.

Henning, K., Jones, A., & Holdford, R. (2005). "I didn't do it, but if I did I had a good reason": Minimization, denial, and attributions of blame among male and female domestic violence offenders. *Journal of Family Violence,* 20(3), 131–139.

Holtzworth-Munroe, A., & Stuart, G. L. (1994). Typologies of male batterers: Three subtypes and the differences among them. *Psychological Bulletin,* 116(3), 476–497.

Kropp, P. R., & Hart, S. D. (2000). The spousal assault risk assessment (SARA) guide: Reliability and validity in adult male offenders. *Law and Human Behavior,* 24(1), 101–117.

Kropp. P., Hart, S., Webster, C., & Eaves D. (1999). *Spousal assault risk assessment guide user's manual.* Toronto, Canada: Multi-Health Systems, Inc. and B.C. Institute Against Family Violence.

Levesque, D. A., Gelles, R. J., & Velicer, W. F. (2000). Development and validation of a stages of change measure for men in batterer treatment. *Cognitive Therapy and Research,* 24(2), 175–199.

Margolin, G., & Foo, L. (1992). *Attitudes about marriage instrument.* Unpublished instrument, University of Southern California, Los Angeles.

Martin, M. (1997). Double your trouble: Dual arrest in family violence. *Journal of Family Violence, 12*(2), 139–157.

McHugh, M., & Frieze, I. (2005). Understanding gender and intimate partner violence: Theoretical and empirical approaches [Special Issue]. *Sex Roles, 52*(11–12).

McMahon, M., & Pence, E. (2003). Making social change: Reflections on individual and institutional advocacy with women arrested for domestic violence. *Violence Against Women, Special issue: Women's use of violence in intimate relationships, Part 3, 9*(1), 47–74.

McNeely, R., Cook, P., & Torres, J. (2001). Is domestic violence a gender issue, or a human issue? *Journal of Human Behavior in the Social Environment, 4*(4), 227–251.

Mignon, S., & Holmes, W. (1995). Police response to mandatory arrest laws. *Crime & Delinquency, 41*(4), 430–443.

Miller, S. L. (2001). The paradox of women arrested for domestic violence: Criminal justice professionals and service providers respond. *Violence Against Women, 7*(12), 1339–1376.

Mills, L. G. (2003). *Insult to injury; Rethinking our responses to intimate abuse.* Princeton, NJ: Princeton University Press.

Pearson, P. (1997). *When she was bad: Violent women and the myth of innocence.* New York: Viking Penguin.

Prochaska, J. O. (1995). An eclectic and integrative approach: Transtheoretical therapy. In A. S. Gurnam & S. B. Messer (Eds.), *Essential psychotherapies: Theory and practice* (pp. 403–440). New York: Guilford Press.

Prochaska, J. O., DiClemente, C. C., & Norcross, J. C. (1992). In search of how people change: Applications to addictive behaviors. *American Psychologist, 47,* 1102–1114.

Rennison, C. M. (2002). Intimate partner violence, 1993–2001. *Bureau of Justice Statistics Crime Data Brief.* Washington, DC: U.S. Department of Justice.

Rosenthal, J. A. (2000). *Statistics and data interpretation for the helping professions.* Belmont, CA: Wadsworth Publishing.

Saunders, D. (1995). The tendency to arrest victims of domestic violence. *Journal of Interpersonal Violence, 10*(2), 147–158.

Schifrin, E. T. (2004). A correlational study of PTSD symptomatology and battered women's readiness for change in residential and nonresidential shelters using the women's safety inventory (WSI). *Dissertation Abstracts International, 64*(8-B), 4062.

State of California. (1999). Report on arrest for domestic violence in California, 1998 (Office of the Attorney General). *Criminal Justice Statistics Center Report Series, 1*(13), 1–20.

Swan, S. C., & Snow, D. L. (2002). A typology of women's use of violence in intimate relationships. *Violence Against Women, 8*(3), 286–319.

Tjaden, P., & Theonnes, N. (2000). Prevalence and consequences of male-to-female and female-to-male intimate partner violence as measured by the national violence against women survey. *Violence Against Women, 6*(2), 142–161.

Victim Services Agency. (1989). State legislation providing for law enforcement response to family violence. *Response, 12*(3), 6–9.

11

Defining Appropriate Stages of Change for Intimate Partner Violence Survivors

JESSICA GRIFFIN BURKE, PATRICIA MAHONEY, ANDREA GIELEN, KAREN A. McDONNELL, AND PATRICIA O'CAMPO

It is estimated that more than 5 million women are affected by intimate partner violence (IPV) each year in the United States and that close to 1.5 million women are raped or physically assaulted by an intimate partner (Tjaden & Thoennes, 2000). A national study found that close to one-quarter of the women surveyed reported having experienced IPV during their lifetime (Coker et al., 2002). Other research among subpopulations of women has found even higher rates. For example, Gielen and her colleagues (Gielen, O'Campo, & McDonnell, 2002; McDonnell, Gielen, & O'Campo, 2003), working with a low-income, mainly African American sample, found that two-thirds of the women reported any lifetime IPV, and 62% reported any abuse within the past year. While the exact estimates of rates of IPV vary depending on the measurement tool employed and the population sampled, there is no doubt that it is a significant public health problem in the United States (Thompson, Basile, Hertz, & Sitterle, 2006). Experiences of IPV, defined as actual or threatened psychological, physical, or sexual abuse (Crowell & Burgess, 1996), have been shown to have profoundly negative consequences on women's physical and mental health (Campbell, 2002; Campbell et al., 2002; Carbone-Lopez, Kruttschnitt, & Macmillan, 2006; Gielen, McDonnell, O'Campo, & Burke, 2005; McDonnell, Gielen, O'Campo, & Burke, 2005; Pallitto, O'Campo, & Campbell, 2005; Plichta & Falik, 2001).

While many professional health care organizations (Family Violence Prevention Fund, 1999; Joint Commission on the Accreditation of Healthcare Organizations, 1995), including the American Medical Association (1992), have called for routine screening of female patients for IPV, additional work needs to be done to develop and implement effective IPV intervention protocols for health care professionals. New work by MacMillan and colleagues (2006) offers guidance on the types of screening tools to be employed in the health care setting, yet little direction exists on how health care professionals should intervene with patients who screen positive for abuse (Rhodes & Levinson, 2003; Wathen & MacMillan, 2003).

Recent research suggests that the transtheoretical model of behavior change (TTM) is a promising approach for interventions addressing abuse (Brown, 1997; Burke, Dennison, Gielen, McDonnell, & O'Campo, 2004; Burke, Gielen, McDonnell, O'Campo, & Maman, 2001; Frasier, Slatt, Kowlowitz, & Glowa, 2001; Zink, Elder, Jacobson, & Klostermann, 2004). This model of behavior change may be particularly appropriate for interventions delivered in the health care setting because it provides a tool to assess an individual's readiness to change and to tailor patient counseling accordingly. The TTM, also known as the stages-of-change model (Prochaska & DiClemente, 1982, 1983), has been successfully applied to a range of health behaviors, including smoking cessation, condom use, exercise, mammography screening, diabetes control, drug use, adherence, and eating practices (e.g., Belding, Iguchi, Lamb, Lakin, & Terry, 1995; Di Noia, Schinke, Prochaska, & Contento, 2006; Gielen et al., 2001; Johnson et al., 2006; Keefe et al., 2000; Keller, Allan, & Tinkle, 2006; O'Campo et al., 1999; Perz, DiClemente, & Carbonari, 1996; Prochaska et al., 1994; Rossi et al., 1994). The TTM originated in the 1980s from an examination of psychotherapy and behavioral change theories and conceptualizes change as a process that occurs in five stages: precontemplation, contemplation, preparation, action, and maintenance (Prochaska & DiClemente, 1982, 1983). According to the TTM, the process of behavior change is often cyclical, with individuals progressing and relapsing between stages before achieving the success of maintenance. The underlying premise of the model is that people in different points of the behavior change process can benefit from different types of interventions tailored to their stage of readiness (Prochaska & Velicer, 1997).

Existing research suggests that the TTM is consistent with how women describe surviving their abusive situations (Brown, 1997; Burke et al., 2001, 2004; Frasier et al., 2001; McDonnell, Burke, Gielen, &

O'Campo, 2006; Zink et al., 2004). Using in-depth qualitative interviews with open-ended questions, Burke and colleagues (2001) asked 78 women who were either currently in or had recently left an abusive relationship to talk about their experiences of IPV. Results from their research showed that women talked about five stages of behavior change in relation to IPV (Table 11.1). For example, some women described a stage in their process during which they were actively engaged in making changes related to ending the abuse, corresponding to the TTM action stage. While leaving the relationship was the most commonly reported behavior for women categorized in the action stage, other behaviors that women talked about included fighting back, contacting family members, and calling the police. This approach for defining action to address abuse is consistent with prior research showing that while leaving appears to be the most effective way for a woman to end IPV (Campbell, 1989; Peled, Eisikovitis, Enosh, & Winstok, 2000), some women are not interested in or able to end the relationship at a given point in time, and some women who do end the relationship still experience abuse (Campbell, 1995). Subsequent qualitative work conducted by the same research team with an additional 23 abused women also supports the development of a TTM stage-based IPV measurement tool and associated intervention (Burke et al., 2004).

Table 11.1

STAGES OF CHANGE FOR INTIMATE PARTNER VIOLENCE

Precontemplation	The woman does not recognize the abuse as a problem and is not interested in change.
Contemplation	The woman recognizes the abuse as a problem and has an increasing awareness of the pros and cons of change.
Preparation	The woman recognizes the abuse as a problem, intends to change and has developed a plan.
Action	The woman is actively engaged in making changes related to ending the abuse.
Maintenance	The abuse has ended and the woman is taking steps to prevent relapse.

Note. From "The Process of Ending Abuse in Intimate Relationships," by J. G. Burke, A. C. Gielen, K. A. McDonnell, P. O'Campo, & S. Maman, 2001, *Violence Against Women, 7*(10), 1144–1163. Copyright 2000 by Sage Publications. Adapted with permission.

Some health care professionals and advocates argue that a TTM approach to women's experiences of abuse is inherently "victim blaming" because ultimately the abusive behavior is that of the perpetrator. However, it is clear that women in abusive relationships do take action to survive, cope with, and end the abuse (Campbell, Rose, Kub, & Nedd, 1998; Farrell, 1996; Moss, Pitula, Campbell, & Halstead, 1997). While some research has addressed the application of the TTM to perpetrators' abusive behavior (Daniels & Murphy, 1997; Levesque, Gelles, & Velicer, 2000), less work has been done to apply the TTM to abused women's experiences. Health care providers caring for abused women need to be armed with appropriate skills and intervention protocols to help women keep themselves safe and free from harm.

Building on the qualitative research of Burke and colleagues (2001, 2004), a quantitative survey was designed to measure a woman's stage of readiness to work toward staying safe from IPV and the factors associated with stage movement. A primary goal of this work was to develop a staging tool. Such a tool is an essential element for determining an abused woman's stage of change and for implementing an appropriate TTM stage-based intervention. For example, prior work (Burke et al., 2004) suggests that intervention activity that includes information about what constitutes abuse would be an appropriate way to help women move from the stage of precontemplation into contemplation for ending the abuse. In addition to being a critical tool for the implementation of stage-based interventions, such a staging tool is critical for the evaluation of TTM-oriented interventions. The development of a sound staging tool for measuring movement from one stage to another will permit examination of the effectiveness of stage-tailored intervention activities.

These exploratory analyses utilized data from a clinic-based sample of abused women to address the following goals: (a) to describe the distribution of women across the stages of change for staying safe from IPV and across the stages of change for leaving an abusive relationship, (b) to examine the relationship between stage assignment and other indicators of a woman's stage (i.e., safety behaviors), and (c) to explore the relationship between stage assignment and desired services.

METHODS

Sample and Recruitment

Between June 2005 and June 2006, 96 women were recruited from six community health clinics serving low-income women in urban Baltimore

City, Maryland. In order to be eligible for the study, women had to be over the age of 17, not pregnant, English speaking, without private insurance, and to have experienced physical partner violence within the past year. Women were screened for current physical abuse status using the following item from the Abuse Assessment Screen (McFarlane, Parker, Soeken, & Bullock, 1992): "Within the last year, have you been hit, slapped, kicked, or otherwise physically hurt by a boyfriend, husband, or someone you were in a couple relationship with?"

Study procedures were approved by the Johns Hopkins Bloomberg School of Public Health Committee for Human Research. Flyers advertising the study were posted in each recruitment site. Women who called the study number were screened for eligibility over the phone. In two settings—an obstetrics and gynecology clinic and an HIV women's clinic—a recruiter worked on-site to introduce the study and screen women while they waited in their exam room (no partners were allowed in exam rooms, making this a confidential setting). Eligible women were asked if they would like to join the study, and those who agreed were administered the staging algorithm (described in the following) prior to scheduling an interview time. Only two eligible women declined to participate.

Data Collection

Data were obtained through a quantitative survey. At the time of the interview, the interviewer described the study and obtained informed consent. Interviews were completed in person in a private office in a university building accessible by public transportation and lasted approximately 1 hour. The interviewers received crisis intervention training from a local domestic violence shelter and were equipped with contact information for community resources, including the local domestic violence shelter and drug treatment facilities, so that women identified as needing immediate help could be referred to appropriate services. After completing the interview, women were paid $20 cash and given a community resource phone list that included IPV services.

Study Variables

Respondent Demographics

These items included the following: age, race, employment status, educational status, federal income support status (food stamps, WIC foods, WIC vouchers, Temporary Assistance for Needy Families, or other support programs).

Relationship Status

Women were asked how they would define their relationship to the abuser (e.g., boyfriend, husband, ex-husband). For the current analyses, responses were dichotomized into current or former partner. Those who described a former partner were asked how long ago the relationship was ended.

Abuse History

Abuse was measured using the Revised Conflict Tactics Scales (Straus, Hamby, Boney-McCoy, & Sugarman, 1996), including the physical, sexual, and psychological abuse subscales. The referent period for frequency was the past year. Additional questions regarding recency of abuse were asked by subscale (any minor physical, any severe physical, any minor sexual, any severe sexual, and any psychological) for the referent period of the past 6 months and past month.

Stage of Change for Staying Safe From Abuse

Based on our previous qualitative research (Burke et al., 2001, 2004) and earlier work by Brown (1997), we developed a series of questions about the woman's most recent abusive intimate partner and a staging algorithm to assess her stage of change for staying safe from abuse (Figure 11.1). Action was defined as behaviors to keep themselves safe from abuse and did not focus exclusively on leaving the relationship, given existing research that indicates that some women take actions to end the abuse while staying in the relationship and that ending the relationship and ending the abuse are two separate processes (Campbell, 1995).

The interviewer referred back to the subject's positive answer on the Abuse Assessment Screen (e.g., "Please think about all of the things this person has done that have physically hurt you when answering the next questions"). Women were then asked the series of questions in the algorithm concerning whether the abuse occurred in the past 6 months, whether they consider their partner's abuse toward them a problem, and whether they have done (or plan to do) things to end the abuse or keep themselves safe. Precontemplation is defined as not thinking that the abuse is a problem. Contemplation is defined as considering the abuse is a problem but not yet thinking about taking any specific actions to keep herself safe. Preparation is defined as thinking about taking specific ac-

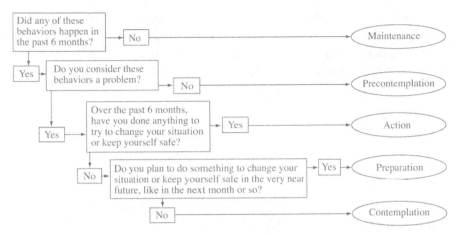

Figure 11.1 Staging algorithm for staying safe from abuse.

tions to keep herself safe in the near future. Action is defined as having taken specific steps to keep safe within the past 6 months. Maintenance is defined as having been free from the abuse for 6 months or more. The 6-month criterion is the most commonly used definition of maintenance in the TTM literature (Prochaska & DiClemente, 1982).

Stage of Change for Leaving the Abusive Relationship

Using information from a woman's definition of the relationship (e.g., boyfriend, ex-boyfriend), separation status, and, when appropriate, her response to "Do you plan to end this relationship in the next 6 months?," a variable for stage of change for leaving the abusive relationship was constructed. The four-category variable describes a woman's stage of leaving: together, no intention to leave (prepreparation, which includes the traditional stages of precontemplation and contemplation); together, intends to leave within 6 months (preparation); left within past 5 months (action); and left 6 or more months ago (maintenance).

Safety Behaviors

Women were asked 32 safety behavior items adapted from work by Goodman, Dutton, Weinfurt, and Cook, 2003, and McFarlane and colleagues, 2002 plus 2 additional items (asking him to move, ending, or trying to end the relationship). Women were asked if they had done each behavior in the past 6 months. The 34 items were later collapsed into groups by the study authors based on content similarity (e.g., all items related to making copies of documents were grouped under "copy documents"), with a total of 15 resulting categories that reflect distinct behaviors (e.g., fought back and called the police).

Desired Services

Because we are ultimately interested in implementing a tailored intervention for abused women in health care settings, women were also asked whether they would want specific abuse-related services available in the clinic they were visiting. This 15-item list was slightly modified from Chang and colleagues (2005).

Data Analysis

This article presents univariate and bivariate explorations of variables of interest. We sought to describe the stages of change that women were in with regard to IPV experiences and also the associations for being in a given stage.

RESULTS

Sample Characteristics

Table 11.2 presents data on the sample characteristics. A majority of the participants were African American (83%) and just over half (58%) had completed high school. This was a low-income sample, with 81% reporting no paid employment and 82% receiving some form of federal income assistance. Women ranged in age from 20 to 54, with a mean age of 40. As one of the recruitment settings was an HIV clinic, 27% of the sample were HIV positive.

As mentioned previously, to be eligible for the study, all women had to have experienced some physical abuse in the past year; most women (78%) reported experiencing any physical or sexual abuse within the past 6 months. The frequency and severity of abuse was high; nearly all women (97%) experienced severe abuse (physical or sexual) within the past year. In addition, 65% of all women reported at least three separate instances of severe abuse within the past year, and more than one-quarter (28%) of all women reported 11 or more instances of severe

Table 11.2

SAMPLE CHARACTERISTICS (N = 96)

	NUMBER	%
Race: African American	80	83
High school graduate	56	58
No paid employment	78	81
Federal income support	79	82
Age	Mean = 40.43; SD = 7.24; range = 20–54	
HIV positive	26	27
Any physical or sexual abuse in past 6 months	75	78
No longer with partner	46	48

abuse within the past year. Just under half the sample reported no longer being in a relationship with the abusive partner.

Stage of Change for Staying Safe From Abuse

Based on the staging algorithm (Figure 11.1) for staying safe from abuse, most of the participants were classified into the action stage (65%). Approximately one-quarter (24%) of the women were in the maintenance stage, and very few were in preparation (9%), contemplation (1%), and precontemplation (1%). Therefore, for the subsequent analyses, we combined preparation, contemplation, and precontemplation into one stage, labeled "pre-action."

Data addressing women's use of safety behaviors within the past 6 months was explored to determine whether use of the staging algorithm appropriately "staged" or categorized women. While women in all stages of change were engaged in a number of safety behaviors (Table 11.3), a greater proportion of women who were categorized in pre-action for staying safe from abuse reported use of most strategies, compared to women in the action stage for staying safe from abuse. For example, 90.9% of women in pre-action reported hiding things, while 85.5% of women in action, and only 52.2% of women in maintenance reported doing so.

Table 11.3

PERCENT OF WOMEN WHO ENGAGED IN SAFETY BEHAVIORS IN PAST 6 MONTHS BY STAGE OF CHANGE

	STAGE OF CHANGE FOR STAYING SAFE FROM ABUSE				STAGE OF CHANGE FOR LEAVING ABUSIVE RELATIONSHIP				
	PREACTION N=11	ACTION N=62	MAINTENANCE N=23	χ^2	PREPREPARATION N=21	PREPARATION N=29	ACTION N=21	MAINTENANCE N=25	χ^2
Avoided or complied with abuser	100	98	74	**	95	93	100	84	ns
Talked to partner about the abuse	100	71	61	*	91	90	57	48	**
Talked to family or friends	91	84	65	ns	91	86	86	60	*
Hid things	91	86	52	**	91	86	81	60	*
Fought back	91	87	61	*	86	86	91	64	ns
Copied documents and important numbers	82	77	52	ns	81	69	71	68	ns
Established plan with family, friends, neighbors	73	58	26	*	54	62	57	36	ns

Talked with professionals	73	65	39	ns	48	69	67	52	ns
Made plan for self	64	79	52	*	67	72	86	60	ns
Ended or tried to end relationships	64	81	35	**	33	66	95	76	**
Called the police	55	48	22	ns	43	48	43	36	ns
Hid or removed weapons	36	42	9	ns	48	35	38	16	ns
Asked abuser to move	36	34	26	ns	19	48	33	24	ns
Sought education or job training	18	52	52	ns	48	31	48	68	ns
Moved to a new location	18	52	30	*	19	38	67	48	*

Note. ns = not significant.
*p < .05. **p < .01.

Stage of Change for Leaving an Abusive Relationship

Results from combined information related to relationship status and intention to leave show that approximately one-fifth of the women (22%) were with their partner and had no plans of leaving (prepreparation), 30% were with their partner and reported planning to leave within the next 6 months (preparation), 22% had been apart from their partner for less than 6 months (action), and 26% had been apart from their partner for 6 months or more (maintenance). Table 11.3 presents the proportion of women reporting safety behaviors within the past 6 months by stage of leaving. Again, it is interesting that the women who are in prepreparation and preparation report engaging in several types of actions. For example, a higher proportion of women in prepreparation than in the other stages of change for leaving an abusive relationship reported having hidden things (91%) and talked to their partner about the abuse (91%).

Stages of Change and Desired Services

Results presented in Table 11.4 show how stages of change are related to preference for select services. While many of the findings presented in Table 11.4 are not statistically significant, they do suggest different trends in service preference by stage of change. Compared to women in action and maintenance for leaving an abusive relationship, a higher proportion of women who are categorized into preaction stages would like informational resources. For example, 90% of women in preparation for staying safe from abuse report that they would like information about the legal steps they can take to stay safe from abuse. On the other hand, a large proportion of women in maintenance for leaving an abusive relationship would like a chance to talk with a peer advocate (84%) about relationship problems. Significant differences in service preference by stage of staying safe from abuse were found for three of the counseling activities (a chance to talk with a counselor about relationship problems, a chance to talk with a peer advocate about how to keep safe, and counseling with a partner focused on relationships).

DISCUSSION

Results from this exploratory study highlight the complexity of the process of ending abuse. While IPV research has begun to examine women's

Table 11.4

INTERVENTIONS DESIRED BY STAGE OF CHANGE

	STAGE OF CHANGE FOR STAYING SAFE FROM ABUSE				STAGE OF CHANGE FOR LEAVING ABUSIVE RELATIONSHIP				
	PREACTION $N=11$	ACTION $N=62$	MAINTENANCE $N=23$	$\chi2$	PREPREPARATION $N=21$	PREPARATION $N=29$	ACTION $N=21$	MAINTENANCE $N=25$	$\chi2$
Information interventions									
Information about legal steps to stay safe from abuse, like protection from abuse orders, or divorce	73	76	78	ns	81	90	62	68	ns
Information about legal steps related to children, like custody and support	36	71	61	ns	71	69	50	64	ns
A domestic violence hotline number	64	77	65	ns	81	86	57	64	ns
Counseling interventions									
A chance to talk with a counselor about relationship problems	46	82	70	*	81	76	67	76	ns
A chance to talk with a counselor about how to keep safe	55	81	65	ns	76	79	67	72	ns

(Continued)

INTERVENTIONS DESIRED BY STAGE OF CHANGE (*Continued*)

Table 11.4

	STAGE OF CHANGE FOR STAYING SAFE FROM ABUSE				STAGE OF CHANGE FOR LEAVING ABUSIVE RELATIONSHIP				
	PREACTION $N=11$	ACTION $N=62$	MAINTENANCE $N=23$	$\chi 2$	PREPREPARATION $N=21$	PREPARATION $N=29$	ACTION $N=21$	MAINTENANCE $N=25$	$\chi 2$
A chance to talk with a peer advocate about relationship problems	55	77	70	*ns*	71	72	62	84	*ns*
A chance to talk with a peer advocate about how to keep safe	46	82	57	**	81	79	62	64	*ns*
Contact with someone from the doctor's office/clinic to see how things are going	46	73	52	*ns*	81	66	48	64	*ns*
Counseling or support groups	46	69	57	*ns*	71	62	62	60	*ns*

Counseling or therapy with a partner focused on marriage/relationships	27	69	52	*	57	72	52	56	ns
Other interventions									
Help getting housing, food, or other needs	91	77	87	ns	81	83	81	80	ns
Help getting a job	36	76	78	*	62	83	71	68	ns
Help with drug or alcohol use	55	61	52	ns	67	69	45	48	ns
Help reporting to the police	27	55	57	ns	52	62	29	60	ns
Help getting child care	0	47	70	**	52	52	29	52	ns

Note. ns = not significant.
*p < .05. **p < .01.

responses to the violence and decision-making processes with regard to enhancing safety and ending abuse (Brown, 1997; Campbell et al., 1998; Campbell & Soeken, 1999), more work remains to be done with regard to the definition of appropriate stages of change for IPV victims and in the development of tailored IPV interventions to most effectively assist women in moving forward on the path to safety.

Using the staging algorithm for staying safe from abuse (Figure 11.1), we were not able to obtain a good distribution of women by stage. The sample distribution was skewed toward the later stages of action (65%) and maintenance (24%). In addition, our findings illustrate the difficulties we had distinguishing between the women in the various stages; women in all the stages were engaged in some form of action to address the abuse. Although there are only 11 women in the pre-action stage for staying safe from abuse, the fact that so many have engaged in safety behaviors within the past 6 months challenges the appropriateness of the staging algorithm addressing "staying safe" and suggests that there may be no single action stage for abused women as it relates to staying safe. Recall that women categorized in contemplation and preparation reported during staging that they had not done anything to keep themselves safe, yet these data show that they had engaged in behaviors related to their safety. These findings call into question the appropriateness of using a staging algorithm that uses one global question about keeping safe.

Our results also suggest that defining a single action stage is very difficult and perhaps not a useful approach to staging IPV victims. Those women who were categorized into the preparation stage of change for leaving an abusive relationship (i.e., reported no intention of leaving their partners) were engaged in a large number of safety behaviors. This is not surprising considering the reality of their situations; women in abusive relationships undertake such behaviors in order to stay as safe as possible while remaining with a partner who has hurt them. When we consider the variety of actions reported by women in this and other studies and the efficacy of these actions on their ability to end abuse in their lives, we are challenged to find a set of actions that would be equally meaningful to all IPV survivors. For some women, ending the relationship ends the abuse; for others, it does not. For some women, one phone call to the police ends the abuse; for others, it does not. Most women who leave have employed various strategies prior to leaving. For example, one woman in Burke and colleagues' (2001) research described her experience fighting back but then finally leaving: "One time I actually fought back and drew blood. He went into shock. He was like 'How could you do this to me?' . . . I got out of it . . . I finally left."

Results presented in Table 11.3 showing that 76% of the women in maintenance for leaving an abusive relationship ended or tried to end the relationship in the past 6 months are curious and noteworthy. Why would women who have ended their relationships at least 6 months ago report that they "ended or tried to end" the relationship within the past 6 months? A detailed exploration of data from those 19 women showed that 63% had ended the relationship more than 8 months prior to study participation. It is possible that some of these women are still being pursued by their ex-partners and have felt as if they are still in the process of ending the relationship, even though they have been apart longer than 6 months. However, it is also possible that these results highlight issues related to recall of the exact timing of events and call into question the use of the specific 6-month time frame for classifying women into action versus maintenance stages.

Other TTM work addressing behavior change is more straightforward than addressing stages of change related to IPV. For example, with regard to smoking cessation, the targeted behavior is smoking, and the stage-based measures focus on movement toward quitting. But it is not as clear what we should be asking in the case of IPV. What behavior should the intervention target? What measure of success should be addressed in a stage-based intervention evaluation?

In their recent work to understand behavior change for women experiencing IPV, Chang and colleagues (2006) acknowledge their struggles with how to define the stage of "action." They ultimately chose to define action as "any behavior the female participants themselves defined as an active attempt to change their situation" and that moved women toward an "improved situation" or "more safety." Utilizing that definition, they were able to map women's stages of change and found that women generally moved in a nonlinear, nonsequential progression toward change and engaged in multiple actions in response to external triggers. Their results suggested that instead of moving from precontemplation to contemplation to preparation to action, women often leapfrogged from precontemplation to action in response to an abuser's behavior. For example, a woman who is in precontemplation who is attacked by her abuser may call the police in an attempt to save her life. Calling police is an action she is taking toward the goal of staying safe, but she has leapfrogged from precontemplation to action because of the actions of her abuser.

Instead of clarifying, these results, in addition to the work of Chang and colleagues (2006), illustrate the true difficulties of designing a stage-based intervention approach for addressing IPV. Unlike other behaviors that have been studied up to this point using TTM theory, IPV is not a health behavior in that it is not an action or an activity that a person engages in. Rather, it is a behavior (in fact, a series of behaviors) enacted on a person by a separate individual. While we know women move through stages in their decision-making process to end the abuse in their lives, the interactive, complex nature of IPV presents new challenges to conceptualizing stages in a way that is standard enough to be useful for all (or most) IPV victims but comprehensive and flexible enough to handle the complexity of IPV.

The results from this study support the significant role of helping relationships with friends, family, and even heath care professionals and the importance of information distribution previously found by Burke and colleagues (2004). A majority of women in all stages of change, both for staying safe from abuse and for leaving the abusive relationship, reported the safety behavior of talking with family and friends (Table 11.3). In addition, close to three-quarters of all the women staged for leaving an abusive relationship stated that they would like a chance to talk with a counselor or peer advocate about relationship problems and about how to keep safe. Results from this study also underline the importance of informational interventions. Women at all stages of change, for both staying safe from abuse and for leaving the abusive relationship, reported wanting a domestic violence hotline number. These findings are consistent with prior work by Chang and colleagues (2005) showing that 81% of the abused women interviewed reported wanting access to such information. One other notable finding is the large number of women (more than 75%), in all stages of change, who reported wanting help with housing, food, and other needs. This finding is consistent with earlier research with low-income urban women (O'Campo, McDonnell, Gielen, Burke, & Chen, 2002) and underscores the importance of acknowledging and addressing the context of women's lives. These findings are supported by a growing wealth of literature encouraging ecological approaches to interventions that attend to an individual's needs, such as those of housing, nutrition, education, and employment (e.g., Cohen, Scribner, & Farley, 2000; Sallis et al., 2006). While we continue to struggle with whether and how to assess a woman's stage of change for IPV, it is clear, based on research findings and on abused women's expressed preferences, that clinic-based intervention programs should include informational resources and opportunities to talk with counselors about their abuse experiences.

The cross-sectional design and small sample size are potential limitations of this study. Our findings would have been strengthened had we had the financial resources available to conduct follow-up interviews with women to capture changes over time. In addition, the small sample size precluded the identification of potentially meaningful statistical differences between stage groups. Another consideration in interpreting the results is that 27% of the women were HIV positive. However, stratified analyses did not suggest any differences by HIV status. Data from other quantitative work have found few differences in abuse experience by HIV status (Gielen et al., 2002; McDonnell et al., 2003).

To our knowledge, this is the first study that has quantitatively addressed the TTM stages of change for women's experiences of ending abuse within intimate relationships. While these findings provide insight into the complexity associated with measuring women's efforts toward ending abuse, much additional work remains to be done to define the appropriate stages of change for IPV survivors and to develop and validate quantitative measures of stages of change.

ACKNOWLEDGMENTS

Supported by the Centers for Disease Control and Prevention, National Center for Injury Prevention and Control, grant number 1 R49 CE000198–01, and the Johns Hopkins University School of Medicine General Clinical Research Center, grant number M01-RR00052, from the National Center for Research Resources/NIH.

REFERENCES

American Medical Association. (1992). Violence against women: Relevance for medical practitioners. *Journal of the American Medical Association, 257,* 3184–3189.

Belding, M. A., Iguchi, M. Y., Lamb, R. J., Lakin, M., & Terry, R. (1995). Stages and processes of change among polydrug users in methadone maintenance treatment. *Drug and Alcohol Dependence, 39,* 45–53.

Brown, J. (1997). Working toward freedom from violence: The process of change in battered women. *Violence Against Women, 3,* 5–26.

Burke, J. G., Dennison, J., Gielen, A. C., McDonnell, K., & O'Campo, P. (2004). Ending intimate partner violence: An application of the transtheoretical model. *American Journal of Health Behavior, 28*(2), 122–133.

Burke, J. G., Gielen, A. C., McDonnell, K. A., O'Campo, P., & Maman, S. (2001). The process of ending abusive relationships: A qualitative exploration of the transtheoretical model. *Violence Against Women, 7*(10), 1144–1163.

Campbell, J. C. (1989). A test of two explanatory models of women's responses to batter-ing. *Nursing Research, 38*(1), 18–24.

Campbell, J. C. (1995). *Assessing dangerousness: Violence by sexual offenders, batterers, and child abusers*. Thousand Oaks, CA: Sage.

Campbell, J. C. (2002). Health consequences of intimate partner violence. *Lancet, 359,* 1331–1336.

Campbell, J. C., Jones, A. S., Dienemann, J., Kub, J., Schollenberger, J., O'Campo, P., et al. (2002). Intimate partner violence and physical health consequences. *Archives of Internal Medicine, 162,* 1157–1163.

Campbell, J., Rose, L., Kub, J., & Nedd, D. (1998). Voices of strength and resistance: A contextual and longitudinal analysis of women's responses to battering. *Journal of Interpersonal Violence, 13,* 743–762.

Campbell, J. C., & Soeken, K. L. (1999). Women's responses to battering overtime: An analysis of change. *Journal of Interpersonal Violence, 14,* 21–40.

Carbone-Lopez, K., Kruttschnitt, C., & Macmillan, R. (2006). Patterns of intimate part-ner violence and their associations with physical health, psychological distress, and substance use. *Public Health Reports, 121*(4), 382–392.

Chang, J. C., Clauss, P. A., Ranieri, L., Hawker, L., Buransoky, R., Dado, D., et al. (2005). Health care interventions for intimate partner violence: What women want. *Women's Health Issues, 15,* 21–30.

Chang, J. C., Dado, D., Ashton, S., Hawker, L., Cluss, P., Buranosky, R., et al. (2006). Understanding behavior change for women experiencing intimate partner violence: Mapping the ups and downs using the stages of change. *Patient Education and Coun-seling, 62,* 330–339.

Cohen, D. A., Scribner, R. A., & Farley, T. A. (2000). A structural model of health behav-ior: A pragmatic approach to explain and influence health behaviors at the population level. *Preventive Medicine, 30*(2), 146–154.

Coker, A. L., Davis, K. E., Arias, I., Desai, S., Sanderson, M., Brandt, H. M., et al. (2002). Physical and mental health effects of intimate partner violence for men and women. *American Journal of Preventive Medicine, 23*(4), 260–268.

Crowell, N. A., & Burgess, A. W. (1996). *Understanding violence against women*. Wash-ington, DC: National Academy Press.

Daniels, J. W., & Murphy, C. M. (1997). Stages and processes of change in batterers' treatment. *Cognitive and Behavioral Practice, 4*(1), 123–145.

Di Noia, J., Schinke, S. P., Prochaska, J. O., & Contento, I. R. (2006). Application of the transtheoretical model to fruit and vegetable consumption among economically dis-advantaged African-American adolescents: Preliminary findings. *American Journal of Health Promotion, 20*(5), 342–348.

Family Violence Prevention Fund. (1999). *Routine screening for domestic violence in health care settings*. Washington, DC: Bass and Howes.

Farrell, M. L. (1996). Healing: A qualitative study of women recovering from abusive relationships with men. *Perspectives in Psychiatric Care, 32,* 23–32.

Frasier, P. Y., Slatt, L., Kowlowitz, V., & Glowa, P. T. (2001). Using the stages of change model to counsel victims of intimate partner violence. *Patient Education Counseling, 43*(2), 211–217.

Gielen, A. C., Fogarty, L. A., Armstrong, K., Green, B. M., Cabral, R., Milstein, R., et al. (2001). Promoting condom use with main partners: A behavioral intervention trial for women. *AIDS and Behavior, 5*(3), 193–204.

Gielen, A. C., McDonnell, K. A., O'Campo, P., & Burke, J. G. (2005). Suicide risk and mental health indicators: Do they differ by abuse and HIV status? *Women's Health Issues, 15*(2), 89–95.

Gielen, A. C., O'Campo, P. J., & McDonnell, K. A. (2002). Intimate partner violence, HIV status, and sexual risk reduction. *AIDS and Behavior, 6*(2), 107–116.

Goodman, L., Dutton, M. A., Weinfurt, K., & Cook, S. (2003). The intimate partner violence strategies index. *Violence Against Women, 9,* 163–186.

Johnson, S. S., Driskell, M. M., Johnson, J. L., Dyment, S. J., Prochaska, J. O., Prochaska, J. M., et al. (2006). Transtheoretical model intervention for adherence to lipid-lowering drugs. *Disease Management, 9*(2), 102–114.

Joint Commission on the Accreditation of Healthcare Organizations. (1995). *Accreditation manual for hospitals.* Oakbrook Terrace, IL: Author.

Keefe, F. J., Lefebvre, J. C., Kerns, R. D., Rosenberg, R., Beaupre, P., Prochaska, J., et al. (2000). Understanding adoption of arthritis self-management: Stages of change profiles among arthritis patients. *Pain, 87,* 303–313.

Keller, C., Allan, J., & Tinkle, M. B. (2006). Stages of change, processes of change, and social support for exercise and weight gain in postpartum women. *Journal of Obstetric, Gynecologic, and Neonatal Nursing, 35*(2), 232–240.

Levesque, D. A., Gelles, R. J., & Velicer, W. F. (2000). Development and validation of a stages of change measure for men in batterer treatment. *Cognitive Therapy and Research, 24*(2), 175–199.

MacMillan, H. L., Wathen, C. N., Jamieson, E., Boyle, M., McNutt, L. A., Worster, A., et al. (2006). Approaches to screening for intimate partner violence in health care settings. *Journal of the American Medical Association, 296,* 530–536.

McDonnell, K. A., Burke, J. G., Gielen, A. C., & O'Campo, P. (2006). Intimate partner violence. In A. C. Gielen, D. Sleet, & R. J. DiClemente (Eds.), *Injury and violence prevention: Behavior science theories, methods and applications.* San Francisco, CA: Jossey-Bass.

McDonnell, K. A., Gielen, A. C., & O'Campo, P. (2003). Lifetime abuse among low income women: Does HIV status make a difference? *Journal of Urban Health, 80*(3), 494–509.

McDonnell, K. A., Gielen, A. C., O'Campo, P., & Burke, J. (2005). Abuse, HIV status, and health related quality of life among a sample of HIV positive and HIV negative low income women. *Quality of Life Research, 14*(4), 945–957.

McFarlane, J., Malecha, A., Gist, J., Watson, K., Batten, E., Hall, I., et al. (2002). An intervention to increase safety behaviors of abused women. *Nursing Research, 51*(6), 347–354.

McFarlane, J., Parker, B., Soeken, K., & Bullock, L. (1992). Assessing for abuse during pregnancy. *Journal of the American Medical Association, 267,* 3176–3178.

Moss, V. A., Pitula, C. R., Campbell, J. C., & Halstead, L. (1997). The experience of terminating an abusive relationship from an Anglo and African American perspective: A qualitative descriptive study. *Issues in Mental Health Nursing, 18,* 433–454.

O'Campo, P., Fogarty, L., Gielen, A. C., Armstrong, K., Bond, L., Galavotti, C., et al. (1999). Distribution along a stages of change continuum for condom and contraceptive use among women accessed in different settings. *Journal of Community Health, 24,* 61–72.

O'Campo, P., McDonnell, K., Gielen, A. C., Burke, J., & Chen, Y. (2002). Surviving physical and sexual abuse: What helps low income women? *Patient Education and Counseling, 46*(3), 205–212.

Pallitto, C., O'Campo, P., & Campbell, J. C. (2005). Is intimate partner violence associated with unintended pregnancy? A review of the literature. *Trauma, Violence and Abuse, 6*(3), 217–235.

Peled, E., Eisikovitis, Z., Enosh, G., & Winstok, Z. (2000). Choice and empowerment for battered women who stay: Toward a constructivist model. *Social Work, 45,* 9–25.

Perz, C. A., DiClemente, C. C., & Carbonari, J. P. (1996). Doing the right thing at the right time? The interaction of stages and processes of change in successful smoking cessation. *Health Psychology, 15*(6), 462–468.

Plichta, S. B., & Falik, M. (2001). Prevalence of violence and its implications for women's health. *Women's Health Issues, 11*(3), 244–258.

Prochaska, J. O., & DiClemente, C. C. (1982). Transtheoretical therapy: Toward a more integrated model of change. *Psychotherapy: Theory, Research and Practice, 19,* 276–288.

Prochaska, J. O., & DiClemente, C. C. (1983). Stages of processes of self-change of smoking: Toward an integrative model of change. *Journal of Consulting and Clinical Psychology, 51,* 390–395.

Prochaska, J. O., & Velicer, W. F. (1997). The transtheoretical model of health behavior change. *American Journal of Health Promotion, 12*(1), 38–48.

Prochaska, J. O., Velicer, W. F., Rossi, J. S., Goldstein, M. G., Marcus, B. H., Rakowski, W., et al. (1994). Stages of change and decisional balance for 12 problem behaviors. *Health Psychology, 13,* 39–46.

Rhodes, K. V., & Levinson, W. (2003) Interventions for intimate partner violence against women: Clinical applications. *Journal of the American Medical Association, 289*(5), 601–605.

Rossi, S. R., Rossi, J. S., Rossi-DelPrete, L. M., Prochaska, J. O., Banspach, S. W., & Carleton, R. A. (1994). A processes of change model for weight control for participants in community-based weight loss programs. *International Journal of the Addictions, 29*(2), 161–177.

Sallis, J. F., Cervero, R. B., Ascher, W., Henderson, K. A., Kraft, M. K., & Kerr, J. (2006). An ecological approach to creating active living communities. *Annual Reviews of Public Health, 27,* 297–322.

Straus, M. A., Hamby, S. L., Boney-McCoy, S., & Sugarman, D. B. (1996). The revised conflict tactics scale (CTS-2): Development and preliminary psychometric data. *Journal of Family Issues, 17,* 283–316.

Thompson, M. P., Basile, K. C., Hertz, M. F., & Sitterle, D. (2006). *Measuring Intimate Partner Violence Victimization and Perpetration: A Compendium of Assessment Tools.* Atlanta, GA: Centers for Disease Control and Prevention, National Center for Injury Prevention and Control.

Tjaden, P., & Thoennes, N. (2000). *Extent, nature, and consequences of intimate partner violence: Findings from the National Violence Against Women Survey.* Washington, DC: U.S. Department of Justice, Office of Justice Programs, National Institute of Justice.

Wathen, C. N., & MacMillan, H. L. (2003). Interventions for violence against women: Scientific review. *Journal of the American Medical Association, 289*(5), 589–600.

Zink, T., Elder, N., Jacobson, J., & Klostermann, B. (2004). Medical management of intimate partner violence considering the stages of change: Precontemplation and contemplation. *Annals of Family Medicine, 2*(3), 231–239.

12

The Transtheoretical Model in Intimate Partner Violence Victimization: Stage Changes Over Time

KELLY H. BURKITT AND GREGORY L. LARKIN

Intimate partner violence (IPV) is a pervasive public health problem (Basile, 2002; Caetano & Cunradi, 2003; Halpern, Young, Waller, Martin, & Kupper, 2004; Kramer, Lorenzon, & Mueller, 2004; Plichta & Abraham, 1996) involving physical violence, sexual violence, threat of physical or sexual violence, or psychological and emotional abuse occurring within the context of victim–perpetrator relationships among current or former intimate partners (Saltzman, Fanslow, McMahon, & Shelley, 2002). Findings from a representative telephone survey of 8,000 women and 8,000 men across the United States showed that as many as 1.9 million women are physically assaulted by an intimate partner each year (Tjaden & Theonnes, 1998). Intimate partner violence is also a substantial burden to the health care system, resulting in an estimated $5 billion to $10 billion a year in physical and mental health care costs, lost productivity, and criminal justice interventions (American Medical Association, 1994; National Center for Injury Prevention and Control, 2003).

As health care institutions struggle to implement or maintain programs to assist IPV victims, it becomes crucial to effectively and cost efficiently match program goals with those of individual victims. Given the multiplicity of backgrounds, resources, and needs of each patient, however, promoting healthy change in patients experiencing partner violence is complex. Behavior change itself is a dynamic, nonlinear process often characterized by short-term gains followed by reversion to previous behavior. Research has demonstrated that smokers, for example, attempt to quit an average of three to five times before quitting permanently (Norcross & Vangrelli, 1988–1989).

Similarly, in the context of partner violence, victims often find it difficult to escape the violence and are recurrently exposed to the abusive trauma during the course of their relationship. Indeed, many people often ask, "Why doesn't she just leave?" but this ill-informed question mistakenly assumes that leaving the relationship leads to instant security and ignores formidable internal and external barriers to leaving, such as money, transportation, police assistance, family and social pressure, personal values and beliefs about relationships, isolation, fear of retribution by the abuser, love for the abuser, and concern for children (Brown, 1997; Grigsby & Hartman, 1997). Thus, for most women in the midst of an active IPV relationship, questions regarding how to decrease exposure to violence (which may include the decision to leave the relationship) are fraught with fear, uncertainty, and, at best, mixed emotions (Davies, 1998). Given the dynamics of IPV, it is not surprising that it often takes years to end the cycle of abuse and begin the process of recovery.

While society often believes that the only solution to an abusive relationship is to extricate oneself from the situation, it should be noted that there are many other alternatives that victims choose. In fact, the true goal is to seek an end to the violence and distress in the relationship, and leaving is not always the safest or most appropriate option (Dienemann, Campbell, Landenburger, & Curry, 2002; Gilliland, Spence, & Spence, 2000). Research has shown that nonviolence can be achieved without leaving the relationship and that even after leaving there is often continued violence (Campbell, Rose, Kub, & Nedd, 1998). Decreasing victimization and recovery of self are central goals for partner violence victims (Landenburger, 1989), and ultimately there are many ways for victims to achieve this outcome.

THE TRANSTHEORETICAL MODEL OF BEHAVIOR CHANGE

The transtheoretical model of behavior change (TTM) proposes that people progress through five stages when attempting to modify health behaviors: precontemplation, contemplation, preparation, action, and maintenance (Prochaska & DiClemente, 1986). *Precontemplation* is a stage of relative denial in which people are not thinking about changing the behavior in question. *Contemplation* involves seriously thinking about changing the behavior. *Preparation* begins when steps are being taken toward the behavior change and when the environment is being set up to support the newly acquired behavior. *Action*, then, is the period of overt change, and *maintenance* involves continuing the new behavior and working against relapse despite temptations to do otherwise. Progression through these stages is not necessarily linear, and relapse to a previous stage is the rule rather than the exception (Prochaska, 1995).

While a large systematic review of stage-based interventions showed mixed results overall (Riemsma et al., 2002), the TTM has utility beyond customizing interventions. In fact, the TTM has successfully predicted both cessation of negative behaviors (e.g., quitting smoking, weight control) and acquisition of positive behaviors (e.g., safer sex, sunscreen use, mammography screening; Prochaska et al., 1994). The TTM presupposes that the "decisional balance sheet" of pros and cons perceived to be associated with the behavior must change if progression toward action and maintenance is to occur (Prochaska, Velicer, Guadagnoli, & Rossi, 1991). Previous research has shown that between contemplation and action, the pros of changing a behavior begin to outweigh the cons (Prochaska et al., 1994). In addition, temptations to engage in the target behavior tend to decrease across the stages. Measures designed to assess TTM-based stages have been used to capture the cognitive trajectory employed in making new life changes.

THE TTM IN IPV

The TTM has been extended to women in abusive relationships (Brown, 1997). Brown identifies an important difference between changing other health behaviors and women attempting to survive a relationship involving IPV: specifically, IPV is not entirely under individual control. Unlike smoking, IPV denotes an interdependent dyad wherein individual behavior must truly be addressed in the context of a two-person relationship. Nevertheless, Brown points out that many service agencies for IPV victims have intuitively developed programs and approaches that respect the stages women go through in making changes in their lives (Brown, 1997). In fact, most programs and institutions working with assault survivors emphasize letting the abused woman take the lead and respecting her timetable and goals (Hadley, Short, Lezin, & Zook, 1995; Herman, 1992; Meichenbaum, 1994; Waites, 1993; Yassen & Glass,

1984). While more precise IPV-based staging may lead to better customized treatment and intervention strategies, a more thorough and basic understanding of the change process in IPV is needed.

Understanding the stage differences of IPV victims may lead to insights regarding both the likelihood of continued exposure to abuse and the important role of barriers in maintaining victimization. Partner factors, abuse intensity, the presence of children, unemployment, isolation, and emotional distress are examples of barriers that may impede progression through any TTM-based stages.

This chapter examines the process of change in IPV victims longitudinally and explores cluster membership using the TTM-based construct of stages of change. As it is standard practice in applying the TTM to cluster analyze response patterns across the five stages, we sought to place individuals into homogeneous groups suggested by the data rather than in predefined categories. Since individuals who are similar on all five stages are grouped together, the cluster groups may have defining characteristics for which specific considerations and possible interventions are appropriate. For example, if a woman is identified as precontemplative and has children living with her, educating her about the effects of witnessing IPV on children may be particularly relevant.

This study was designed to test the following hypotheses: (a) IPV victims map into distinct stage-based clusters; (b) the clusters correlate with abuse exposure and other psychosocial variables, including the use of community resources, social support, and emotional distress; and (c) IPV victim stage-based cluster membership is prone to change over time.

METHODS

Participants

Study Population and Inclusion–Exclusion Criteria

All participants were enrolled at the time of presentation for treatment to the emergency department (ED) of an inner-city, level I trauma and burn center in Western Pennsylvania. Women were included if they were 18 years or older and identified themselves as being currently involved in an abusive relationship.

Women were excluded if they could not speak English, were unable to answer questions while in the ED, were intoxicated, or were already in a shelter at the time of enrollment. In addition, to help control for other stressful life events that might affect the variables of interest, women were excluded if they had experienced trauma unrelated to their abuse within the past year.

Sample Characteristics

One hundred and ninety-nine women were referred for participation in the study. Of those, 102 (50.8%) enrolled in the study. The majority of the women who did not enroll were ineligible either because they experienced non-IPV trauma in the past year (n = 15, 15.5% of those not enrolled) or because they did not meet study criteria for experiencing IPV (n = 18, 18.6%). Of the 199, 22 women (22.7%) declined participation, citing lack of time or interest. Data on the remaining women were unavailable. Of the 102 women enrolled in the study, 53 (51%) completed follow-up at 3 to 4 months. Thirty-three (32.3%) of the 102 women enrolled but did not complete data collection at enrollment (time 1), and 16 (15.6%) did not complete data collection at follow-up. Of the 49 women who did not complete data collection, 29 (59.2%) were unable to be recontacted because of an address change, disconnected telephone numbers, being in a shelter, or not responding to messages or letters. Another 18.4% (n = 9) were recontacted but were not interested in continuing with the study. After enrollment by a research assistant, one person (2%) who had been enrolled was deemed ineligible by the project coordinator (KHB) because her reported abuse experience did not meet study criteria. Data were not available on the remaining 10 women (20.4%) who did not complete follow-up.

Demographics of the final sample are presented in Table 12.1. The final sample of 53 women was relatively young (mean age 31) and Black, non-Hispanic (60.4%). The participants were also highly educated; 37.7% graduated high school or received their general equivalency diploma (GED), and 49.0% had postsecondary education in either college or technical school. Despite the education level attained, the sample was primarily low income: 18.9% earned less than $5,000 per year, and 49.0% earned less than $20,000 per year. Most of the women in this sample (56.6%) identified themselves as "single but involved in a relationship." The second-highest relationship category was "married or living together as if married" at 30.2%. The majority of participants had at least one child (84.9%), with the mean number of children being approximately two. For 37.7% of the sample, the abuser was the father of at least one of the participant's children. Of those women with children, most did not worry about the safety of their children with regard to their partner's behavior (64.3%).

Table 12.1

DEMOGRAPHICS OF FINAL SAMPLE (*N* = 53)

VARIABLE	MEASUREMENT SCALE
Age	31.1 ± 8.7 (range 18–48 years)
Income	
$0–$10,999	43.4% (*n* = 23)
$11,000–$20,999	24.5% (*n* = 13)
$21,000+	32.1% (*n* = 17)
Education	
Less than high school	11.3% (*n* = 6)
High school or GED	37.7% (*n* = 20)
Part college	24.5% (*n* = 13)
Completed college/technical school	24.5% (*n* = 13)
Ethnicity	
White, non-Hispanic	30.2% (*n* = 16)
Black, non-Hispanic	60.4% (*n* = 32)
White, Hispanic	3.8% (*n* = 2)
Missing/unknown	5.6% (*n* = 3)
Marital status	
Single but involved	56.6% (*n* = 30)
Married or living together as if married	30.2% (*n* = 16)
Separated/divorced	13.2% (*n* = 7)
Length of relationship (number of months)	48.0 ± 42.4 (range 2–182)
Children (% yes)	84.9% (n = 45)
Abuser children's father (% yes)	37.7% (n = 20)
Frequency of abuse	
1 time	7.5% (*n* = 4)
2–5 times	35.8% (*n* = 19)
6–10 times	22.6% (*n* = 12)
11+ times	34.0% (*n* = 18)
Recency of abuse	
<24 hours	75.5% (*n* = 40)
2–7 days	9.4% (*n* = 5)
2–4 weeks	5.7% (*n* = 3)
Relationship ended at time of enrollment (% yes)	26.4% (*n* = 14)

Of the final sample, 75.5% had been physically assaulted within 24 hours of enrollment in the study, and most had experienced physical assault by their partner on more than one occasion (92.4%). Most had suffered injury from their partner (81.1%) and had received medical care for their injuries (67.9%) at some point in time. In addition to the physical abuse, 32.1% reported that their partner had sexually assaulted them.

For many women, this was the first partner who had physically assaulted them (49.1%). However, an equal number of women had at least one prior partner physically assault them (45.3%), and 17.0% reported being sexually assaulted by a prior partner. In addition, 37.3% of the women in this sample reported experiencing other physical assault by a parent or guardian, a relative, an acquaintance, or someone like a stranger or coworker, while 28.3% reported being sexually assaulted by someone other than an intimate partner.

Independent sample t tests revealed no significant differences between women who completed follow-up and those who did not with regard to recency of last physical assault ($t[1, 97] = .69, p = .49$), frequency of abuse ($t[1, 97] = .33, p = .74$), length of relationship ($t[1, 96] = .68, p = .50$), or whether the abusive relationship had ended at least 24 hours prior to study enrollment ($\chi^2[1] = .85, p = .36$). With regard to demographics, White women were significantly less likely to complete the study than women of color ($\chi^2[1] = 6.36, p < .01$). No other demographic differences were observed between those who completed data collection and those who did not.

Procedure

The hospital's Human Subjects Review Committee approved the study prior to initiating data collection. The ED routinely screens all women 18 years of age and older for IPV regardless of presenting complaint. Thus, many of these women did not present to the ED because of injuries directly related to IPV. On identification of a victim during routine screening for IPV in the ED, the health care provider contacted the researcher on call by pager. When the female researcher arrived at the hospital, she approached the woman and explained the purpose of the study in a private room. If she indicated that she would be interested in participating, informed consent was obtained, and further information regarding the perpetrator and IPV history was acquired to ensure that she met inclusion criteria. If the woman indicated that she was not interested, the patient was referred to the social worker on call, the standard hospital procedure. Patients then completed the study questionnaires and were recontacted at 3 to 4 months and scheduled for an appointment at the hospital for retesting and completion of the follow-up assessment. Participants were paid for their time at the initial session and again at follow-up.

This study was nested inside of a randomized trial in which patients were also assigned one of two different types of victim advocates during their time in the ED. During the course of their visit, participants were randomized to either Emergency Department Victim Advocacy (EDVA) or Standard Social Service (SSS) intervention. A local women's shelter employee who was stationed at the hospital conducted EDVA, while SSS was conducted by a hospital social worker trained in IPV. Both interventions involved empathic support, immediate safety assessment, and linkage with community resources; however, EDVA also provided empowerment counseling, education about IPV, safety planning for the future, and follow-up support and assistance after leaving the hospital. There were no actual differences between these two subgroups in either demographics or other covariates at enrollment or follow-up, so the subgroups have been combined for purposes of analyzing the TTM.

MEASURES

Abuse and Trauma Screening

The Domestic Safety Assessment (DSA) (Salber & Taliaferro, 1995) was used for initial screening by the ED. Questions on the DSA include the following: (a) Do you feel safe at home? (b) We all have disagreements—when you and your partner or a family member argue, have you ever been physically hurt or threatened? (c) Do you feel your partner or a family member controls your behavior too much? (d) Does he or she threaten you? (e) Has your partner (or other family member) ever hit, pushed, shoved, punched, or kicked you? (f) Have you ever felt forced to engage in unwanted sexual acts or contact with your partner or other family member?

The DSA-Revised built on these original questions and included the following: (a) Have you ever in your lifetime been hit, shoved, punched, kicked, or otherwise physically hurt by someone, such as your current partner, an ex-partner, a parent or guardian when you were younger, a relative, an acquaintance, someone like a stranger, or coworkers? (b) Have you ever had a partner control your actions, put you down, or threaten you? (c) Have you had any unwanted sexual acts or contact by someone else such as a partner, a parent or guardian when you were younger, a relative, an acquaintance, someone else like a stranger, or coworker? Research assistants were trained to follow-up with specific information regarding the perpetrator, dates, frequency, and date of last contact with the person. The detailed information was completed for each relationship mentioned. Eligible participants indicated that with their current partner they felt "threatened and controlled" and reported experiencing at least one incident of physical or sexual assault within the past 2 months.

"Other Trauma" Screening

During the screening process, people were also asked about other stressful or disturbing experiences they might have encountered in the past year. The question was based on the posttraumatic stress disorder introduction from the Structured Clinical Interview for the *Diagnostic and Statistical Manual of Mental Disorders,* 4th ed. (First, Spitzer, & Gibbon, & Williams, 1996) and included events, such as fires, physical assault or rape by strangers, and other types of disaster. Patients were excluded if they reported "yes" and described an event similar to those described.

Stages of Change

The TTM was measured using the Process of Change in Abused Women Scales (PROCAWS; Brown, 1998). This measure is designed to systematically measure the process of change that IPV victims go through to obtain a violence-free life. As Brown (2001) notes, the measure is "not meant to imply that an abused woman should change her behavior. Rather, it is meant to describe the changes and cognitive shifts that do occur as abused women begin to look at themselves, their relationships, and their partners differently" (p. 1).

The PROCAWS was developed on 300 women ages 18 to 78 (mean 34); 57.0% of these women were in a shelter, 24.7% from a support group, 12.7% from court, and 5.7% from an ED. In this sample, 27.9% of the women had less than a high school degree, 68.7% were White, 34.4% were married or living as if they were married, 42.7% were separated or divorced, and 21.7% were single or never married. The income for 65.7% of the sample was less than $20,000 per year. The PROCAWS includes 25 items designed to measure stage of change, 12 items measuring the pros and cons of change, and 7 items measuring temptations. Additional scales measuring self-efficacy and confidence were not included in the present study.

Stage of Change

The questions measuring stage of change are rated on a Likert-type scale from 1 (strongly disagree) to 5 (strongly agree). Factor analysis identified five factors, each with five items, related to stages of change: Precontemplation, Contemplation, Letting Go of the Hope He'll Change (i.e., Letting Go), Action, and Autonomy/Separate Self. Letting Go of the Hope He'll Change and Autonomy/Separate Self are not traditional TTM stages, but in Brown's original sample, Letting Go appeared pivotal and accounted for the most variance, while Autonomy can be considered the functional equivalent to maintenance. Precontemplation includes items such as (a) my partner is the boss, and that's how it should be, and (b) if I do what my partner wants, the abuse will stop, while Contemplation includes items such as (a) I would like to figure out some ways to end the abuse, but I need help, and (b) I might like to talk to someone who could tell me how to deal with an abusive partner. Letting Go of the Hope He'll Change includes items like (a) I have less and less hope that my partner will ever change and (b) I'm beginning to realize that my partner doesn't want to change. Action items identify clear behavior changes on the victim's part and include (a) I am actively taking steps to keep myself safe from abuse and (b) anyone can talk about ending abuse in their life; I'm actually doing something about it. Finally, Autonomy/Separate Self includes items such as (a) I have learned the pleasure of making choices for myself and (b) I am doing things to live my life the way I want to. Reliability for the five subscales ranged from Cronbach's alpha of .70 to .86. For each subscale, a mean factor score was determined for each respondent and converted to t scores for cluster analysis.

Decisional Balance

The 12 decisional balance items are also rated on a Likert-type scale from 1 (not important) to 5 (extremely important). The decisional balance scale is comprised of two factors, pros and cons, with subscale reliabilities of alpha of .82 and .85. Items describe factors associated with the cons or the "Pull of the relationship" and the pros or the "Strain of the Abuse." Examples of con items include (a) I would be lonely without my partner; (b) the relationship has its good times, I don't want to lose those; and (c) I would feel like a failure if my relationship ended. Pro items include (a) I'm tired of walking on eggshells around my partner, (b) the abuse is getting worse and worse, and (c) remaining in this relationship is harmful to me. It is expected that as women progress through the stages, the pros of figuring out a way to end the violence would increase, and the cons of the pull of the relationship would decrease.

Temptations

The seven temptation items range from 1 (not at all tempted) to 5 (extremely tempted). It asks the participant to rate "how tempted you may be to remain, or return, in each situation." The items include (a) when I feel like I'm the only one who can help my partner, (b) when I remember the part of my partner that I fell in love with, (c) when my partner promises to change, and (d) when my partner enters a treatment program.

Relationship Status

At each time point, participants were asked if they were currently involved in the relationship and when it ended. If it was greater than 24 hours, the relationship was considered to have ended. While 24 hours is often not long enough to define the end of a relationship, the 24-hour time period was chosen for practical reasons to separate those women who appeared to be directly reacting to the most recent violence incident versus those who had taken action prior to the violent incident. For example, a woman who presented to the ED within hours of an assault and indicated that the relationship is over as of now would not constitute leaving by our definition. This information was used as an outcome variable in subsequent analyses.

Use of Community Resources

The items regarding use of community resources were developed in consultation with the local women's shelter. Questions were dichotomous, and participants were asked follow-up questions for any positively endorsed answer. The measure was comprised of six questions asking participants if they engaged in any of the following activities in the past 6 months (or since enrollment at follow-up): telephoned anyone or participated in counseling services; called the police for partner abuse; contacted a lawyer, attorney, or other legal service regarding IPV; requested a restraining order or protection from abuse (PFA); received shelter from the local women's shelter; or were involved with any drug or alcohol rehabilitation programs.

Mental Health

The Symptom Checklist-90–Revised (Derogatis, 1992) is comprised of 90 psychological symptom items rated on a 5-point scale (0–4) ranging from "not at all" to "extremely." High symptom reporting is indicative of increased distress and is associated with other self-report and physiological indicators of distress. This measure provides nine subscales as well as a global index of symptom reporting, and reliability coefficients range from .84 to .90. The Global Severity Index (GSI) represents the best single indicator of the current level or depth of psychological distress and combines information on numbers of symptoms and intensity of perceived distress. The GSI score is created by summing the distress scores for the 90 items and dividing by 90, such that the GSI then ranges from 0 to 4, as in the case with each individual item.

Social Support

The Interpersonal Support Evaluation List (ISEL) assesses perceived availability of general and specific kinds of social support, including tangible support, belongingness, and availability of a person to talk to (Cohen & Hoberman, 1983). The ISEL is comprised of 40 true or false items that participants rate as "generally true or not true" for them. Items include such things as (a) I regularly meet or talk with members of my family or friends; (b) if I were sick and needed someone to drive me to the doctor, I would have trouble finding someone; (c) I don't often get invited to do things with others; and (d) most people I know think highly of me. Internal reliability (alpha coefficient) ranged from .88 to .90, and subscale alphas range from .62 to .92. The ISEL correlates between .21 and .62 with other measures of social support and adjustment, indicating some overlap and some differentiation. Scores on the ISEL are related to psychological and physical symptomatology (e.g., Beck Depression Inventory, Langer Symptom Checklist, and Coben-Hoberman Inventory of Physical Symptoms), and high levels of support as measured by the ISEL may buffer the effects of life stress (Cohen, Mermelstein, Kamarck, & Hoberman, 1985).

Statistical Analyses

Cluster analysis is currently the recommended statistical technique for describing the patterns of responding on the PROCAWS. Cluster analysis places individuals into homogeneous groups that are suggested by the data rather than in predefined categories (the clusters are derived empirically rather than theoretically). Thus, the different clusters are similar or dissimilar in significant ways. The clusters can then be analyzed to identify the characteristics of individuals in each cluster, thus providing further information about applicability of the identified clusters in the real world.

We used cluster analysis to group the participants along the PROCAWS subscales and then relate these groupings to differences in demographic and outcome measures. After calculation of the five subscale scores (i.e., Precontemplation, Contemplation, Letting Go, Action, and Autonomy), the Ward method of hierarchical agglomerative cluster analyses was used to identify participant profiles. This method of clustering was chosen based on previous work both by the developer of the PROCAWS (Brown, 1998) and by other researchers studying the stages of change (McConnaughy, DiClemente, Prochaska, & Velicer, 1989; McConnaughy, Prochaska, & Velicer, 1983). Descriptive summaries of clusters and significant demographic, abuse, and outcome variables that were related to cluster membership are presented. These cluster profiles summarize the differences between the clusters on key variables.

Following cluster analyses, participants were categorized as to whether their cluster profiles changed over time and, if so, to what degree and in what direction. After identification, labeling, and ordering the clusters at enrollment and completion, a change score was calculated by subtracting the numerical cluster score at enrollment (i.e., 1–5) from the score at completion.

RESULTS

Preliminary analysis examined three- through seven-cluster solutions. After considering the possible combinations, a five-cluster solution for each time point was retained. The five-cluster solution was chosen because it resulted in the most logical theoretically interpretable solution— the more expansive solutions resulted in a loss of distinctions between groups, while a more parsimonious solution collapsed conceptually distinct subgroups. The cluster profiles were labeled to reflect salient characteristics of the clusters answers on the PROCAWS: Reluctance, Precontemplation, Uninvolved/Ambivalent, Engagement, and Action.

The results regarding the TTM are presented in four sections. First, the profiles of the stage cluster groups are presented at enrollment and completion. Second, the relationship between the clusters and decisional balance and temptations is reviewed. Third, the relationship between the clusters and background and outcome variables is presented, providing a practical understanding of the differences between the clusters. Fourth, changes in cluster status over time are presented and discussed.

Cluster Profiles

Mean *t* scores at each stage of change (Precontemplation, Contemplation, Letting Go, Action, and Autonomy/Separation) for identified clusters at enrollment and completion are presented in Figures 12.1 and 12.2.

Clusters at Enrollment

For the five-cluster solution, clusters at enrollment generally fit the five-stage theoretical PROCAWS model.

The Reluctance cluster comprised about 1 in 10 (11.5%) of the sample. The pattern with regard to staging shows Precontemplation scores two standard deviations above the mean, Contemplation and Letting Go of Hope scores approximating the mean, and Action and Autonomy scores 1.5 standard deviations below the mean. These women endorsed items such as "My partner is the boss and that's how it should be," "If I do what my partner wants, the abuse will stop," and "Being really jealous means my partner loves me."

The women who made up the Precontemplation cluster constituted approximately one in four (23%) of the women in the sample. The pattern reflects average scores at 50 for all stages except for Letting Go of Hope, which is 1.5 standard deviations below the mean. These women held on to the beliefs that their partners would change and that their partners desired change. Because of the low scores on Letting Go of Hope, this could potentially also be considered that the woman is essentially holding on to the hope that he will change, and therefore she remains in the Precontemplation phase.

A middle cluster, the Uninvolved/Ambivalent cluster, also comprised approximately one in four (27%) women in the sample at enrollment. Stage scores for these women tended to center around the

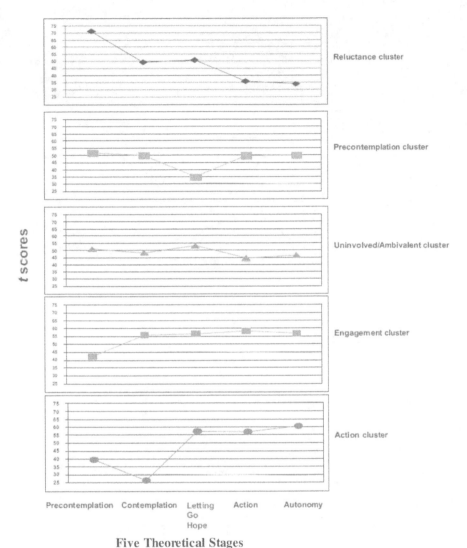

Five Theoretical Stages

Figure 12.1   Five clusters at enrollment.

mean with less than .5 standard deviation departure at any given stage. These women tended to endorse neither earlier stages or later stages of change—they were apathetic or passive regarding their relationship.

At enrollment, the largest cluster was the fourth, or Engagement, cluster (32.7%; Figure 12.1). Women in this cluster were below the mean on Precontemplation and slightly above the mean on the other stages. These women tended to endorse both items, indicating that they

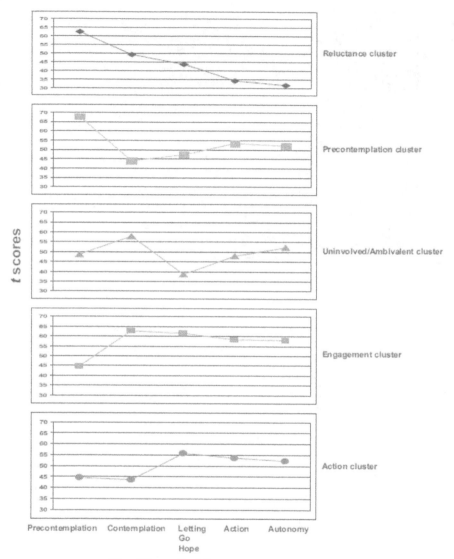

Five Theoretical Stages

Figure 12.2 Five clusters at completion.

were ready to make changes but felt that they needed help to do so and that they were taking action to end the abuse in the relationship.

The final cluster identified at enrollment, Action (Figure 12.1), is characterized by Precontemplation scores one standard deviation below the mean and Contemplation scores more than two standard deviations below the mean, while at the same time elevated scores for Letting Go of Hope,

Action, and Autonomy. At enrollment, this group comprised the fewest number of women (6%) and endorsed somewhat similar item scores as the Engagement cluster with the notable exception of the Contemplation scores. These women were clearly stating that they did not need help to end the relationship or maintain the changes that they were making.

Clusters at Completion

As mentioned, the five-cluster solution at completion contained similar but slightly different patterns to those at enrollment (Figure 12.2).

As at enrollment, the Reluctance cluster at completion was characterized by elevated Precontemplation scores and average scores for Contemplation and Letting Go of Hope, with very low (two standard deviations) scores for Action and Autonomy. This cluster can be conceptualized as women who are reluctant to think about or take action to change the current situation. Approximately one in six women constituted this cluster at completion.

The Precontemplation cluster at completion was comprised of 8% of this sample. The Precontemplation cluster at completion was characterized by women with very high Precontemplation scores ($t = 67.6$) with other scores centering around the mean. Unlike the women in the Reluctance cluster, these women had elevated Precontemplation scores but only average scores for the other stages. This profile contrasts with this cluster at enrollment, which was characterized by average scores for most scales with low scores for Letting Go of the Hope. However, it is our belief that both profiles are characteristic of precontemplative thought.

One in four women made up the Uninvolved/Ambivalent cluster at completion. This cluster appears somewhat similar to the Precontemplation profile at enrollment. However, these women had average scores for Precontemplation, Action, and Autonomy with above average scores for Contemplation and below average scores for Letting Go of Hope. Thus, these women were holding on to the hope that he would change while beginning to indicate that they wanted to change their current situation but needed help.

One-third of the sample at completion made up the Engagement cluster. These women were similar to the Engagement sample at enrollment in that the scores on Precontemplation were below average and scores on the other four scales were above average.

The pattern for the women in the Action cluster was similar to that observed at enrollment. While only 6% of the sample fell into this cluster at enrollment, this cluster grew significantly, comprising 42% of the entire sample at completion.

Decisional Balance and Temptations on the PROCAWS

Table 12.2 presents the means and standard deviations for the decisional balance and temptation scores at enrollment and completion.

Decisional Balance

As an example, Figure 12.3 shows the mean level of endorsement of pros and cons of the relationship by cluster membership at enrollment. The hypothesized relationship holds at both enrollment and completion. At enrollment, as women move from Precontemplation to Uninvolved/Ambivalent, the pros of ending the relationship begin to outweigh the cons associated with the strain of staying. While not as clean, the decisional pattern at completion indicates that, in general, as women move from Ambivalent Contemplation to Engagement, the pros begin to outweigh the cons.

Temptations

As expected by the TTM, temptation scores tended to decrease across clusters at both enrollment and completion. Temptation t scores are consistent with the TTM and indicate that temptation is inversely re-

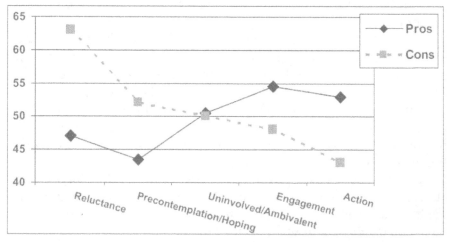

Figure 12.3 Mean pros and cons scores by stage clusters at enrollment.

MEAN *T* SCORES AND STANDARD DEVIATIONS FOR DECISIONAL BALANCE AND TEMPTATIONS BY CLUSTER MEMBERSHIP AT ENROLLMENT AND COMPLETION

VARIABLE	RELUCTANCE	CLUSTER PRECONTEMPLATION	UNINVOLVED/AMBIVALENT	ENGAGEMENT	ACTION
Pros					
Enrollment	49.1 ± 11.1	45.3 ± 12.2	51.9 ± 8.2	51.5 ± 9.8	53.90 ± 2.4
Completion	46.8 ± 8.8	41.8 ± 11.4	50.2 ± 7.7	58.7 ± 4.11	50.0 ± 11.2
Cons					
Enrollment	67.4 ± 10.1	51.1 ± 10.4	46.7 ± 5.8	47.2 ± 6.4	12.3 ± 2.0
Completion	57.6 ± 9.9	52.5 ± 19.2	54.7 ± 9.0	48.6 ± 9.3	44.6 ± 5.2
Temptations					
Enrollment	61.2 ± 7.6	52.7 ± 7.8	51.7 ± 9.1	44.9 ± 8.5	36.1 ± 0.0
Completion	59.4 ± 9.4	49.5 ± 15.8	54.2 ± 9.7	45.5 ± 7.6	45.4 ± 7.0

Table 12.2

lated to stage progression in that women reported being less tempted to remain with or return to their abusive partner across cluster stages.

Relation of Cluster Membership to Abuse and Other Psychosocial Variables

Demographic and outcome variables were examined by cluster at each time point to identify distinguishing features of cluster membership. Tables 12.3 and 12.4 present detailed information and significance levels regarding variables that were found to be different across clusters at either time point (enrollment and completion, respectively).

Enrollment

At enrollment, the frequency of physical assault, perceived social support–appraisal, and perceived social support–self-esteem were significantly different by clusters. With regard to physical assault, women who reported being assaulted 1 to 10 times were more likely to fall into the Precontemplation, Engagement, or Action categories, while women who were assaulted 11 or more times were more likely to be in the Uninvolved/Ambivalent category ($p < .01$). The primary difference with social support by cluster was that the women who made up the Reluctance cluster were much less likely to report appraisal ($p < .05$) or self-esteem ($p < .01$) support as compared to those in the remaining clusters.

Completion

Interestingly, only social support–self-esteem and frequency of physical assault were not related to cluster membership. Women in the Reluctance cluster were more likely to report having children ($p < .01$) and that the abuser was the father of their children ($p < .05$), while women in the Engagement and Action clusters reported that they had children but the abuser was not the father of their children. At completion, more women in the Engagement and Action clusters reported that the relationship had ended ($p < .01$) and that they had made use of community resources ($p < .01$). Women in both the Uninvolved/Ambivalent cluster and the Action cluster reported less distress than the other clusters ($p < .01$). This may be related to the women in both of these clusters also reporting more social support–appraisal ($p < .01$) and social support–tangible ($p < .05$) than the other clusters.

Table 12.3

VARIABLES CORRELATED WITH CLUSTER MEMBERSHIP AT ENROLLMENT

			CLUSTER		
VARIABLE	RELUCTANCE $N = 6$ (11.5%)	PRECONTEMPLATION $N = 12$ (23.1%)	UNINVOLVED/ AMBIVALENT $N = 14$ (26.9%)	ENGAGEMENT $N = 17$ (32.7%)	ACTION $N = 3$ (5.8%)
Children (% yes)	100.0 ($n = 6$)	75.0 ($n = 9$)	85.7 ($n = 12$)	82.4 ($n = 14$)	100.0 ($n = 3$)
Abuser children's father (% yes)	100.0 ($n = 6$)	40.0 ($n = 4$)	38.5 ($n = 5$)	25.0 ($n = 4$)	50.0 ($n = 1$)
Frequency of physical assault**					
1–10 times	50.0 ($n = 3$)	75.0 ($n = 9$)	35.7 ($n = 5$)	88.2 ($n = 15$)	66.6 ($n = 2$)
11+ times	50.0 ($n = 3$)	25.0 ($n = 3$)	64.3 ($n = 9$)	11.8 ($n = 2$)	33.3 ($n = 1$)

(Continued)

Table 12.3

VARIABLES CORRELATED WITH CLUSTER MEMBERSHIP AT ENROLLMENT (*Continued*)

| | CLUSTER | | | | |
| | RELUCTANCE | PRECONTEMPLATION | UNINVOLVED/ AMBIVALENT | ENGAGEMENT | ACTION |
VARIABLE	N = 6 (11.5%)	N = 12 (23.1%)	N = 14 (26.9%)	N = 17 (32.7%)	N = 3 (5.8%)
Relationship ended (% yes)	0.0 (n = 0)	25.0 (n = 3)	28.6 (n = 4)	29.4 (n = 5)	33.3 (n = 1)
Community resources total	.83 ± 1.2	2.0 ± 1.5	1.7 ± 1.4	1.6 ± 1.4	0.7 ± 0.6
Global Severity Index	1.5 ± 1.2	0.8 ± 1.0	0.9 ± 1.0	0.9 ± 0.7	0.6 ± 0.6
Social support–appraisal*	3.5 ± 1.4	6.8 ± 1.8	5.9 ± 2.9	6.8 ± 1.9	5.7 ± 2.1
Social support–self-esteem**	3.7 ± 2.8	7.3 ± 0.9	5.7 ± 3.0	7.6 ± 1.5	8.0 ± 2.7
Social support–tangible	3.2 ± 3.5	6.4 ± 2.1	6.8 ± 2.9	6.1 ± 3.7	7.3 ± 3.8

Note. Community resources total scores range from 0 to 6, Global Severity Index scores range from 0 to 4, and Social Support subscale scores range from 0 to 10. All are presented as mean ± standard deviation.
* p < .05. ** p < .01.

Table 12.4

VARIABLES CORRELATED WITH CLUSTER MEMBERSHIP AT COMPLETION

	CLUSTER				
VARIABLE	RELUCTANCE $N=8$ (15.4%)	PRECONTEMPLATION $N=4$ (7.7%)	UNINVOLVED/ AMBIVALENT $N=12$ (23.1%)	ENGAGEMENT $N=6$ (11.5%)	ACTION $N=22$ (42.3%)
Children (% yes)**	100.0 ($n=8$)	25.0 ($n=1$)	75.0 ($n=9$)	83.3 ($n=5$)	95.5 ($n=21$)
Abuser children's father (% yes)*	100.0 ($n=6$)	40.0 ($n=4$)	38.5 ($n=5$)	25.0 ($n=4$)	50.0 ($n=1$)
Frequency of physical assault**					
1–10 times	25.0 ($n=2$)	50.0 ($n=2$)	100.0 ($n=12$)	66.6 ($n=4$)	63.6 ($n=14$)
11+ times	75.0 ($n=6$)	50.0 ($n=2$)	0.0 ($n=0$)	33.3 ($n=2$)	36.4 ($n=8$)

(*Continued*)

Table 12.4

VARIABLES CORRELATED WITH CLUSTER MEMBERSHIP AT COMPLETION (*Continued*)

VARIABLE	RELUCTANCE	PRECONTEMPLATION	CLUSTER UNINVOLVED/ AMBIVALENT	ENGAGEMENT	ACTION
	N = 8 (15.4%)	*N* = 4 (7.7%)	*N* = 12 (23.1%)	*N* = 6 (11.5%)	*N* = 22 (42.3%)
Relationship ended (% yes)**	28.6 (*n* = 2)	50.0 (*n* = 2)	41.7 (*n* = 5)	100.0 (*n* = 6)	95.5 (*n* = 21)
Community resources total**	.25 ± 0.5	1.0 ± 8.2	1.3 ± 1.2	3.0 ± 1.4	1.9 ± 1.4
Global Severity Index**	1.2 ± 1.0	1.7 ± 1.3	.6 ± .7	1.9 ± .9	.6 ± .7
Social support–appraisal**	4.3 ± 3.0	5.8 ± 1.7	6.8 ± 2.8	5.5 ± 2.4	7.6 ± 1.7
Social support–self-esteem	4.9 ± 2.9	5.3 ± 4.3	7.7 ± 2.5	4.7 ± 3.4	7.5 ± 2.6
Social support–tangible*	4.0 ± 3.6	5.3 ± 4.3	7.7 ± 2.5	4.7 ± 3.4	7.5 ± 2.6

Note. Community resources total scores range from 0 to 6, Global Severity Index scores range from 0 to 4, and Social Support subscale scores range from 0 to 10. All are presented as mean ± standard deviation.
*p < .05. ***p* < .01.

Progression Through the Stages of Change Over Time

Overall, from enrollment to completion, women tended to move toward the Action cluster. This statement holds true more for the later stages than the earlier stages. For example, of the three women who made up the Reluctance cluster at enrollment, two remained in Reluctance. Interestingly, the majority of participants in the Uninvolved/Ambivalent cluster (8 of 14, or 57%) at enrollment moved to Action, while the remainder were evenly distributed throughout the other clusters. Of the 17 women making up the Engagement cluster at enrollment, 8 (47%) moved to Action at completion, 3 (18%) stayed in Engagement, and 4 (24%) dropped one level to Ambivalent. All three women in Action at enrollment remained in Action at completion.

The calculated change score resulted in a new dependent variable with a range of –3 to 3, a mean of .59, and a median of 1.0, indicating that, in general, women were more likely to move in a positive direction across stages over time and that the majority of them moved one level. The second-highest frequency was 0, indicating that these women did not move through the stages over time.

The stage change score was related to total use of community resources and ending the relationship at completion. The change score analysis with the factor covariates explained 37% of the variance with regard to use of community resources ($R^2 = .37, p < .001; \beta = .56, p < .001$). Thus, progression through the stages was significantly related to use of more community resources; however, other demographic and psychosocial variables were not significantly associated with stage change scores.

Logistic regression predicting the end of the relationship at completion ($\chi^2 = 15.28, p = .004$; odds ratio = 2.58 [confidence interval = 1.36–4.92]) showed that those who progressed through the stages were 2.58 times more likely to end their relationship at completion. These findings are consistent with the TTM of change that as women move through the stages from Precontemplation to Autonomy, they are likely to engage in actions consistent with becoming free of the abuse.

DISCUSSION

Many authors have examined cognitive states associated with abusive intimate relationships (Dienemann et al., 2002; Landenburger, 1989;

Wuest & Merritt-Gray, 1999). The clusters identified in this prospective cohort are consistent with those described by the TTM (Precontemplation, Contemplation, Preparation, Action, and Maintenance) as well as those suggested by previous researchers using retrospective data (Dienemann et al., 2002; Mills, 1985; Moss, Pitula, Campbell, & Halstead, 1997; Wuest & Merritt-Gray, 1999). There appears to be a common progression of thought among IPV victims as they move from a violence-filled life to a violence-free life. For example, Dienemann and colleagues (2002) identified five states that women tend to go through in IPV relationships, including being committed to continuing, being committed but questioning, considering and preparing for change, breaking away or the partner changing, and establishing a new life, apart or together. These cohere more closely with our five clusters, even though we studied an ED-based rather than a shelter-based sample.

When examining the TTM stages in our sample, one important stage appears to be what we term "uninvolved ambivalence." This appears to be the crossroads between what Landenburger (1989) describes as "enduring" and "disengaging" and is similar to Brown's (1998) "letting go of the hope he'll change." In our sample, women making up the Uninvolved cluster had children who were the sons and/or daughters of the abuser, and a number of them had taken steps to end the relationship or the violence. However, their scores on all TTM subscales tended to fall around the mean, indicating that they were not strongly endorsing statements reflective of Precontemplation (e.g., "If I do what my partner wants, the abuse will stop") or of Autonomy/Separate Self (e.g., "I am doing things to live my life the way I want to"). This crossroad may categorize people in different stages of action who are still sorting through their cognitions about their current life circumstances.

While we did not find cluster membership to be predictive of relationship termination, we did find termination to be associated with directional movement across the stages. Specifically, victims who progressed through the stages were significantly more likely to end their relationship at study completion. These findings are consistent with the TTM of change that as women move through the stages from Precontemplation to Autonomy, they are likely to engage more in behavioral than in cognitive processes (Burke, 2004). Future IPV research should focus on dynamic stage movement over time rather than more static conceptions of cluster membership.

Understanding characteristics of the women making up our clusters may provide valuable information for tailoring interventions. For example, the Reluctance clusters at enrollment and completion were comprised of women who had children and for whom the perpetrator was the father of the children. They also perceived less social support in their environment than women in other clusters. These women endorsed items indicating that jealousy equals love and that, if they do the right thing, the abuse will end. For these women, basic education about the definitions of abuse and the effects on children may be the most effective. In addition, increasing their perceived social support by offering child care so that they could gain easier access to community resources may be a helpful adjunct to service provision. Similarly, the Engagement clusters exemplify victims who endorsed items indicating that they were making changes in their relationship but that they needed help to continue and maintain these changes. These women were the most likely to be actively engaged in using community resources and the most likely to have ended their relationship between the time of enrollment and study completion. They also reported experiencing the most global distress of all the clusters. Tailored intervention for these women may include education regarding normative experiences of women ending abusive relationships, encouragement, and stress management. Finally, victims in the Action clusters were making changes (or had made changes) and did not perceive the need for further assistance. Consistent with this, these women reported the least use of community resources of all clusters. However, these women also reported the lowest distress and the highest levels of perceived social support. For these women, a tailored intervention may focus primarily on assessing perceived barriers and difficulties they may encounter in the future, reinforcement of the changes already made, and encouragement for continued self-growth and self-preservation.

While the TTM has received much attention and has been successful when applied to interventions in some populations, it may be an insufficient basis on which to formulate effective interventions. Indeed, a systematic review of the effectiveness of stages-of-change-based interventions in promoting individual behavior change yielded mixed results (Riemsma et al., 2002). Of 37 different stage-based interventions reviewed, only 10 showed a positive association with the outcome. There were no significant differences between stage-based and nonstage-based interventions in 17 trials, but the authors of this review readily admit that most of these trials suffered from design and measurement issues and that there continues to be a great need for accurate stage measurements in order to permit evolving and optimal stage-specific interventions in the future.

The present work is one step forward in generating useful measures of readiness for change in victims of IPV. The cluster profiles identified women with different levels of engagement in thinking about and implementing change. The factors reflected those women who are already taking action, those who are not yet taking action but are not comfortable with the current situation, and those who are not yet engaged in thinking of changing their current situation. These three factors may be more important when tailoring an intervention for IPV victims than the five-stage TTM theory. Further research will be required to extend these findings to other samples and determine their specific utility for designing more tailored, customized interventions for victims of IPV in the future.

There are several important limitations to this work, including the focus on women who were already going to a health care facility for treatment; this may have biased the sample toward those already engaged in help seeking, threatening the generalizability of the results to women who are not active help seekers. Fortunately, the measures employed were previously developed in a larger and more diverse IPV population, but our efforts suggest that they are also valid in the subpopulation of women seeking emergency health care.

Another limitation is our small sample size and the attrition from the original sample, although there were few significant demographic or baseline psychosocial differences between those participants who completed longitudinal follow-up and those who did not. Future work should attempt to follow victims more closely and for longer periods of time; however, there are inherent dangers in such surveillance, and close follow-up may constitute an intervention in and of itself. Thus, the ED-based interventions employed here must also be carefully controlled when tracking stage changes over time.

Our time frame for follow-up was rather limited (3 months) when compared to the length of many abusive relationships. Interestingly, even in this short time frame, we saw movement across the stages. This movement may be the result of having a sample of already active help seekers, many of whom, in addition to coming to the ED for medical care, were connected to community resources focused on providing assistance to IPV victims. It is hoped that future research will allow for greater follow-up and provide more detailed information of changes over time.

Despite these limitations, examination of stage movement over time provides new information that contributes to our understanding of the process of change in IPV victims. This is one of the first quantitative studies to apply the TTM to a cohort of IPV victims. It is also unique in that our sample consisted of women who are presenting to an ED and not already in shelter. The utility of the TTM in describing cluster membership may have implications for clinicians who attempt to screen, treat, and refer victims of conjugal violence in practice.

REFERENCES

American Medical Association. (1994). 4,000,000 women abused annually. *Hospitals and Health Networks, 68,* 15.

Basile, K. C. (2002). Prevalence of wife rape and other intimate partner sexual coercions in a nationally representative sample of women. *Violence and Victims, 17,* 511–524.

Brown, J. (1997, July). Working toward freedom from violence: The process of change in battered women. *Violence Against Women, 3,* 5–26.

Brown, J. (1998). *The Process of Change in Abused Women Scale (PROCAWS): Stages of change, pros and cons, and self-efficacy as measurable outcomes.* Paper presented at Program Evaluation and Family Violence Research: An International Conference, Durham, NH.

Brown, J. (2001). *Information on PROCAWS.* Unpublished data and manuscript.

Burke, J. G. (2004). Ending intimate partner violence: An application of the transtheoretical model. *Journal of Health Behavior, 29,* 122–133.

Caetano, R., & Cunradi, C. (2003). Intimate partner violence and depression among Whites, Blacks, and Hispanics. *Annals of Epidemiology, 13,* 661–665.

Campbell, J., Rose, L., Kub, J., & Nedd, D. (1998). Voices of strength and resistance: A contextual and longitudinal analysis of women's responses to battering. *Journal of Interpersonal Violence, 13,* 743–762.

Cohen, S., & Hoberman, H. M. (1983). Positive events and social supports as buffers of life change stress. *Journal of Applied Social Psychology, 13,* 99–125.

Cohen, S., Mermelstein, R., Kamarck, T., & Hoberman, H. (1985). Measuring the functional components of social support. In I. G. Sarason & B. R. Sarason (Eds.), *Social support: Theory, research and application* (pp. 73–94). The Hague: Martinus Nijhoff.

Davies, J. (1998). Safety planning with battered women: Complex lives/difficult choices. In *Sage series on violence against women* (Vol. 7, pp. 50–52). Thousand Oaks, CA: Sage.

Derogatis, L. R. (1992). *SCL-90-R: Administration, scoring and procedures manual—II.* Towson, MD: Clinical Psychometric Research.

Dienemann, J., Campbell, J., Landenburger, K., & Curry, M. A. (2002). The domestic violence survivor assessment: A tool for counseling women in intimate partner violence relationships. *Patient Education and Counseling, 46,* 221–228.

First, M. B., Spitzer, R. L., Gibbon, M., & Williams, J. B. W. (1996). *Structured clinical interview for DSM-IV Axis I disorders, research version* (Patient Edition, SCID-I/P). New York: Biometrics Research, New York State Psychiatric Institute.

Gilliland, M. G., Spence, P. R., & Spence, R. L. (2000). Lethal domestic violence in eastern North Carolina. *North Carolina Medical Journal, 61,* 287–290.

Grigsby, N., & Hartman, B. R. (1997). The barriers model: An integrated strategy for intervention with battered women. *Psychotherapy, 34,* 485–497.

Hadley, S. M., Short, L. M., Lezin, N., & Zook, E. (1995). WomanKind: An innovative model of health care response to domestic abuse. *Women's Health Issues, 5,* 189–198.

Halpern, C. T., Young, M. L., Waller, M. W., Martin, S. L., & Kupper, L. L. (2004). Prevalence of partner violence in same-sex romantic and sexual relationships in a national sample of adolescents. *Journal of Adolescent Health, 35,* 124–131.

Herman, J. L. (1992). *Trauma and recovery.* New York: Basic Books.

Kramer, A., Lorenzon, D., & Mueller, G. (2004). Prevalence of intimate partner violence and health implications in women using emergency departments and primary care clinics. *Women's Health Issues, 14,* 19–29.

Landenburger, K. (1989). A process of entrapment in and recovery from an abusive relationship. *Issues in Mental Health Nursing, 10,* 209–227.

McConnaughy, E. A., DiClemente, C. C., Prochaska, J. O., & Velicer, W. F. (1989). Stages of change in psychotherapy: A follow-up report. *Psychotherapy, 26,* 494–503.

McConnaughy, E. A., Prochaska, J. O., & Velicer, W. F. (1983). Stages of change in psychotherapy: Measurement and sample profiles. *Psychotherapy: Theory, Research and Practice, 20,* 368–375.

Meichenbaum, D. (1994). *A clinical handbook/practical therapist manual for assessing and treating adults with post-traumatic stress disorder (PTSD).* Ontario: Institute Press.

Mills, T. (1985). The assault of self: Stages in coping with battered husbands. *Qualitative Sociology, 8,* 103–123.

Moss, V. A., Pitula, C. R., Campbell, J. C., & Halstead, L. (1997). The experiences of terminating abusive relationships from an Anglo and African-American perspective. *Issues in Mental Health Nursing, 18,* 433–444.

National Center for Injury Prevention and Control. (2003). *Costs of intimate partner violence against women in the United States.* Atlanta, GA: Centers for Disease Control and Prevention.

Norcross, J. C., & Vangrelli, D. J. (1988–1989). The resolution solution: Longitudinal examination of New Year's change attempts. *Journal of Substance Abuse, 1,* 127–134.

Plichta, S. B., & Abraham, C. (1996). Violence and gynecologic health in women < 50 years old. *American Journal of Obstetrics and Gynecology, 174,* 903–907.

Prochaska, J. O. (1995). Why do we behave the way we do? *Canadian Journal of Cardiology, 11*(Suppl.), 20A–25A.

Prochaska, J. O., & DiClemente, C. C. (1986). Toward a comprehensive model of change. In W. R. Miller & N. Heather (Eds.), *Treating addictive behaviors: Processes of change* (pp. 3–27). New York: Plenum Press.

Prochaska, J. O., Velicer, W. F., Guadagnoli, E., & Rossi, J. S. (1991). Patterns of change: Dynamic typology applied to smoking cessation. *Multivariate Behavioral Research, 26,* 83–107.

Prochaska, J. O., Velicer, W. F., Rossi, J. S., Goldstein, M. G., Marcus, B. H., Rakowski, W., et al. (1994). Stages of change and decisional balance for 12 problem behaviors. *Health Psychology, 13,* 39–46.

Riemsma, R. P., Pattenden, J., Bridle, C., Sowden, A. J., Mather, L., Watt, I. S., et al. (2002). A systematic review of the effectiveness of interventions based on a stages-of-change approach to promote individual behaviour change. *Health Technology Assessment, 6*(24), 1–242.

Salber, P. R., & Taliaferro, E. (1995). *The physician's guide to domestic violence: How to ask the right questions.* Volcano, CA: Volcano Press.

Saltzman, L. E., Fanslow, J. L., McMahon, P. M., & Shelley, G. A. (2002). *Intimate partner violence surveillance, uniform definitions, and recommended data elements.* Atlanta, GA: Centers for Disease Control and Prevention, National Center for Injury Prevention and Control.

Tjaden, P., & Theonnes, N. (1998). *Prevalence, incidence and consequences of violence against women: Findings from the national violence against women survey* (Research Brief No. NCJ 172837). Washington, DC: National Institute of Justice, Centers for Disease Control and Prevention.

Waites, E. A. (1993). *Trauma and survival: Post-traumatic and dissociative disorders in women.* New York: Norton.

Wuest, J., & Merritt-Gray, M. (1999). Not going back: Sustaining the separation in the process of leaving abusive relationships. *Violence Against Women, 5,* 110–133.

Yassen, J., & Glass, L. (1984). Sexual assault survivors groups: A feminist practice perspective. *Social Work, 29*(3), 252–257.

Index

CPSIA information can be obtained
at www.ICGtesting.com
Printed in the USA
LVHW031731100619
620741LV00008B/127/P